FINANCIAL MODELS AND SIMULATION

Financial Models and Simulation

Dimitris N. Chorafas

St. Martin's Press

First published in Great Britain 1995 by
MACMILLAN PRESS LTD
Houndmills, Basingstoke, Hampshire RG21 2XS
and London
Companies and representatives
throughout the world

A catalogue record for this book is available
from the British Library.

ISBN 0-333-63419-5

10   9   8   7   6   5   4   3   2   1
04   03   02   01   00   99   98   97   96   95

Printed and bound in Great Britain by
Antony Rowe Ltd
Chippenham, Wiltshire

First published in the United States of America 1995 by
Scholarly and Reference Division,
ST. MARTIN'S PRESS, INC.,
175 Fifth Avenue,
New York, N.Y. 10010

ISBN 0-312-12630-1

Library of Congress Cataloging-in-Publication Data
Chorafas, Dimitris N.
Financial models and simulation / Dimitris N. Chorafas.
p. cm.
Includes bibliographical references and index.
ISBN 0-312-12630-1
1. Corporations—Finance—Mathematical models. 2. Financial
services industry—Technological innovations. 3. Fuzzy systems.
I. Title.
HG4012.C47 1995
658.15—dc20   95-2012
                                                    CIP

Contents

v

List of Figures

xi

List of Tables

Preface

Financial analysis and *auditing* have many things in common but they also have several differences. Progress in auditing comes by taking things apart, and in financial analysis by putting things together. Therefore:

- The term *analysis* is a misnomer.
- What is really meant is *synthesis* of analytical results.

A common element of financial analysis and of auditing is that of *modeling*. Whether done through a formal, structured approach using mathematics and computers or by means of analogical reasoning by the expert, modeling can be instrumental in revealing hidden relationships which help to analyze and synthesize pertinent information elements.

A good deal of these information elements come through databased accounting procedures, market input, time series and other data streams. Sometimes the input is quantitative but quite often it presents both quantitative and qualitative aspects. Hence the approach which characterizes the 15 chapters of this book.

*   *   *

This is a *how to* book written for business executives and management, accounting and finance students. Though it involves financial models it requires no background in mathematics. Every term is explained in the text in a way which is fully comprehensive. Practical examples permit the reader to gain insight into the way modern financial analysis is done.

The book divides into four parts, each addressing one major area of interest. Part One explains the practice of financial modeling and gives *applications examples* from both financial institutions and manufacturing organizations.

As an introduction to the leading edge of financial analysis, Chapter 1 presents ways and means currently in use, aimed to simplify a world of complexity in the handling of financial data, starting from the contribution of Luca Paciolo in the late 15th century, and proceeding to the modern management accounting standards.

Modeling concepts in finance and accounting is the theme of Chapter 2, which also introduces the basic notions of financial modeling. This presentation stresses the need for interdisciplinary approaches and leads to a comprehensive definition of the modeling domain in Chapter 3.

Chapter 4 examines the organizational prerequisites to the successful development and implementation of financial models, including the quality of inputs and what might constitute an acceptable error level in management accounting. In the background is the concept that financial analysis is done for decision support reasons and that it has to integrate with management accounting practices.

Models for budgeting and budgetary control are the focal point of Part Two, which is applications oriented. Chapter 5 addresses the issues connected with financial planning and budgeting procedures, examining the budget as a short-term financial plan and linking its observance to the notion of *management accountability*.

The effective development of budgets, their expression in an algorithmic form and plan versus actual evaluation, requires a budget analyzer. This is the theme of Chapter 6, which also discusses the prerequisites to a budgetary model. Chapter 7 explains how to build financial models in order to control costs, as well as how to use cost standards.

A whole methodology and associated procedures for control over costs and budgets is presented in Chapter 8, which also underlines the importance of getting acceptance of financial plans by those who will be responsible for implementing them. Both quantitative and qualitative approaches are presented, and through practical examples it is explained how they can be put into practice.

$$*\qquad*\qquad*$$

Contrary to what many books suggest, accounting is not a process which obeys strictly quantitative rules. Accounting is both qualitative and *judgmental*. Who is to say:

- The appropriate allowance for bad debt?
- The reserves which should be made for law suits?
- The right presentation of accounting results for management control reasons?

In very large measure, accounting rules include a great deal of judgmental interpretation. The presentation of results is itself an art whose heterogeneity can reach significant proportions. But decisions require a level of homogeneity, hence the need for models and standards.

Part Three is structured in this frame of reference. Chapter 9 addresses the issues related to models for balance sheet reporting. It explains the organizational and technological impact on the company's balance sheet and presents applications which involve 'What-if' experimentation.

By contrast, Chapter 10 covers the new and burgeoning domain of financial instruments for Off-Balance Sheet transactions: Options, Futures, Forwards, and Swaps. It explains the role of the financial analyst in connection with derivatives, presents the role models play in volatility and hedging, and discusses why derivatives are really marked-to-model — while every bank says that its instruments are marked-to-market.

The theme of Chapter 11 is cash flow and its management. After defining the many meanings of 'cash flow', the text looks into cash flow as a critical resource, explaining the prerequisites for a dynamic financial analysis and the sense of non-traditional financial research. This is carried further in Chapter 12 which focuses on ways and means for judging profitability – from the customer mirror to the organizational prerequisites for accurate and timely management reporting.

Part Four exploits the background which has been developed through the first twelve chapters, and serves as a conclusion. Chapter 13 presents practical examples on how the use of financial ratios can serve as a thermometer of the enterprise's finances. Ratio analysis is discussed under the perspective both of manufacturing companies and of financial institutions.

There are of course more powerful means for analysis and control than ratios, and Chapter 14 presents the creative use of algorithmic solutions – both with balance sheet and off-balance sheet instruments. Chapter 15 focuses on the role of visualization in connection with financial analysis. It is not enough to obtain quantitative results. These must also be presented in a comprehensive manner.

*   *   *

When we think about what underpins *success in finance*, we find that there is a strong relationship between the level of our knowhow and our professional performance. In this simple sentence lies the aim of the present book. The new perspectives it opens to its readers will be an integral part of a person's career advancement and his or her professional survival.

Since this book has been based on an extensive research project, I wish to express my appreciation for the collaboration received from 244 senior managers, systems designers, computers and communications specialists and finance experts in America, England, Germany, Austria, Sweden, Denmark, and Japan.

Eighty-nine computer manufacturers, communications companies, financial institutions, service companies and university laboratories participated in this effort. A personalized list can be found in the Acknowledgments on pp. 348–50.

Let me close by expressing my thanks to everybody who contributed to this book: to my colleagues for their insights, to the company executives as well as university faculties who reviewed selected parts of this book for the assistance which was given, and to Eva-Maria Binder for the drawings, typing and index.

Valmer and Vitznau   DIMITRIS N. CHORAFAS

Part One

The Practice of Financial Modeling

1 The Leading Edge of Financial Analysis

INTRODUCTION

If one asks ten different persons what is meant by *financial analysis* he will most likely receive an equal number of different replies, many of them fuzzy. The term does not mean the same thing to all people, and it is often interpreted from each person's own professional interests.

- Some think that financial analysis is synonymous with the use of *mathematics* in finance and accounting.

For many years, the study of time series and the use of critical ratios played a major role in analysis, and so did business statistics. Then came spreadsheets, simulators, expert systems and nonlinearities.

- Others believe that the main ingredient is *macro*economics, an opinion not generally shared – particularly by those who think that *micro*economics is more important.

Studies in macroeconomics have a longer standing both in academe and in some parts of the business community. But, more recently, microeconomics has gained considerable momentum and became largely synonymous with analytics.

- Still others underline the leading role *analysis* plays in management policies, including the use of new technology such as expert decision systems.

The irony is that all these definitions are correct, but none is in itself complete. The approach which we take in regard to the analysis of financial statements and accounting records must be polyvalent. It should reflect *both* senior management policy and the fine print, making the best possible use of mathematics.

Models have been employed since accounting began. Science itself took off out of the need for quantification in agriculture. Numbers are necessary in any endeavor, in order to analyze or predict. However,

- What sets financial modeling apart from accounting is that it goes beyond mere quantification.

- It brings into the picture *qualification* enriched through expert systems, simulators and other knowledge artifacts.

This does not set the usage of financial models apart from what has so far been done through accounting and other quantification procedures. On the contrary, it integrates different disciplines into one well-knit system which can serve in a polyvalent manner the current needs of its users and their developing requirements.

THE EFFORT TO SIMPLIFY A WORLD OF COMPLEXITY

It is an ancient paradox that the rules of nature are simple but the world itself is complex. The universe is populated by a rich variety of physical and logical entities in a myriad of patterns. There is an evident diversity, yet all these forms are generated and even propelled by the same underlying laws.

Over the years, the analytical powers obtained through models and computers have led to a growing interest in the old questions of *complexity*. But in what may seem to be a contradiction, businessmen as well as mathematicians, physicists, engineers and computer scientists have for about four decades primarily used the computer for trivia and administrative data processing chores.

- Administrative-type functions were handled prior to the 1950s and 1960s by means of much simpler engines, the relay-based accounting machines.
- Computers and realtime processing of business models enabled us to do something more sophisticated – and therefore to gain a competitive position.

Clear minds have seen this contradiction and, in their way, have given warning signals. As early as the early 1950s, Dr Robert Oppenheimer prophetically suggested that the computer is much more than a glorified accounting machine and can offer a totally different level of insight and foresight. But then he added that it would take two or three decades to realize the difference.

At the heart of Oppenheimer's hypothesis was the fact that with a programmable general purpose computer, in principle, we can simulate any real life system. This parallels the original thoughts of Dr Alan Turing and his 'Turing machine', a hypothetical device which is the conceptual forerunner of modern computational procedures.

Whether in business or in science, what really matters in attacking the problem of complexity is not the physical form a Turing machine might take but the notion of *computability*:

- By following a programmable course, a man-made device can perform what are normally regarded as mental manipulations.
- This is a process which accountants and financial experts have been using

all along. In fact it constitutes the core of their business, as we will see in the following paragraphs.

The concept of computability has underpinned many of the more recent developments in information technology. But most significantly it constitutes the foundations on which lies the edifice of mathematical models – from simple algebraic equations to nonlinearities, stochastic processes, simulators and fuzzy engineering.

As many successful implementations in finance and in industry at large help document, mathematical models allow more freedom of expression than a verbal description could do. As with accounting, every procedure has its place. But:

- Whereas modeling programs are designed to encourage tinkering with the data, hence to experimentation.
- Accounting programs are designed primarily to prevent unauthorized tinkering with financial information.

This is the point underpinning many of the concepts in this book; a book written for professionals in finance and accounting, but also in engineering and management.

For all professional people, continuing on-the-job performance requires a comprehensive view of models and modeling. Through examples which are defined from daily experience, we will build little by little towards this goal.

Since every chapter is self-explanatory and requires no *a priori* knowledge of business administration, it addresses itself to a range of professionals from accountants and financial analysts to engineers and scientists whose work requires an understanding of economics and finance.

- What professionals from all walks of life have in common is the drive to simplify the complexities confronting them in their daily work.
- Whether consciously or unconsciously, in so doing they abstract and simplify – and hence they model the real world.

Abstraction and idealization also underpin the act of management. Therefore, managers can greatly profit from analytics, by learning how to use their background to master what might look like complex and esoteric issues – but in reality, after we get to know them, they tend to become quite simple procedures.

THE NEW WAVE OF FINANCIAL ACCOUNTABILITY

Financial models can range from the elementary, such as the use of ratios, to the fairly complex, for instance, simulators and knowledge engineering constructs. Modeling software generally permits on-the-fly changes in data and allows numerous evaluations of oncoming information. The more classical accounting software is not designed for this type of free expression.

Combined with computer technology and enriched with artificial intelligence (AI) (see Chorafas, 1987), modeling offers online interactive manipulation as well as an extensive graphics representation. Visualization makes it feasible to spot both *macro* and *micro* anomalies quickly, permitting us to concentrate on the underlying factors that make the market tick.

- Modeling and graphics make it easy for the user to spot trends from historical data, and carry them forward into the future.
- If the computed trend line varies remarkably from a historical pattern, there should be a good reason *why*.
- This goes further than the *What-if* capability spreadsheets permit, and it makes prediction feasible.

On the bottom line, prediction and experimentation are tools of management. The improvement of the practice of management should be a constant preoccupation of all executives as it is part of their responsibility for the survival of the organization for which they work.

- Whether in a financial institution or in an industrial company, the exercise of managerial and professional functions means *accountability*.
- The notions underlying accountability are generally valid, irrespective of the particular branch of industry in which a person or a company operates.

The concept of accountability is generic, but it can be further strengthened through appropriate tools. For instance, financial planning models have been developed to assist managers and professionals in preparing a *forecast of income*, in *controlling costs* and in elaborating *cash flow* estimates – three issues which constitute the pillars of financial management.

Originally, this work has been made through data processing by programming the accounting practices which we have inherited from the past. No better example can be given regarding this reference than the one provided through the practice of budgeting, described in detail in Part Two of this book.

More recently, past procedures are being revamped and restructured to permit experimentation, optimization and plan versus actual control. This is being achieved by blending the power of analytics with the tools provided by information science.

A reference to new tools and methods does not just mean any use of computers. Both the term *information science* and the practices associated with it have evolved over time and they will continue doing so in the years to come.

- From the batch environment of the 1950s, to the timeshared applications of the late 1960s and the realtime implementation of the 1980s.
- From the mainframes of the 1960s, to the dedicated departmental computers of the 1970s and the client-server models of the 1990s (see also Chorafas, 1994a).
- From the accounting oriented routines of the first two decades of computer usage, to the expert decision support systems of the last fifteen years.

There has been a steady evolution in computer usage, spearheaded by the cutting edge of technology and the steadily increasing competition, also by the imaginative work done by managers and rocket scientists in the more advanced financial institutions and manufacturing companies in the First World. Known as *agents*, knowledge artifacts are now running both on personal computers and on high performance computers, providing their users with market leadership.

OVERCOMING THE PROBLEM OF INNUMERACY

Paraphrasing Mark Twain who once stated that 'If Homer didn't write the *Iliad*, it was written by another man of the same name' – if managers did not develop models, models were nevertheless developed for managers. But are all professionals able to use them, and if not, why not?

- The answer is that there has been what John Allen Paulos (1990) calls the heavy cost of *innumeracy*.
- That is, the aftermath of mathematical illiteracy and its consequences in business and professional life.

The social costs of innumeracy, says Paulos, range from unfounded government policies to belief in different pseudosciences. A similar statement can be made about pseudoproblems in business.

We usually address the real problems through planning. Management planning is a way of avoiding many false starts and a score of unrewarding investments. But attention! 'The plan is nothing,' Dwight Eisenhower once said. '*Planning* is everything.'

The concept which lies behind this statement is that the process of planning is much more important than any given plan developed in response to a specific situation. The same is true of the processes of:

- Financial analysis, and
- Accountability.

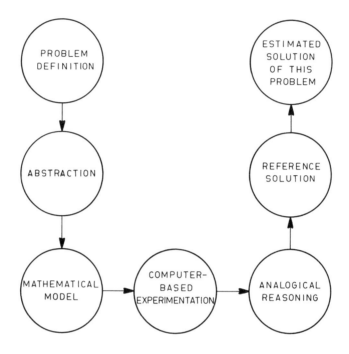

Figure 1.1 A common ground in DP, DSS and AI

Situations change and therefore a valid experimentation procedure – which is supported through *modeling* – should be flexible and adaptable to the environment as it evolves. This, however, requires doing away with innumeracy.

The notions of *analysis*, *planning* and *accountability* are intimately related. They also connect to the process of *computability*. Such convergence brings to the foreground the need for integrative studies which search to combine into one system:

• Most of what has been achieved so far in legacy-type data processing, with
• The new perspectives in advanced information technology enriched with knowledge engineering.

Such integration is not only logical and necessary but also a sequel to that which has taken place during the late 1970s and early 1980s in terms of transaction oriented data processing and decision support systems (DSS).

The use of mathematical approaches in *finance* reveals a common ground which exists between data processing, decision support and knowledge engineering which is being explained in Figure 1.1. This common ground is made of analogical reasoning, which underpins all financial judgment, most of the accounting procedures, as well as the act of management.

BASIC CONCEPTS UNDERPINNING ACCOUNTING PROCEDURES

Accounting has often been characterized as a *business language.* More exactly, it is the language used to communicate financial information. A very important issue for any executive is the need to know about the company's *current financial status* as well as to appreciate the *future outlook.*

Prior to extending credit to a company, bankers and suppliers appraise its financial soundness and weigh the associated risks. US Government agencies such as the Securities and Exchange Commission (SEC), and the Internal Revenue Service (IRS) are concerned with the financial activities of business for purposes of:

- Regulation, and
- Taxation.

Employees are also vitally interested in the stability and the profitability of the organization for which they work, and evidently this is even more true of the stockholders. All these people need quantifiable evidence on which to base their decision.

Through accounting the company's management is kept informed of its operations: from debits and credits, to profits and losses, also of financial plans and budgetary control measures.

- The management of a relatively small firm may be intimately familiar with all operating and financial details and, hence, requires comparatively little accounting information.
- But as the size of the business increases, management loses its direct contact with day-to-day transactions and needs formal channels of timely reporting.

Much of the required information is financial, and accounting helps in providing a track of essential events affecting the organization. This information, however, has to be interpreted in terms of success or failure in helping in day-to-day control as well as in planning future action.

Accounting procedures aid in obtaining these objectives. They help in recording, classifying, and summarizing in terms of money, transactions and events which are at least in part of a financial character.

- Models provide the means for interpreting the results being obtained in a business.
- Models may be used in recording entries or notations, as well as in ensuring that they are correct.
- Models are also involved in classifying and sorting the transactions in an orderly and systematic manner.

A mass of isolated transactions conveys little meaning when considered as a heap. The information elements stored in the database become useful only when they are properly classified and then managed through appropriate algorithms and heuristics.

The models which we use in connection with finance and accounting try to simplify our perception of daily events. But whenever problems of complexity are being dealt with, the work which needs to be done tends to raise some questions about the link between:

- Mathematics, and
- The business world.

The interest is akin to that of the physical sciences, and their assumption that nature conforms to certain mathematical laws, such as Newton's inverse square law of gravitation. As we will see in the following section, the concept which dominated the work of Luca Paciolo was quite similar.

- The reason why science works is that the real world can be modeled using computable mathematics.
- When the physicist's mental faculties become strained, he can enlist the help of computers and thereby tackle problems of ever greater complexity.*
- In a similar manner, when the businessman faces a tougher world – one which judges him more harshly than before on his effectiveness – he can rely on mathematics and on computers.

This is done by means of *analytical approaches*. The organizations of today are more and more places of brains, not muscles. And brains can be greatly assisted through knowledge engineering (see also Chorafas, 1991a).

But how can we be sure that the real world always avails itself of computable mathematics? *What if* some of its laws are non-computable? As we will see in the present book, by shooting for the 100 percent such queries miss the point. Even if only 80 percent is computable, we can do lots of useful work by starting with a really *valid methodology*.

THE CONTRIBUTION OF LUCA PACIOLO

A valid methodology is really what accounting is all about. Luca Paciolo has been the man who put in place the accounting system of signs and rules which we are using today. Paciolo was a Franciscan monk of the order of

---

* The author wishes to express his awareness that professionals of both sexes will be the readers and users of this book. Every effort has been made to use language that avoids gender discrimination. 'He or she' was not written because its frequent repetition can be awkward to the reader and disruptive. 'He' stands for 'he or she'.

the 'Minor Observants,' who lived in the 15th and 16th centuries.

- A theologician and mathematician, Luca Paciolo taught mathematical sciences in many Italian cities as well as abroad.
- His most notable work was 'Summa de Arithmetica Geometria Proportioni et Proportionalita,' published in 1494 and in a second edition in 1521.

A chapter of this book, entitled 'Tractatus de computis et scripturis' is wholly dedicated to *accounting*. Luca Paciolo was not the inventor of double-entry accounting, which was already in use in his time, and he himself defines it as of Venetian origin. But he was the first to structure the double-entry approach in a mathematically meaningful sense.

Historically, the concept behind double-entry accounting seems to have originated about a century and a half prior to the publication of Paciolo's book. This is suggested from evidence which exists in the archives of the state of Genoa and dates back to 1340, crediting the Genoese rather than the Venetians with this invention.

Other references regarding nonstructured double-entry accounts have been found in Florence, dating from 1395, and also in the archives of the state of Venice, where the accounts date from 1406 and 1434. Historians think that the most ancient journal which provides practical evidence is that of Andrea Bargarigo, who operated in Genoa in 1430.

All business operations, from the simplest to the most complex, have benefited from this mathematical formalization – and, therefore, normalization – of double-entry. *Delivery versus payment*, one of the currently most advanced ways of handling securities transactions, would have been impossible without the ability to simultaneously:

- Debit cash, and
- Credit securities

in two different accounts – or vice versa. This is what Figure 1.2 suggests by exhibiting, as an example, double-entry through electronic bookkeeping into the accounts of Client *A* and Client *B*. This involves a simultaneous operation into four books which are databased.

This is a modernization through information technology of an existing infrastructural procedure, on which rests the whole tradition of modern accounting. But it is always rewarding to look at the beginnings of the accounting system. In his writings, Luca Paciolo suggests that three accounting books should be kept:

- The memorial,
- The journal, and
- The general ledger.

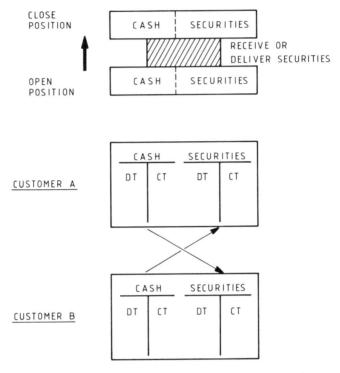

Figure 1.2 Delivery versus payment means that we do the operation simultaneously on four books which are databased

The *memorial* is a type of first entry and voucher on which must be entered all accounting operations 'day-per-day and hour-per-hour,' that is, in a chronological order. In the memorial are registered, as well, all the entries which represent operations without classification into debits and credits (Both the practice and the name *memorial* remain today. For instance, they are part of the law in the Grand Duchy of Luxembourg).

In the *journal*, the operations described in the memorial are entered in separate credit and debit accounts with indication of foreign currency operations. In the Paciolo tradition, which continued till the end of the 17th century, neither balances nor reports were made in the journal.

It is in the *general ledger* that each entry which was made in the journal will be divided with precision in credit and debit columns with balances on each page and appropriate reports to the continuation of the account. Paciolo seems to have been the first to define that the total of *credits* and of *debits* should correspond.

• The methodology he established includes the definition of the need of keeping subsidiary books, such as books for inventories.

• It also specifies that all books should be validated by the merchants' corporation, in the city where the enterprise resides.

As a mathematician Luca Paciolo essentially did the general ledger's normalization. Available evidence indicates that a sort of general ledger was kept in Sienna as far back as in 1255. By the mid-15th century a similar concept seems to have been used by merchants and financial institutions all over North Italy, in Genoa, Milan and Venice, but they followed no standard layouts.

It is interesting to notice that the first systematic approach to mercantile accounting is to be found in a book on practical arithmetic. Paciolo also seems to have structured the teller procedures, but the most important contribution which he made is the mathematical theory which explains the mechanism of double-entry and its importance in keeping under control transactions and the economic results of management.

POSTING, ACCUMULATION AND COMMUNICATION OF FINANCIAL DATA

Since its normalization in 1494, the function of accounting includes the posting, accumulation, and communication of financial data concerning economic activities. This data is typically expressed in monetary units while, as a process, accounting is concerned with the translation of financial transactions into business records:

• Collecting information about transactional operations of different types,
• Recording such data in a homogeneous and dependable manner, and
• Transmitting financial results to interested persons, in a comprehensive way.

Accounting reports aim to meet the need for objective reporting. This involves different presentation services which may serve a great number of purposes, but each one rests on a mathematical infrastructure.

Yet, the underlying concept is so flexible that it can be used in many other applications than general accounting, for instance in contracting a bill of materials (BOM) which must be updated by product, by due date and by manufacturer as shown in Figure 1.3.

Whether we talk of money, engineering products or any other goods, proper accounting procedures permit us to tally valuables entrusted to custodians, and also to compare results against the stewardship expected of them.

• They show the disposition of properties given over for administration to the executor or trustee of an estate, and

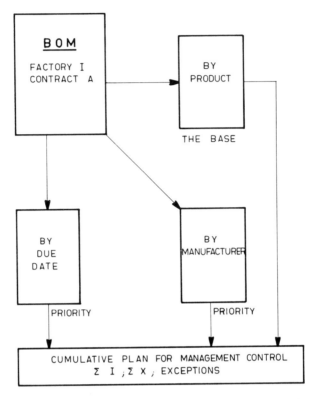

Figure 1.3   Normalized accounting procedures may be used not only with money but also with goods, such as the bill of materials (BOM)

- Help accumulate and present financial figures to explain what has happened to resources entrusted to individuals and institutions.

This reinforces the notion of accountability of which we spoke on p. 8 and provides a sound basis for accounting practices and associated financial reports. The concept underpinning the whole procedure rests on the need for reflecting and demonstrating trust in:

- Expressing the value of assets and liabilities,
- Measuring profits and losses,
- Meeting the requirement of custody, and
- Accounting for all changes that have taken place due to transactions or other events.

Accounting reports serve many more uses than this. The information presented in financial statements assists in formulating judgments as to the course of action which has been pursued in acquiring, holding, or disposing of interests – whether this is done by a person or an organization.

Accounting results present a basis for making decisions as to whether money or other resources should be advanced on credit. We employ accounting reports to judge whether or not loans are justified, authorize the further payment for goods and services, decide on deferred payments to avoid undue risk of loss, and so on.

As Luca Paciolo noted 500 years ago, the fundamental use of accounting is to *justify* legal requirements as well as bylaws. During the last few decades another very important use of accounting has been closely connected with management decisions. The effective usage of financial information reflects on managerial ability and serves for:

• Management control purposes,
• Plan versus Actual evaluations, and
• As a basis for further plans.

Part of accounting is the accumulation of financial information relevant to taxation. Another part is the evaluation of company assets. Still another important use is the presentation of facts and figures that serve to make up statistical information used both for control and for making projections.

HOW THE FINANCIAL ACCOUNTING STANDARDS BOARD LOOKS AT ACCOUNTING PRACTICE

Accounting, the professionals of the Financial Accounting Standards Board (FASB)* stated in the course of our research, is not a science which obeys strictly *quantitative* terms. Accounting is both *qualitative* and *judgmental*. Who is to say:

• The appropriate allowance for bad debt?
• The level of reserves which should be made for lawsuits?
• The proper presentation of accounting results for management control reasons?

There are many judgmental issues coming into accounting and the analysis of financial results. From Luca Paciolo onwards, normalization has largely dealt with the fundamentals, while the interpretation of the facts is left to management.

For instance, in terms of the fundamentals, the methods and procedures

---

* FASB is an American normalization institute, which is an offshoot of the Securities and Exchange Commission (SEC) and the Institute of Public Accountants. It has been chosen as an example of the standard-setting required in finance, business and industry.

supported by an accounting system help in preparation of basic debit or credit documents commonly referred to as *vouchers*. They are designed to:

- Keep the accounting department informed as to the transactions which have taken place, and
- Ensure a way of documentation which makes auditing and certification feasible.

Vouchers are the basis for all accounting records and tabulations. They support the different entries as classified, inscribed and presented in various ledgers – and can be seen as a loose-leaf version of Paciolo's memorial. Analyses of reports can be meaningless unless there exists evidence underpinning a system of internal checks and controls.

Because there is a multiplicity of functions to which accounting data is put, the content, objectives, and procedures being involved must be considered from at least two different viewpoints:

1. Recording, classifying, and presenting the financial effects of all transactions.
2. Establishing procedures which make feasible the measurement of expenses, income, assets, liabilities and other financial results.

Seen under this dual perspective, accounting reports comprise not only conventional income and expense statements in the general ledger – but also balance sheets, profit and loss statements, fund accounts, assets and liability reports.

- Each one of these may be accompanied by additional analyses, and
- Details of changes need to be presented in specific asset or equity accounts, over a given timeframe.

Supporting classification and subclassification of accounting data may be necessary, related to income statement, balance sheet items, and comparative ratios. These and other relevant data can be presented in *tabular* or *graphic* form – but it is wise to recall the FASB's dictum that to a very large measure accounting rules include judgmental interpretation.

- The presentation of results is itself an art whose heterogeneity can reach significant proportions.
- But decisions require a level of homogeneity, hence the need for norms and standards.

Standards can only be set after appropriate research, involving the ability to reach a consensus and the virtue of presenting results in a comprehensive manner. These prerequisites pose a series of challenges which, from FASB's viewpoint, include:

- Identifying the most significant standards issues that require resolution,
- Establishing appropriate priorities when tackling those issues,
- Achieving general acceptance of what the standards are to be, and
- Maintaining support for the process of setting standards.

Seen under the dual perspective of the private and public sectors, a whole range of issues needs to be steadily treated in terms of normalization. (Issues concerning the public sector are addressed by the activities of the Government Accounting Standards Board (GASB), a parallel organization to FASB which was established in 1984). FASB is constantly deliberating far-reaching standards that are connected with financial reporting models. It also devotes time to more narrow-scope practices concerning some of the mechanics of the financial accounting profession itself.

PRINCIPLES UNDERPINNING MANAGEMENT ACCOUNTING

While the classical accounting system and associated activities relating to the books and records of the firm deal with a large mass of detail, the managerial version of such information is different. Its goal is to assist in establishing policies, strategies, plans and controls. Rather than precision, the prerequisites to management accounting are:

- Accuracy, and
- Analytics.

The management accounting system can be a complex set of procedures and models closely integrated with operations, but designed to accomplish a number of objectives not associated directly with the precision necessary for balance sheet reporting or income statements.

Financial analysis is based on general ledger, income statement and other accounting data. But it aims at the *interpretation* of information through extrapolation or other methods which provide:

- Insight, and
- Foresight.

As Sam Walton (1992) aptly remarked:

'Nowadays you hear a lot about fancy accounting methods. But back then we were using the ESP method which really sped things along when it came time to close those books. It's a pretty basic approach. If you can't make your books balance, you take however much they are off by and enter it under the heading ESP which really stands for 'Error Some Place!'

The goal should be to eventually locate the error source and wipe it out – a principle just as valid for corporate finances as it is for personal financial and accounting issues. 'I usually felt that if a fellow could manage his own finances he would be more successful managing one of our stores,' Walton suggested.

Contrary to the way of keeping the general ledger which is centrally regulated, the handling of management accounting data can be customized according to management culture and prevailing needs. This statement is true all the way:

- From classification procedures,
- To presentation policies.

Flexibility is necessary as the detailed classification of information can be demonstrated in a variety of ways, depending on purposes and situations which are ad hoc, recur from time to time, or are constantly present.

Flexibility is particularly important when we deal with ad hoc views and exceptions. One of the challenges is to get a maximum of readily available information very fast and with a minimum of manual work. This can be achieved through communications, computers, software, algorithms and heuristics.

Managerial accounting is also concerned with systematic collection of *qualitative* facts about the operations within and outside the enterprise. It calls for procedures which can handle vagueness and uncertainty:

- The preparation and administration of budgets is a quantitative exercise which also has qualitative aspects – such as are exemplified through the practice of alternative budgets.
- The interpretation of cost and revenue data by units of organizational responsibility also has qualitative aspects.
- The provision of evidence for the detection and elimination of waste or fraud is mainly quantitative, but judgemental evidence can be subjective.

The identification of problems from managerial decision may involve several issues which are not crisp at all. (A crisp answer, for example, is 'yes' or 'no.' 'May be' is not crisp.) While the orderly handling of operations from the standpoint of systematic standard procedures is not disputed, exception reporting is done by thresholds which may be subjective and quite flexible in terms of implementation.

MANAGEMENT ACCOUNTING AND FINANCIAL STANDARDS

The procedures followed by management accounting include provisions for meeting objectives, comparing actual versus planned expenditures, deriving

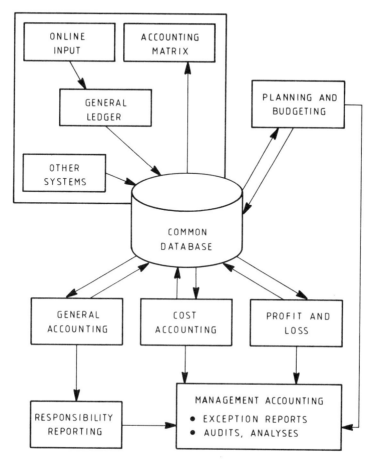

Figure 1.4   A common distributed database serves both general accounting and management accounting

conclusions from business activities, and leading to corrective action. We saw on p. 17 that all this has both quantitative and qualitative aspects.

As Figure 1.4 demonstrates, the information employed by general accounting and by management accounting comes from a common pool. But the interpretation is different, with management accounting addressing:

• Exception reports, concerning management control and leading to corrective action,
• Formal audits and their presentation under standard and flexible forms,
• Financial analyses using a growing inventory of tools, as subsequent chapters will demonstrate.

One of the differences between general accounting and management accounting can be seen in the unit of measurement being employed. This is normal since the metrics we employ should be representative of planning and control action needed in an organizational sense.

- Decisions about the allocation of financial and other resources rely heavily on credible, concise, and comprehensive accessing information.
- This statement is applicable to both general accounting and management accounting.

For financial reporting of a general accounting nature, the organization is viewed as an integrative entity in terms of which the financial data are marshalled to show the current position, and also to demonstrate the effects of operations on the firm as a whole. This is the classical procedure.

For management purposes, however, the notion that the enterprise is a single entity is not very useful. The only exception to this statement regards companies which:

- Are of very small size, and
- Have a narrow scope of operations.

Many of the decisions of management are not necessarily of organization-wide scope, but relate to profit centers and cost centers. Each one of these centers may operate as an independent business unit to be judged on the basis of obtained results.

Therefore, each one operating unit has to be shown separately in terms of plans, actions, profits and losses. Summation which is possible and very useful in classical accounting may be meaningless in managerial accounting where other, more flexible and often ad hoc means of aggregation, are needed.

- Channels of managerial accounting information have to be differentiated, for instance by product, by client, or by market.
- This is necessary to control credit risk in a way which makes sense not only globally but also individually.

For these reasons, there is no way to develop a unique framework for management accounting, much less to formalize it. This contrasts to the need for standards addressing general accounting – which are essential both for legal reasons and for the proper functioning of an enterprise and of the economy as a whole.

Reliable information about the operations and financial position of individual organizations has many uses in the management of the economy as well as for regulators and control authorities. Also for the public in making investment decisions. The usefulness of financial reporting can be improved by focusing on the:

- Primary characteristics of relevance and reliability,
- Timeliness of information so that it reflects actual conditions,
- Evaluation perspectives through comparability and consistency.

At the general accounting level the FASB in America, and normalization boards in other countries aim to keep standards current to reflect changes in methods and ways of doing business. To account for changes in the economic environment they promptly consider any significant areas of deficiency in financial reporting that might be improved through new standards.

In management accounting, by contrast, the norms are not being set by national or international bodies but the company itself. Query and reporting norms are usually settled within the perspective of a *management information system* (MIS). They aim to provide a homogeneous basis for evaluation, decision support and corrective action.

Whether for management accounting reasons, for experimentation purposes, for the realtime handling of input data or for any other, *simulation* is a very helpful procedure. It rests on the mathematical modeling of a given:

* Situation
* Process, or
* Business environment.

Simulation is essentially a *working analogy*. Analogy means similarity of properties without identity. When we are able to construct analogous systems, measurements or other observations made on one of them can be used to predict the reaction of the others. In this book, mathematical modeling and simulation are used as practically synonymous terms.

2 Introducing Modeling Concepts in Finance and Accounting

INTRODUCTION

Two of the basic objectives of a properly implemented financial information system are to provide control over the accounting books and assure compliance with regulatory requirements. A third goal is management oriented: reporting accurately information showing the financial position of the company, for the use of management.

Management accounting, for example, may involve information which aids in evaluating how a subsidiary performs and/or an individual executive performs. Other management accounting reports focus on return on investment (ROI) decisions which were made, a product's profitability or a market's response, the ability of meeting financial goals, or other criteria.

Chapter 1 has explained the concept of modeling and how important are the analytical tools in evaluating *profitability*. Profitability evaluation may consider a product or service; a customer account; or some other frame of reference. Models are also written for:

- Transferring charges and credits between products or profit centers regarding funds provided and used,
- Measuring an account's profitability in comparison to other accounts and to internal standards,
- Highlighting discrepancies which exist between different production (or sales) units, and so on.

Modeling and experimentation are necessary inasmuch as the ultimate goal of financial reporting by enterprises rests on the need to provide information that is useful to present to potential investors, creditors and the management of the organization.

It takes a certain amount of moral authority to do almost anything beyond the routine. But action can be so much better focused when the information which is necessary can be presented ad hoc, in realtime and in a comprehensive manner. All these issues are supported through modeling.

BRIDGING THE GAP BETWEEN FINANCE AND MATHEMATICS

It is a cheering fact that during the last few years there has been considerable progress in bridging the gap between finance and mathematics. Today we can say that a common ground between the two disciplines has been found on which the specialists of each work without feeling entirely out of their element.

As we will see in this and subsequent chapters, financial *models* might be termed first approximations to an actual economic situation in which deliberate simplifications are made in order to obtain an unambiguous and valid formulation of a problem. This is done by means of *algorithms* and *heuristics*.

In the 8th century AD, Muhammed Ben Musa, called *Alkhawarizmi*, wrote the first book on Algebra. Later on, his name was corrupted to *Algorithmus*. At present, the word 'algorithm' is used to designate a process of calculation which:

- Leads from variable input data
- To results determined through a step-by-step procedure.

For over 100 years economists and financial experts have typically worked with algorithms. They do so because there is excellent historical precedent, in the physical sciences, regarding the validity of algorithmic models in processes involving calculation.

The mid-1930s saw a major contribution in the field of theoretical economics. It came in a series of papers by Abraham Wald who analyzed the economic factors and structured equations for determining *prices* and *production* levels at economic equilibrium.

However, only during the years after the Second World War did the use of mathematics in finance accelerate, through operations research, linear programming, simulation and more recently knowledge engineering. Both quantification and qualification are approached by means of modeling, not unlike what has been seen in the physical sciences:

- Newton's first law of motion, that in the absence of external forces a body continues to move with constant velocity, cannot be verified by terrestrial experiment.
- Yet without the idealization of a frictionless universe the science of mechanics could not have been born. Today, we are at a similar threshold in economics and in finance.

Economic factors have been related to production possibilities – the latter meaning information on what goods can be produced, in what quantities and by what processes. How much steel, wiring, plastics, rubber, labor, and so on, is required to build one automobile? Or, how much in terms of calories and vitamins is necessary to produce one able-bodied laborer?

- This information can often be given quantitatively in the form of production functions, or
- Can be expressed in relations which tell in a concise manner what processes of production are technologically possible.

What is more, fuzzy engineering principles (see pp. 39 and 40 below) can help to enhance the scope of financial analysis. They can be employed in a number of domains, including budgeting, investment advice, securities trading, portfolio management, currency exchange, options and futures (derivatives are studied in Chapter 10).

Not only complex activities but also other operations benefit from models and knowledge-enriched approaches. For instance, the relatively simpler calculation of financial ratios and the determination of debt to meet end-of-year cash-on-hand requirements.

- Desired financial ratios can be embedded into a system which works interactively with the company's own databases and with public databases.
- The mission of the model may be to recalculate according to alternative criteria the income and cash flow statements or to do cash flow forecasting.

Timeshared computer programs and linear programming models have been developed since the 1970s to assist in controlling and monitoring the daily money transactions among cash accounts, coordinating with incoming cash and financial obligations. (A rigorous presentation on cash flow is made in Chapter 11.)

One of the available linear programming applications uses the short-term forecasts of sources of funds, fund requirements, and interest rates to develop a cash-flow model that sets various cash balance targets for the coming week. It:

- Schedules the cash coming from the banks,
- Maintains the required reserve balances, and
- Selects an optimum plan for the purchase and sale of short-term funds.

A comparison between actual balance and target balance allows the treasurer to allocate income and outgoing cash more efficiently, and do so on a factual and documented basis. (In Chapters 11 and 12 we will see practical examples of how this is done.)

Based on professional knowhow which has been mapped into the machine we can effectively support functions which range from analysis to optimization. There is value differentiation through this approach which, more recently, is moving to a higher level of sophistication as well as it addresses interdisciplinary problems.

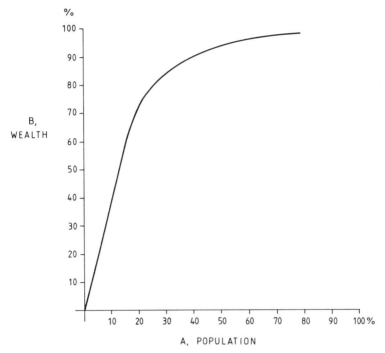

Figure 2.1   Pareto's Law suggests that a small part of variable *A* controls a big part of variable *B*

THE NEED FOR INTERDISCIPLINARY APPROACHES

If we look at the developments in physics, engineering, economics and finance, over the past two centuries, we are struck by the lack of interplay between disciplines. The number of theoretical economists who have had any sort of command of advanced mathematics has been extremely small.

At the same time, with only minor exceptions, up until the last few decades one can hardly name a top-rank mathematician who interested himself in problems of economics and finance, although there are exceptions such as Vilfredo Pareto, the Swiss-Italian mathematician and economist.

Some 100 years ago, at the turn of the century, Vilfredo Pareto developed a mathematical relation which has had wide applicability, not only in finance but also in many other industrial sectors.

- Studying wealth distribution in the Swiss economy, Pareto found that, as the 19th century came to a close, 1 percent of the population controlled 35 percent of the wealth.
- A study done in 1992, practically a century later, in the American economy has shown precisely the same statistic: 1 percent of the population controls 35 percent of the wealth.

When laws like the one shown in Figure 2.1 are discovered, they can be used in a very constructive manner in shaping policies and decisions. But even less fundamental or more ephemeral laws can have salutory results in terms of financial operations because they help in guiding our thinking.

The state of affairs which over long stretches of time kept finance and mathematics as alien entities, contrasts with the very close relation that has always existed between mathematics and the physical sciences. However, it is not difficult to account for such discrepancy.

- Only since 1945 have we started to appreciate the need for mathematical approaches as a precondition for a science of economics.
- The advent of Input/Output analysis in the 1940s, operations research in the 1950s and of digital simulation in the 1960s (see also Chorafas, 1965) opened the mind of financial analysts towards the able use of mathematical models, and
- Since the late 1970s spreadsheets have become widely available on personal computers – leading to mathematics 'with a human face' and at an affordable cost.

The use of spreadsheets in finance gained real momentum by the mid-1980s and did much to alter the way in which financial analysts work. As the latter developed computer oriented skills, they looked for further advances. But to successfully exploit the potential of systems expertise a whole *methodology* had to be developed. Step-by-step, Figure 2.2 shows its infrastructure.

A valid methodology – particularly one which is interdisciplinary – starts with the conceptual definition of a problem in economics or finance. After accounting for analytical requirements, this leads to specifications, with the logical expression of a financial problem providing the basis for modeling. That is the phase of mathematical design.

This path is often taken by mathematical economists. But, as we will see, it has more recently been enriched by knowledge representation, which makes feasible the structuring of rules as a way of implementing flexible, intelligence-enriched modeling.

- The organization and structure of the approach which we take should be subject to prototyping.
- Such a prototype should be tested not only *per se* but also by integrating it into the real world situation.

The results of the tests will lead to evaluation and adjustments – hence *tuning*. Every step in model development should have a feedback permitting us to backtrack and effect necessary modifications. No system lasts forever.

This can be said in conclusion: mapping the problem into the computer leads to the possibility of working towards a comprehensive situation which

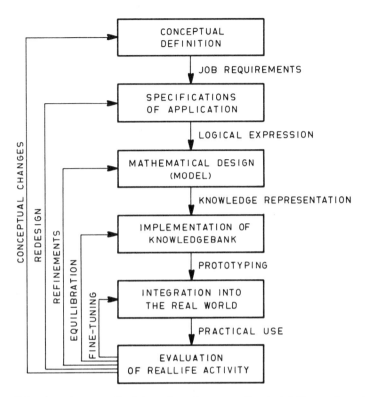

Figure 2.2   A systems methodology is not necessarily straightforward, as it includes loopbacks

can be structured and optimized. Economic problems are always of such urgency that there is tremendous pressure on the financial expert to get immediate results. Other things being equal, the better the tools being used, the better the results obtained.

THE MISSION OF DEVELOPING AND PROVIDING FINANCIAL INFORMATION

Mapping a real world situation into the computer by means of a financial model might be an exciting exercise which opens up lots of possibilities. But left on its own, even the most perfect model will do precious little. Some 80 percent of the problem in analysis is not the model, but the data which it will use.

We can better appreciate the importance of data if we understand the concept of *targetting*. To succeed, any human enterprise must have targets. If the target is clarity in financial statements and meaningful analysis, then different models are necessary to meet specific accounting requirements and nearly all of them must be customized. The chances are that such models will fall within the following major domains:

- General ledger accounting
- Planning and budgeting
- Asset and liability management
- Profit and loss evaluation
- Cash flow and cash management
- Evaluation of funds and investments
- Cost accounting, and
- Responsibility and profitability reporting.

From accounting to statistics and beyond, every one of these applications areas requires lots of information to be collected, filtered, stored, retrieved, manipulated (through models) and reported in a comprehensive form. The more comprehensive are the results we want, the better must be our models.

Analytical financial reporting has a growing range of uses, because practice has demonstrated how critical it is in making investments, and allocating credits. Also for many other decisions concerning a particular business.

Cash flow analysis is an example. Since investors and creditors are interested in receiving cash from the company, financial studies should provide information to help them assess the amounts, timing, and possible uncertainty of prospective cash flows which:

- Directly impact on the prospects for receiving loans, or
- Provide investors with information on the company's business perspectives.

Analytical financial reporting should respond to user needs by providing information about the economic resources of the company, the claims to those resources, its current obligations to transfer resources to other entities, owners' equity, and the effects of transactions.

Events and circumstances constantly change the assets and liabilities landscape and the claims to available resources. Therefore, not just an analytical but also a timely and effective method of evaluating performance is vital in today's dynamic business environment.

- Like profitability, performance can only be evaluated in relationship to a standard or plan, against which it may be gauged.
- Models are necessary to enhance organizational responsibility by comparing income and expense items, as well as assets, liabilities and equity accounts.

Financial models help to elaborate not only accounting data but also statistics – for instance current information in connection with the approved plan or budget. Models will be noting any variances, bringing under perspective background reasons.

Responsibility accounting is a systematic method of reporting revenues and costs within the organization which can be tailored to express ad hoc needs. A model, for instance, will allow costs to be accumulated and reported by varying levels of responsibility in both a quantitative and a qualitative way:

- The behavioral aspects of a responsibility control system involve people and entail motivational considerations as well as standards of performance.
- Planning and control cannot be successful unless the individuals on which it impacts accept the standards of performance, therefore both motivating and imposing a degree of control.

The process of providing financial information is indivisible from the structure of a responsibility accounting system. This differs in several respects from traditional accounting as all relevant references are such that they can be expressed in performance characteristics.

Management comprehension of accounts, statistics and patterns can be improved through graphical representation, particularly an interactive *visualization* – the turning of data into graphics and figures. Visualization is the most effective way of financial reporting – made feasible by means of online access to databases, intelligent networks, personal computing and graphics packages available as commodity software. We will discuss this issue in Part Four.

BASIC NOTIONS BEHIND FINANCIAL MODELING

Financial modeling has been practiced for a long time by budgeting practitioners, using largely manual procedures. With computers, a natural development is the construction of mathematical artifacts which reflect the ways and means underpinning financial operations. Conceptually, this is not difficult and there are now numerous illustrations in quantiative practice:

- These provide important references on the organizational aspects regarding the development and use of financial models.
- An example is the analysis of income statements aiming to determine the true components of revenue and expense.

Quite often, conceptual modeling starts by identifying the physical activities causing income items to increase or decrease. An appropriate mathematical relationship can be developed for each account, followed by equations written to produce the total net income for the company.

The study and analysis of financial ratios is another example of financial modeling (see also Chapter 13). For many years ratio analysis has been a valuable tool for measuring performance, whether comparisons are made against:

- An established industry standard
- Our own company's prior results
- Some desired objectives set by management, or
- New industry values which are developing.

Financial officers keep track of key ratios on an historical basis so that trends can be established as an early warning system. Trends and ratios pinpoint potential problem areas for management decision, and lead to timely corrective action.

As many financial institutions and other organizations have found through experience, well-focused models can be used to set targets during the profit planning process. For instance, goals regarding:

- Return on assets (ROA), and
- Return on equity (ROE).

These are two frequently used ratios that have proved to be of assistance in the planning process. Professionals interpreting such ratios are typically divided into two camps: those who see difficulties everywhere and those who see the opportunities.

Managers and accountants who understand the opportunities presented by modeling have seen to it that during the 1980s more powerful analytical and conceptual tools than the simpler concepts reflected in ratios were implemented.

- The foremost banks and the more progressive treasurers of manufacturing organizations are eager to put sophisticated financial models into daily practice.
- They do so not just because such solutions are feasible, but for the reason that the *knowledge revolution* obliges us to proceed in that way to remain competitive.

Frederick the Great once said he could excuse one of his generals being defeated but never being surprised. Financial modeling permits us to avoid surprises by gathering, massaging and reporting personalized intelligence. Three forces are in the background of this process:

1. The evolution of the workforce,
2. Deep market changes, and
3. Rapid technological innovations.

All three have sharpened the cutting edge of competition. They have done so not only in terms of the inherent power they provide but also because they have synergy and, therefore, bring to bear a compound effect.

A practical example in knowledge engineering is the best way for appreciating how the process of modeling works. In the years to come, intelligent artifacts known as *agents* will characterize all advanced implementations of information technology – while applications depending on classical data processing will end up in a cul-de-sac.

FINANCIAL ANALYSIS AND KNOWLEDGE ENGINEERING

Wise financial executives today understand that a sound approach to business opportunity should not exclude any reasonable possibilities in the development of new products and services. This reference is the more valid with the new vistas being opened up by artifacts, particularly if we can successfully integrate our knowledge constructs with the databased information accumulated over the years.

A review of the fundamentals underpinning financial models will reveal that they can be of many types – some specific to the situation or problem subjected to analysis, others more generally applicable to different problems and their variations. One of the better ways of looking at financial models is to separate them into two classes:

- The one reflects an interrelation and interaction between the different factors which, once established, cannot be changed automatically because of lack of rules which would make realtime adjustments possible.

The matrix which has been classically used with Input/Output analysis for macroeconomic purposes, also known as the Leontief model, is an example. Two other examples are those of linear equations and of critical ratios.

- The other class is much more flexible because it does not map a given situation once and for all, but has embedded into it decision rules based on heuristics. These permit automatic adjustments as the situation develops.

Knowledge engineering is the process by which a systems expert, usually known as a knowledge engineer, will carry out the investigation and acquisition of, say, a financial analyst's knowhow. The domain may be budgeting, the approval of loans, investment advice, currency exchange, operations in futures, options, bonds and equities, or strategic planning.

Knowledge engineering involves many stages of which the first two are vital to the development of a financial model. At the very start is the *discovery* of knowledge generally known as knowledge acquisition.

1. *Knowledge acquisition* (see also Chorafas, 1990a)

Knowledge needed can be gained from public sources – not excluding books, articles, house rules and bylaws. Usually, however, the knowledge engineer acquires a working understanding of the rules prevailing in a given field through the *domain expert* or, less cryptically, the professional who has mastered that field.

The contribution of the domain expert to the discovery of knowledge is to advise about the fundamental aspects of *his* professional knowhow, and the rules which he uses. He does so by answering specific questions concerning this knowledge and the way it is put to work:

- The financial expert's challenge is that of making conscious the thoughts, decisions and moves which are often subconscious – because they have become second nature to him.
- The challenge of the knowledge engineer is to elicit the conceptual, screening and decision making processes proper to the domain expert.

Having done this, the knowledge engineer must understand the rules the financial expert uses and map them – through the appropriate tools – into the computer's memory. In other words, though it is very important, knowledge acquisition alone will not create the knowledge-based system. This will be done through the process of knowledge representation.

2. *Knowledge representation*

Knowledge representation consists of the writing of the software necessary to map the acquired knowhow into computer memory. More precisely, the rules the domain expert uses in his daily work.

The outcome of knowledge representation is an *expert system*; that is, a software construct that experts in the specific field which it addresses have enriched with their knowledge. Based on such knowledge, expert systems give advice to their users and *justify* the opinion which their offer. This is characteristic of the new practices in modeling, discussed in this book.

CAPITALIZING ON INTERACTIVE COMPUTATIONAL FINANCE

The best way of looking at what has been so far obtained in terms of the implementation of analytical models and expert systems in finance, as well as in industry at large, is in terms of the industrialization of knowhow. Of particular interest is the knowhow possessed by a few talented people. However, contrary to monolithic data processing:

- The acquisition of professional experience is an iterative and steady process, and
- It requires close collaboration between the domain expert and the knowledge engineer.

Mapping of the knowledge obtained is successfully done through rapid prototyping followed by successive refinements of the resulting model. Such process is the cornerstone of what has become known as *interactive computational finance*.

First, a *prototype* – and hence a tentative model – is constructed, which reflects the expert's knowhow in the specific area of his work. As the financial analyst who contributed his professional knowledge sees the system functioning, he is able to add to the knowledge representation. This he does by commenting, many times in a matter-of-fact way, on rules representing his experience.

- Through this process is constructed a *knowledgebank* which resides in computer memory and is executable in realtime.
- The model in the knowledgebank operates on facts, states and values – that is on data – and does so through heuristics and algorithms.

Since we aim at using existing resources rather than reinventing them, apart from the subjects of knowledge acquisition and representation, the knowledge engineer should also master the integration of the expert system with existing software facilities, for instance, spreadsheets which have been extensively used in connection with financial analysis.

Access to rich databases is necessary to enhance the inferencing capability of the knowledge artefact and enrich the applications being developed. While ten years ago expert systems were a novelty, today they are only one of the fields of interest in the growing range of applications regarding financial problems – where the field of implementation of knowledge engineering is steadily expanding.

As Figure 2.3 suggests, in the field of finance and more generally of management, current developments go well beyond rule-based expert systems and involve a number of disciplines which can be applied either individually or in unison. For instance:

- Fuzzy engineering
- Genetic algorithms
- Neural networks
- Pattern recognition
- Language understanding
- Realtime language translation, and
- The mapping of financial markets into the computer.

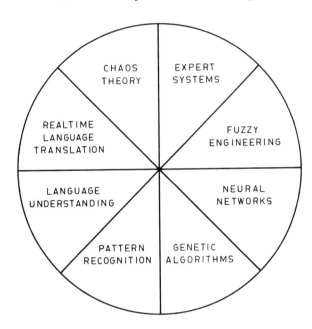

Figure 2.3   Applications domains of artificial intelligence in finance

The tools which we need to represent such processes in an able manner come under the cumulative name of the *new mathematics*. The way it has shaped up during the 1980s, this is a *concept*, but also a bunch of *artifacts* and a *technology*.

Interactive computational finance has come of age because analytical models enable computers to understand and manipulate information much more directly than is possible with conventional programming techniques. At the same time, seamless access to distributed deductive databases provides the necessary raw data from which meaningful information will be extracted (see Chorafas, 1994b).

Interactive computational finance means *knowledge* readily available at workstations, though the background work may be done in number crunching supercomputers. The issue to appreciate is that an industrialization of knowledge transforms the work of professionals:

• From opinions which are often incongruent,
• To a factual and documented diagnosis.

It permits the development of alternative hypotheses and assumptions, making feasible their testing and weighting. It is also possible to include the subjective judgments which may exist but often are not exploited because the old tools cannot handle them.

The integration of subjective judgment and number crunching by processing complex financial models on high performance computers is an integral part of interactive computational finance. Both are essential elements in today's computational arena at Wall Street and other major financial centers.

- In the race to buy low/sell high, securities houses who do not master high technology are frozen out at the switch or jump in with incomplete knowledge and get burned.
- They also lose business opportunities in many of their financial operations, from currency exchange and investment advice to treasury functions.

While models and modeling will not correct organizational ills and personality clashes, other things being equal they offer their users very significant competitive advantages. In an industry accustomed to shopping for both price and value, lack of appropriate supports has serious consequences – from short-term financial losses to falling behind competition in the long term.

CONCEPTS UNDERPINNING MODERN APPROACHES

The first basic concept underpinning modeling solutions is that the general understanding of financial statements will be promoted by abandoning ill-defined terms and non-standard reporting practices. Companies with experience in this new line of thinking suggest that four main advantages can be anticipated:

1. Clarity of financial statement contents and their captions,
2. Professional thinking freed from a confusing ambiguity,
3. A more generally transferable knowledge acquired from experts, and
4. Ability to appreciate accounting algorithms by non-accountants.

Not only are these benefits within reach, but also once properly established the financial modeling practice can be to a large extent automated. Once the policy decision is made by top management, implementation becomes an issue of networks, databases and sophisticated software.

Intelligence-enriched software has been available to leading-edge organizations since the mid-1980s. Expert systems established themselves in financial and other industrial practices in the 1984–6 timeframe. Since then, they have made very significant strides.

The better way of looking at knowledge artifacts is to view them as *a new type* of software: never before the wave of change which started in the mid-1980s have we programmed the *heuristic* processes in the mind of the:

- Financial analyst,
- Investment advisor, or
- Foreign exchange trader.

The edge that makes a knowledge artefact truly 'expert' is the private knowledge or *heuristics* that the expert possesses and applies in actual analysis. (See also p. 41 below on the work of rocket scientists.) This kind of knowledge is constituted by his training and sharpened by his professional experience.

Only heuristics can effectively represent the trial and error approaches which professionals use in their daily work. Automating significant chunks of the thinking processes, particularly those which are more standard, permits the professional to devote more time to astute fine-tuning of that part of his knowledge which is more stochastic.

Systems specialists, too, have a great deal to gain from the implementation of models and knowledge engineering. Programming for computer processing should no longer be done through obsolete languages like Fortran or Cobol, but:

- By means of 5th generation languages, known as expert systems *shells*.
- These are based on the primitives of the intelligent machine's basic software (see Chorafas, 1990a and Chorafas and Steinmann, 1991).

Many shells are user-friendly, thereby making feasible enduser programming. This is significant not only because it breaks the current programming bottleneck and long delivery delays, but also because on-the-job acquired knowhow permits the execution of the finer details associated to a given profession – from the analysis of facts all the way to how decisions are being made.

The acquisition of knowledge which leads the professional and the manager to a certain action is key to the ability of developing sophisticated man-made systems able to assist their users in their job.

- This goes well beyond data collection and tabular representation,
- It requires involving the expert's insight and foresight in connection with his personal work.

However, not only the *product* – that is, the knowledge artifact – but also the *process* itself imposes new demands and requirements. Many of these requirements are novel, since in the past the processes which were connected to financial analysis were neither appreciated in their fundamentals nor kept dynamic to meet rapid changes.

Financial modeling does not solve everything. Many business goals are, and probably will ever remain, at least partially intangible. But even in these instances a model can serve to clarify the interdependency of several fields, thus providing a better guide to evaluation and decision.

THE FLEXIBILITY REQUIRED FOR FINANCIAL MODELING

The use of analytics in finance spread among banks, manufacturing companies and merchandizing concerns not because of reasons of scientific curiosity but due to the fact that tough management and high technology are necessary to fend off competitors. Hence, the interest which needs to be paid both to:

• The product, and
• The process.

First, in regard to the *product*, the emphasis on the acquisition of knowhow and its dissemination through modeling helps dramatize the fact that over the years technology has increasingly assisted the executive task through the development of appropriate tools.

This reference is valid even if for nearly forty years the priorities which have been followed have resembled an inverted pyramid rather than the most urgent needs in executive functions. Figure 2.4 helps to explain the message this paragraph conveys:

• Since the early 1950s, data processing chores have skewed the priorities, as the main attention in computer implementation has been paid to the clerical level.
• Support at the middle management and at the professional levels of reference has been scarce, and even then often deficient.
• Very little or no attention at all was paid at the top management level, yet here is where the greatest benefits to be derived from technology may lie.

The *products* of technology to be delivered to managers and other professionals must be properly focused on their job. They should also be of an advanced nature in regard to what was done as recently as last year, and is currently possessed by the competition.

At the same time, great attention should be paid to the *processes* used in delivering the needed results: their time-to-market, fine mechanics, adaptability, timing and costs. It takes wings to fly. But it profits little having the wings if we do not use them to gain competitive edge.

Why, then, has there been for so many years a distortion in terms of processes and priorities? Several reasons have contributed to this effect, one of them being that when in the 1950s computers were introduced by their vendors as glorified accounting machines, clerical jobs were already subject to a certain degree of mechanization.

Another more deep-rooted reason for the misdirection of information technology processes is that it is much easier to automate routine procedures than to address issues which involve a significant degree of knowhow.

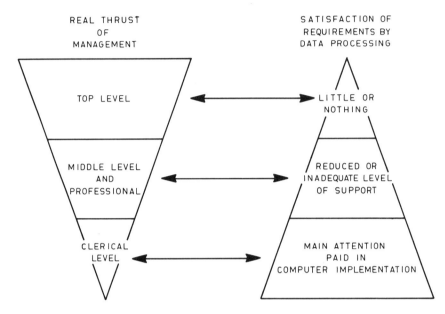

Figure 2.4 Data processing is not answering top management's requirements, knowledge engineering should do better

- The skill needed to automate routine jobs is minimal.
- But to tackle non-routine jobs we must understand their intimite characteristics.

For instance, a distinctive characteristic of financial analysis is the ability to report information by management level in order that decisions can be reviewed and evaluated within the context of organization and structure. As far as processes are concerned:

- Responsibility reporting relationships must be kept fluid, and
- They should be reviewed frequently to reflect evolving lines of authority rather than a rigid structure.

The management oriented information provided by means of analytical models must be presented in a flexible manner, according to the ad hoc requirements of the enduser. It must also be accessible online in realtime and fit the changing environment of the services provided to the market.

All organizational solutions are subject to changes. These may be as simple as altering a cost center's identification, expanding or refining the current chart of accounts, adding a new department or subsidiary, or ensuring that a new region or division receives some of the reports other cost centers normally get.

While simple in concept, all of the foregoing examples on procedural changes have a direct bearing on the analytics – as they impact the management accounting and reporting system. The degree of impact will depend upon the number of program revisions and amount of procedural maintenance required to implement the changes. Therefore, it is wise that all developments be:

- Flexible,
- Modular,
- Parametric.

By providing the system with a set of instructions, we can automatically generate the necessary maintenance procedures in connection with the process of financial reporting. Models help in eliminating the need for laborious manual changes even if the requirements for modifications are rather steady.

THE ROLE PLAYED BY FUZZY ENGINEERING

The algorithmic models of operations research and the heuristic approaches of expert systems both contrast with and complement one another. Contrary to the step-by-step progress towards a solution normalized by Alkhawarizmi, a *heuristic* approach proceeds by trial and error guided by a process of judgment.

- This resembles the way the human mind often works in difficult decision situations.
- Hence it is particularly useful in relatively diffuse and fuzzy problem areas.

Underlying concepts in heuristics are: 'may be,' 'rather greater,' 'about equal,' 'not so sure'... These are qualitative notions which we are able to map through *fuzzy engineering* (see also Chorafas, 1994c). In finance, there is a vast domain of applications with fuzzy sets; applications which cannot otherwise be tackled.

Figure 2.5 provides an example through a case which is typical of budgeting problem. A small laboratory has three sources of income, each relating to one of the key projects it is conducting. Done together with another partner, Project *A* has a 70 percent chance of being renewed. If it does, the budget would vary between $5 and $8 million at different *degrees of certainty.*

It is sure that the company to which the lab belongs will contribute a budget for Project *B*, which can be anywhere from $10 to $14 million with equal certainty. As for Project *C*, its chances to get funded are 50–50. If it is funded, the budget will be at least $20 million with a decreasing likelihood to the $30 million level.

Not only all this can be expressed graphically, as in Figure 2.5, but fuzzy

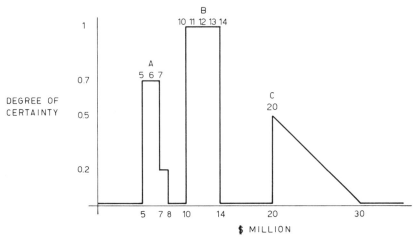

Figure 2.5 A typical budgeting problem presented in a fuzzy engineering graph

engineering also provides the tools for aggregation – which deterministic mathematics cannot do. Neither can algorithmic solutions be of help when the decision maker is confronted with vagueness and uncertainty, as in the present case. Fuzzy engineering:

• Permits building-up a budget with dollar amounts corresponding to different levels of certainty and their *possibilities*.
• This is a better alternative than mixing figures and possibilities in the head of the lab director.

When solving problems, people generally use some intuitive models, if for no other reason than that the world is just too complex and too full of details to comprehend without abstracting or simplifying it in some way. The trouble with these intuitive models is that they embody a host of implicit, hidden assumptions.

Classically, such assumptions have been manipulated inside one's mind where the ablest investigators integrate different approaches, examining and correcting any errors their models may possess. By contrast, enriched with the appropriate tools, computer-based models provide a normalized frame of reference.

• Even if not precisely correct, a fuzzy engineering model may suggest gaps and opportunities which are not immediately apparent.
• Filling these gaps leads to fruitful lines of action which could otherwise have gone unnoticed or been poorly represented.

In the final analysis, heuristic and algorithmic, macroeconomic and microeconomic models are used because they *work*. Over several decades heuristics and algorithms have been employed in the development of *predictive systems* in the physical sciences and in engineering, and there is no surprise that finance and economics want to benefit from such acquired experience.

CROSS-FERTILIZATION PROVIDED BY ROCKET SCIENTISTS

Cross-fertilization comes by way of a transfer of skills. Today, aeronautical engineers and nuclear scientists are very much in demand in banking, due to their modeling experience. Known as *rocket scientists*, they have contributed a great deal to the market competitiveness of the financial institutions which employ them.

Precisely because of interdisciplinary reasons, the rocket scientists' work is at a premium. Synergy between formerly discrete domains of science and finance, can produce surprising results. However, a word of caution is also in order:

1. The model builder must be careful not to oversimplify while *abstracting*.

While it can be easier to understand a complex market situation through major simplifications, this can also be counterproductive because it tends to leave out of the equation obscure but critical factors in experimentation.

2. The best results are obtained through *close collaboration* of rocket scientists and domain experts.

The new breed of computer scientists should avoid the pitfalls and weaknesses of the old generation, for instance, working in glass houses was separated from the man with the problem.

3. For *processing* purposes, the rocket scientist must have his own computer resources.

Confronted with backwards-thinking data processors, both bankers and rocket scientists may give in by accepting static systems solutions, batch-type model handling and months or years of delay in programming. When this happens, the results are not just suboptimal but can also be destructive. Contrary to the old practices of mainframers and other inefficient data processors:

• Financial models must be developed in a very rapid timeframe through visual programming,

- Then, they should be run in realtime using seamless access to databases.

Static solutions and modeling projects which take years, rather than days or weeks, end in dry holes. Rocket scientists understand this, but lulled by the obsolete data processors and mainframe vendors in full conflict of interest, management is not always aware of what lies behind some people's resistance to move forward.

Time delays, batch processing, closed systems solutions and oversimplification have disastrous aftermaths. They tend to eliminate an entire class of competitive moves and actions. Yet such moves might be basic in effectively completing a given study or in providing valid grounds for greater profitability.

Because these risks are real, there should always be a possibility for quantitative measurement and qualitative evaluation. Testing the model in a factual and documented manner and doing so without any loss of time is as important as knowing what we do and what we are after.

- Algorithms and heuristics are not god-given; they are man-made,
- It must be possible to steadily collect data relevant to the problem area, and
- Criteria should exist by which the results of alternative action programs can be compared.

Any successful approach to banking, commercial, industrial and engineering problems starts by stating the criteria. The objectives or goals of the work being done should be explicitly outlined – even if goal-setting is no easy, straightforward job, as it calls for skill and patience. We will see why this is so in Chapter 3, where the modeling domain is defined.

3 Defining the Modeling Domain

INTRODUCTION

Information about money and the ability to manage financial resources are every bit as important as money itself. As bankers know from experience, the overriding effort is that of locating the best or most favorable degree, amount, condition or product mix. This constitutes an *optimum*, under an acceptable level of risk. The notion of optimization is present in all sciences and many tools in mathematics address this issue. But in terms of the goals we are after, from one domain to another the notion of an optimum varies:

- In *biology*, for instance, an optimum is the amount of light, heat, moisture and food best promoting reproduction and growth.
- In *finance*, it is the most favorable choice which we make in order to balance *risk* and *return* – controlling the former and enhancing the latter.

The real challenge in money management is one of determining the best possible asset mix with regard to a given investment horizon. This investment horizon may be short-, medium- or long- term; in each case it will be based on criteria which are partly quantifiable and partly qualitative.

There are no miracles to be had in terms of controlling risk and improving return on investment. However, the best bet is that the winners in the equity and debt markets are usually the players who have:

- Timely information, and
- Superior decision models.

The goal we seek to reach through optimization and other uses of mathematical models is that of approximating the highest level of what could be called *community intelligence*. None of us is really as smart as all of us, that is as intelligent as the market.

In this case, the market is the *domain*. What is done through modeling is to map the domain, which we have defined, into the machine. In this sense, the domain is much larger than the model which, in principle, should be specific and focused.

We use applied mathematics in order to aid discovery. We make hypotheses, and hence tentative statements, and test them. Through analysis, we also hope to improve our cognitive ability, in terms of the perception and understanding of complex financial problems – and most particularly the domain within which they develop and have to be solved.

CAN WE DEFINE THE DOMAIN WE ARE MODELING?

Realistic modeling of natural phenomena like clouds, rain, fire, of man-made structures like robots, plants, or cloth drapery, is not only possible but has been successfully executed, sometimes leading to novel theories, for instance, *Chaos Theory* developed through hypotheses of laws underlying the behavior of clouds (see also Chorafas, 1994c).

The modeling of natural phenomena reflects the fact that free or connected particles are generated by the system, move and change form within the system, and die from system actions. In the case of man-made systems, such actions are initiated and executed by artifacts which play a key role in the model.

A domain model consists of several properties, such as attributes, relations and methods. An aspect of a specification included in that model is considered structural:

- If it is composed of names, types, operations, and variations of these constituent elements, or
- If it is possible to decide whether it describes an object properly, based on the mathematical representation of key aspects.

Domain modeling is being extensively used in financial analysis and forecasting. Over the years it has become a competitive advantage, because leading-edge organizations find it critical to obtaining a good analysis of:

- Problems, and
- Potential solutions.

Most models used in finance are offspring of one of four types: *Time series*, *structural* or analog methods, *nonlinearities* and *knowledge-enriched* approaches which are becoming increasingly popular.

Whether used in the emulation of a real life domain or in a specific, more limited implementation, *mathematics* is a game of *signs* and *rules* employed to represent a situation or reach a specific goal:

- The signs have a semantic meaning,
- The rules describe behavior, and most particularly constraints.

The analysis of time series is one of the oldest examples of the use of mathematics in finance. Most often, the objective is to examine historical price movements in an effort to predict future prices.

Within a given domain, time series approaches are usually connected to *technical analysis* and much of their success depends on the absence of noise in the data. Graphics plays a key role in this approach, permitting us to describe the appropriate domain in an easily comprehensible form.

Structural models attempt to forecast some type of behavior. For instance, they focus on future prices based upon historical relationships of *fundamental*, usually macroeconomic, *variables* and current information.

However, a number of studies have shown that structural models have a poor track record of predicting certain events such as future foreign exchange prices. In this case, *nonlinear* systems representing behavior at the edge of chaos can give far better results, hence their recent popularity.

Quite similarly, since the mid-1980s leading-edge financial institutions and companies in other industries have increasingly employed knowledge engineering. In the mid-1990s, emphasis has been particularly placed on fuzzy sets, genetic algorithms and neural networks, since they offer a much better basis for prediction.

Therefore, financial analysts start to appreciate that among the best modeling techniques are the development and use of knowledge artefacts. Not only does the use of expert systems shells contribute to the improvement of software productivity, it also permits a better experimentation perspective.

Figure 3.1 suggests a procedure which I have followed in my professional practice and found to be rewarding. It consists of four, well-defined steps. Notice that verification follows implementation. The final test of any system is: "Does it *really* work?"

This approach can be used in a variety of modeling domains, leading to comprehensive applications on management planning and control, or other prediction-type problems. It has been, for instance, successfully applied in areas such as:

- Revenue and expense forecasts
- Cash flow projections and income analysis
- Income tax optimization and reporting
- Product line profitability studies
- Trend analysis in the main lines of business
- Market penetration and market share
- Detailed cost control evaluations
- Different procurement studies, and
- Balance sheet and off-balance sheet reporting (see Chorafas and Steinmann, 1994a).

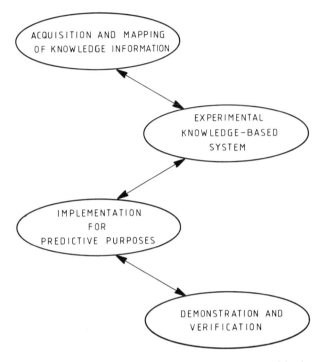

Figure 3.1   Knowledge-based systems and the enhancement of basic technologies

The models used in these domains can be *deterministic* or *stochastic*, *crisp* or *fuzzy*, *linear* or *nonlinear*. But they must be realistic, fitting as close as possible the real world situation which they represent. Short of this, the domain description will be partial and the results suboptimal.

DEVELOPING OPTIMISTIC AND PESSIMISTIC SCENARIOS

Domain modeling and mathematical experimentation permit us to create a number of scenarios and analyze the effects of assumptions on the financial position of an account, a balance sheet, an asset or a liability. The outcome of a course of action or a market trend can be tested under a range of scenarios:

- Optimistic, and/or
- Pessimistic.

The results of an experimentation enable us to learn about the assumptions which we made, as well as the most likely behavior of financial instruments and markets. For instance:

- Banks are experimenting on maturity distributions, growth targets, legal or refinancing restrictions.
- Industrial companies experiment on the evolution of operating expenses, ways and means to cut overheads, and sales forecasts.

Mathematical simulation and experimentation are valuable tools for every company's budgeting and profit planning processes. Projections can be made on future financial performance using, for example, a balance sheet analysis framework. This is a process which has been employed many times with commendable results.

In pessimistic scenarios, models have been used to study *bubbles* and *panics*. Bubbles are ugly when they burst and markets are in a free-fall. Some financial markets acquire that label because they can:

- Rise several hundred or even a thousand percent in a short time,
- Catch the imaginations and wallets of investors who miscalculate the risk involved, and
- Continue on their upward flight paths – right up until the moment that the crash comes.

Bubbles usually follow the line of an explosive curve which can be mathematically expressed. The bubble analogy carries a sense of alienation because it is so often forgotten that inevitably dazzling booms must end in calamity.

A pessimistic scenario suggests that there is a sense of tragedy about bubble markets. The fatal flaw among investors is a virtual absence of concern that a collapse can occur, even though it has happened so many times before. Most often, optimistic scenarios forget to integrate in themselves *lessons learned* in the past from bubble bursting.

The realistic modeling of a financial domain can benefit from the fact that, as experience helps to demonstrate, there are different economic signs of a bubble in the making. High inflation, tightening of credit, a disproportionate number of foreigners investing in the market, and too many new issues coming too close together are examples.

- Bubbles form and burst for a number of technical and fundamental reasons which can be analyzed before they happen leading to predictive results.
- They are often being set on their way by grand societal or financial changes, as well as when there is plenty of money chasing few investment opportunities.

As stock markets hedge against inflation and currency devaluation, valuations may become distorted. This happens not only in booms but also when markets have gone through pretty lean times and start recovering. The problem is overconfidence, which leads to markets that overshoot.

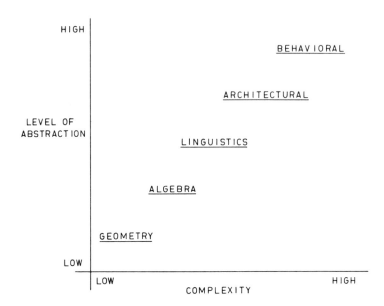

Figure 3.2   Domain modeling goes beyond the mathematical frame and involves several important behavioral issues

The weight of money thrown at a given market makes it move upwards by a wide margin. Scenarios which take this into account are often called pessimistic. By contrast, they are realistic. The best scenario analysis is the one which focuses on the *worst case*. Once the worst case is understood, everything else which can happen is rather positive.

ACCOUNTING FOR VALUATION ERRORS

The hypotheses which we make and the scenarios we develop are not meant to be infallible. One of the roles of domain modeling is to appropriately reflect this possibility, and do so at the behavioral level of reference. As Figure 3.2 suggests, mapping *behavioral* factors into the computer is an activity which goes well beyond basic mathematics such as geometry and algebra. Linguistics and architectural issues are already complex, but behavioral modeling:

- Requires a higher level of abstraction, and
- Involves a greater amount of complexity than any other activity.

Artifacts involving behavioral representation require knowledge engineering and contrast with the much simpler models like those which can be described by graphical means or algebraic equations concerning physical quantities. Market reactions are behavioral.

Higher levels of abstraction have inherent in themselves the possibility of semantic and other errors. This happens not only with modeling but also with guesses about market developments made by domain experts without using a technological support.

When misjudgments happen, the predictions which are made develop what is often called *valuation errors*. Bubbles form when valuation errors take place in massive form reflecting a halo effect. Rather than recognize the overvaluation, investors and financial analysts speculate on overoptimistic scenarios for earnings and economic growth that cannot possibly be met.

- The higher the market goes, the more bullish the sentiment.
- At this stage, an event occurs that proves the forecasts wrong.

When we have a market that is overheated, the correction which comes shows up very sharply. Eventually bubbles burst. A market that has gone up in a straight line tends to fall in a straight line leading to panics, as every pessimistic scenario would tell.

People versatile in prediction theory know that a panic usually shows a sharp vertical drop at some point in the market's development. This pattern occurs because market psychology can change very rapidly:

- From a situation in which there are no sellers, thus leading to a one-way market going up,
- To one in which there are no buyers, which brings the market all the way down.

Investor behavior often reverses direction. For instance, if interest rates begin to rise, bond buyers can face a rude shock. Given the experts' track record as crystalball gazers, the risk will be bigger than many people realize when the behavioral change is detected only a short time prior to the selling panic.

As we will see on p. 50, there are reasons why market actions and reactions are included into modeling. A market behavior module can concentrate on prices of commodities, wages, interest rates and other sources which impact on market response.

Other factors influencing behavior are also important. A legal structure module will reflect on property laws, commercial laws, trading restrictions, prevailing bankruptcy procedures and the role of regulatory agencies in finance and other industries.

To a considerable extent, the references made in these paragraphs reflect issues which are not always considered – yet they are important. The same is true of modules designed to handle specific variables. The more focused these are on the problem at hand, the better the results to be expected.

BEHAVIORAL ASPECTS OF INVESTORS AND LENDERS

Investors should appreciate that both selling and buying are driven by expectations. So long as the expectation is that there will be higher prices, it is rational to buy. Once this expectation changes, it ceases to be rational to buy and it becomes rational to sell. This is the reason why markets are usually much more volatile than the economics which underlie their values.

As earlier sections of this chapter indirectly suggested, most investors and financial analysts bet on optimistic scenarios. Apart from this, there is more experience in emulating technical and fundamental market reactions than in reflecting on *psychological behavior*.

With the art of financial modeling undergoing steady development this reference starts to change. New tools come up which permit us to overcome what in the past used to be a barrier in mapping the market and its behavior into the computer.

- The use of *fuzzy engineering* is one of the best examples which are currently available in this connection, because it permits us to handle vagueness and uncertainty.
- *Genetic learning algorithms* also constitute a valuable tool, since they permit us to emulate the development of market sentiment through models.
- Another good example of the study of market behavior is the work which has been done through *Monte Carlo* in connection with *securitization* (regarding the practical use of fuzzy engineering, genetic algorithms and Monte Carlo, see Chorafas, 1994c).

Since the early 1980s, banks have been keen to package their mortgages and sell them as securities to investors, thereby recovering their capital. Investors, however, are asking for an estimate of *option adjusted spread*. As rocket scientists began to calculate the probability of consumers repaying their mortgages, they discovered that this varied according to:

- Where the mortgage holders lived,
- The length of time their home loan was outstanding, and
- The size of this loan in monetary terms.

The trick in estimating option adjusted spread is to be able to establish beforehand what is the probability that the loans in a pool will be repaid prior to their maturity. Also what distribution this repayment pattern may follow: the latter helps in projecting the cash flow over the pool's lifecycle.

- The behavioral pattern of investors, mortgage holders and lenders is of great interest to the financial community.

- On this pattern depends a great deal of yet unearned profits as well as unrealized losses.

Rocket scientists also chart how homeowners behave in response to changes in interest rates. Once the financial analyst is satisfied that a given group of homeowners is likely to behave *irrationally* – for instance paying off low interest rate mortgages – he passes this finding to the traders who buy their mortgages.

- Traders in mortgage-backed financing have adopted an alternative to the cash-flow method of pricing that accounts for the call risk in the securities.
- The best traders, and the foremost investment firms, can very well understand the message they get from rocket scientists – and they act upon it.

Experience gained from mortgage-backed financing is now passing to other domains. While the corporate bond market has been slower to respond to the new wave of analysis, there is much to do in this area, and asset-backed financing is now using powerful mathematical tools.

With the realization that many of the callable corporate bonds may be overpriced and that *event risk* further lessens their appeal, a revolution in *how* bonds are priced has come about. The end result is that corporations may have to pay higher yields than they now do, for example, for bonds with call features or subject to possible takeover uncertainties.

The message is that not only mortgage pools but other securities as well can benefit from treatment through algorithms and heuristics. Behavioral aspects can be added to account for panics, though current studies hardly scratch the surface of the complex behavioral issues which are involved.

ARE THE BEST MODELS OF A GENERAL OR A SPECIFIC NATURE?

Within the domain to which it is addressed, the model we build can be of a more general or of a more specific nature. The former presupposes that different applications areas possess common characteristics. This is a hypothesis which cannot very often be accepted.

The more successful modeling approaches are focused on the characteristics of a given domain or part thereof. Knowledgeable financial analysts do not develop an artifact which might be used for different purposes, in each case in a quite approximate manner. By contrast, they specialize:

- For *corporate debt securities*, for example, it is advisable to use a family of options pricing models to be applied not to the options book as a whole but to the different positions in it.

- With *indexing*, as in the case of short-term interest rates, options pricing models can also be employed, but their structure has to be tuned to different requirements and their risk management perspectives.

Similar statements can be made about other applications areas. Amortizing debt securities, for instance, repay principal on a periodic basis rather than at maturity.

Amortizing is an issue which merits special attention and can best be addressed through custom-built models. All subjects we consider to be particularly important need to be handled carefully. Amortizing practices may be subject to lower duration weights. Therefore:

- Decisions have to be based on an assessment of the typical amortization profile of a given item.
- Even better, amortizing debt securities should be broken down into their individual tranches and be included in the maturity ladder.

However, for reasons of expediency this is often done together with non-amortizing items, on the basis of other common characteristics. This leads to approximations and, sometimes, to loss of focus.

In this manner, a fixed rate loan of, say, $100,000, repayable in two equal annual instalments, could either be subject to a lower duration weight or included in the standard maturity ladder as two separate loans of $50,000:

- One of one year's maturity,
- The other of two years' maturity.

The Monte Carlo method has been effectively used in connection with this type of calculation, particularly in studying the decay of individual items in the pool. Reference to this was made on p. 50 in connection to mortgage-backed financing.

- Within the same domain of application, there can be a specialization of models in order to obtain greater accuracy.
- Specialization is definitely necessary when we deal with domains which have different characteristics.

A different type of model will be developed and used in connection with portfolio design than for amortization purposes. Within this portfolio model, some modules may vary, based on the premise that each client has a different investment profile.

These examples call attention to the need for customized choices to serve not the average or typical person but *each client* in the most appropriate

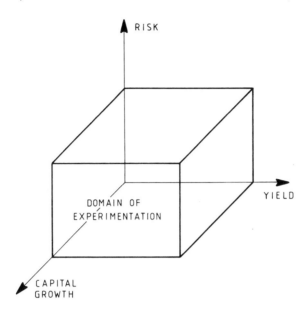

Figure 3.3 Investment decisions are usually situated within the framework of an all-embracing system

way. It takes more time and greater skill to follow this approach – but the results are also much more rewarding.

Investment choices are typically situated in a 3-dimensional coordinate system which, as Figure 3.3 shows, includes the *risk* level the client is willing to take on, the *yield* (regular income) the client desires from the portfolio and the *capital growth* which, in one way or another, is required. These factors are usually closely related. The ideal of a:

- Low risk,
- High yield,
- High growth

portfolio is not feasible in real markets. To optimize according to client wishes, it is necessary to describe a set of investment constraints, for instance, with reference to categories of stock to which these constraints may be related – such as no investments in the computer industry or in weak currency markets.

A microeconomic model designed to serve in the investment advisory domain will tend to include four main modules, each addressing one of the key factors entering into an optimization:

- The price system

- Market behavior
- Legal issues, and
- Specific variables.

In the case of a general type model, the price system module will cover the markets for all *goods* and *services*, factoring those issues which impact on financial assets. By its nature, this approach will be approximate.

In contrast, a custom-made model will only focus on *the* product under study and attempt to fine-tune market behavior in connection with that product. Other products will be included in case they overlap in market appeal to the one we target, but they will have relatively lower weights.

DOMAIN MODELING, MACROECONOMICS AND MICROECONOMICS

The best example of a very general model which covers the whole domain of the economy and its services – from manufacturing to finance – is one which reflects the productive capabilities of a nation. Clearly, knowledge of the factors of production, and the way these relate to one another, is essential for any realistic economic analysis.

Such models are fairly complex, have been used for many years and cover the agricultural, manufacturing and service sectors of the economy. Emphasis is slowly shifting to the factors with the greatest weight. For instance, in the First World services today represents more than 50 percent of employment.

While pioneering work in economic modeling started by the end of the 19th century, the breakthrough essentially came in the immediate years after the Second World War when interdisciplinary research in mathematics and economics permitted us to develop fairly realistic models of the economy. With this, the branch of *macroeconomics* was born.

The *Input/Output* model by Wassily Leontief capitalized on the work which had been done 60 years earlier by Leon Walras, a French economist and mathematician, who also made outstanding contributions in macroeconomics. Insight and foresight have also been contributed by the seminal work of von Neumann and Morgenstern, and by other economists and mathematicians whose contributions enriched the basis of this discipline.

The general model provided by macroeconomics can be sustained and specialized through more focused *microeconomics* models which address specific issues such as pricing and market elasticity. Whether macroeconomic or microeconomic,

- The process of modeling assists in separating the problem into its quantitative (numerical) and judgmental elements, exploring the former through mathematical equations and the latter with knowledge engineering.

- Solutions provided through experimentation help in formulating alternatives and analyzing effects of decisions before they have been implemented.

Whether more general or of a specific nature, a mathematical model does not represent every conceivable facet of a problem. However, if it has been well specified, it will focus on the key features. This is what is done both in macroeconomics and in microeconomics. In principle, we need to study the behavior of both:

- The national economy, and
- The market forces.

Their financial problems are interrelated. Macroeconomics particularly addresses the overall economic background. Microeconomics is a more minute and more polyvalent interdisciplinary effort, with the market's pulse in mind.

In both cases, models are used to forecast the way financial decisions influence an organization – whether this is the national economy as a whole or a private company. Both cases address economic potential and its exploitation. *Risk* and *profit* are the two elements in the bottom line.

Which are the earliest computer-based modeling alternatives, which can run at an affordable cost, and which are the newest versions? As the preceding sections underlined, we have plenty of quantitative tools today.

- Since the early 1950s, George Danzig's linear programming has opened new horizons in business planning. During the following decade, operations research came of age.
- If we look back into the 1950s and subsequent years, we will see a number of important and successful operations research projects (see also Chorafas, 1958). But we will also uncover many skeletons hidden in time closets.

Projects failed not because the tools were deficient but because the people using them were secretive, non-communicative, with no interdisciplinary background. This proved to be a bad policy which, over the years, was duplicated in electronic data processing creating the so-called *legacy* systems. Dissatisfaction with such results saw to it that:

- Since the mid-1980s, the emphasis has shifted towards the use of knowledge engineering and rule-based models.
- More recently, second generation expert systems and tools like fuzzy engineering, genetic algrorithms and neural networks permit us to incorporate behavioral issues into the model (see also Chorafas, 1992).

Fuzzy engineering provides the ability to handle vagueness and uncertainty. This corrects a major shortcoming connected with operations research, where available techniques were suited for dealing only with issues that could be expressed in a quantitative form.

Little was offered by way of implementation in domains which were judgmental and therefore qualitative. But, as stated, this has been corrected through expert systems.

ACCOUNTING OR NON-ACCOUNTING FOR INFLATION?

We said that whether we deal with macroeconomic or microeconomic models, the better are our hypotheses and assumptions, the better will be the results. This statement is true not only with mathematical modeling but also with any profession and with any enterprise. Accounting provides an example.

Rightly or wrongly, one of the conventions underlying corporate accounting is the assumption that fluctuations in the value of money may be ignored. Business transactions are recorded in terms of a nominal monetary unit. Accounting statements exhibiting business results and financial position employ this monetary unit: dollar, yen, pound, Swiss franc, German mark and so on, as the common denominator. But:

- Accounting is itself a financial model.
- Hence, leaving out inflation leads to an
  imperfect model.

Similarly, however, reference is rarely made to an inflation-adjusted presentation. The usual gimmick is that by not being adjusted for inflation sales and profit figures tend to be bigger – and hence, superficially they look better.

This is a valuation error which starts at the level of basic assumptions. As traditionally measured, accounting net income expresses the excess of periodic revenue over the cost of the capital. Under the most frequently used monetary postulate:

- The costs charged against revenue help in measuring gross income,
- But monetary costs reflect the amount of money initially invested, and due to inflation they understate current amounts.

With changing price levels, the value of money does not remain stable. Within the economy as a whole its average purchasing power fluctuates continuously, usually downwards due to inflation.

The problem is that in practically all countries general accounting rules and standards do not reflect the fluctuation of money and therefore lead to a significant misrepresentation. Company management should know better and take care of inflationary (or deflationary) results. It rarely does so, therefore, significantly reducing the accuracy of reporting.

- This is not an issue of mathematical formalisms.
- It is a matter of top management decision and, hence, an issue of policies and procedures.

Under the impact of price level changes, challenges arise as to the adequacy of the conventional method of measuring net income. For many purposes, management policies are inadequate and the result is wrong guidance provided by the accounting model.

Some accountants contend that the principal significance of money lies not in the numbers but in the purchasing power. Therefore, when the value of the dollar changes, accounting measurements of business costs should be modified accordingly.

These accountants propose that the orderly evolution of the profession now requires, as an extension of present practices, the reflection in financial statements of all items of revenue and cost on a *steady* monetary value basis. This means accounting for the results of inflation and dynamic change in monetary terms.

This amounts to a significant improvement over the current model, both in general accounting and in management accounting terms, because it makes the reporting basis more accurate.

- Current experience amply demonstrates that money as a standard of value is *an unstable variable.*
- Hence, in many cases the balance sheet represents the assembly of basically non-additive amounts.

Due to these factors, income calculations are distorted by the failure to place all financial references on a uniform monetary value basis. This is particularly true when higher inflation rates lessen the reliability of nominal accounting criteria. The argument is also valid with transnational accounts involving many currencies and fluctuating exchange rates.

PITFALLS WITH ECONOMIC REPLACEMENT COSTS

Let's always remember that, as we saw in Chapter 1, 500 years ago Luca Paciolo and the Florentine merchants were sophisticated enough to account for the changing value of foreign currencies. Any financial analysis worth its salt should reflect not only economic cost issues but also the value of different currencies in relation to one another.

Even if a firm's net income increases faster than the rate of inflation or the depreciation of local money, a portion of the increase in income is spurious. It does not reflect:

- Improved performance, or
- Ability to pay dividends.

Rather, it mirrors changes which are beyond management's control – though they are used to cover deficiencies or as excuses for a substandard performance. Financial analysis should shed light on these cases, and the model which we build should have the appropriate modules to compensate for their effects.

For instance, by applying inventory valuation and capital consumption adjustments to reported earnings, accountants can arrive at a profit figure that reflects current period accounting rather than historical costs. This differs from conventional income statements which include realized income from price appreciation, such as inventory profits, and from underdepreciation of assets. The discrepancies between:

1. Economic replacement cost, and
2. Accounting or historical cost

become most apparent during periods of rapid change in monetary values. Relatively low inflation had kept the two measures fairly close. But the onset of double-digit inflation (as in the late 1970s and early 1980s) pushed reported earnings to almost twice the amount of real profits.

Policy and procedural changes are therefore necessary and should be reflected into the model. A way to cope with this situation is the creation of accelerated depreciation schedules. Another example is a policy which establishes *real book value* calculated with tangible assets valued at replacement instead of historical cost.

- During periods of severe inflation, the difference between the two methods of measurement can increase dramatically.
- In such times, the distortions caused by historical cost accounting can lead to a serious misinterpretation of book values.

The proponents of modifications, however, are not in agreement as to the methods by which the effects of variation in the value of, say, the dollar should be measured. Or as to the manner in which these effects should be disclosed in corporate financial statements. I bring these issues into perspective because they are important in domain modeling.

Accountants who oppose modification contend that the conventional treatment is deep-rooted in practice, in law, and in general understanding. At the same time, they suggest, the significance of the inflation problem is exaggerated as the variations in the value of money are compensated for in part by other factors.

- According to this school of thought, any change in practice not supported by general demand would result in irregularity among applications, and in confusion.
- There is also the problem of establishing objective inflation factors which can help all industries, therefore leading to comparable results.

Included in this argument is the reflection that as far as different inflation rates among countries and currencies are concerned, at a time of fluctuating exchange rates these are taken care of by the relative value of one money against another. This is a weak argument because there are many other factors than inflation, some of them political, which come into exchange rate-setting.

As these examples help document, while we may all agree on the wisdom of properly defining the modeling domain, the more we get into the details of how this should best be done, the more we appreciate that there are disagreements. Models are made by people and therefore they show people's strengths and weaknesses. Let's keep that in mind when we talk of modeling domains.

THE CHALLENGE CONFRONTING FINANCIAL ANALYSIS

As a result of the issues we have just discussed, financial analysis is confronted with the challenge of having to untie more than one Gordian knot. Not just with the selection of 'this' versus 'that' model, but also a number of other tangled issues, from economic replacement costs to the use of monetary standards as a common denominator.

- From a practical viewpoint, there is significant merit in promoting international comparability of accounting standards, greatly improving the usefulness of financial reporting.
- Associated to this is, however, the mission of bettering the nature and quality level of the information contained in financial reports, with a view to better decision making.

Figure 3.4 is an attempt to reconcile the viewpoints we have seen in the previous two sections. The principles being used bring both *consistency* and *accuracy* into management reporting. This is done by means of a two-tier system.

In the inner tier composed of balance sheet and general ledger (see also the discussion of the balance sheet in Part Three) as well as of eight component parts (taken as an example) accounting follows current, noninflation adjusted practices. By contrast, in the outer two layers which constitute the management accounting system, the entries are adjusted for inflation and for fluctuating foreign exchange rates.

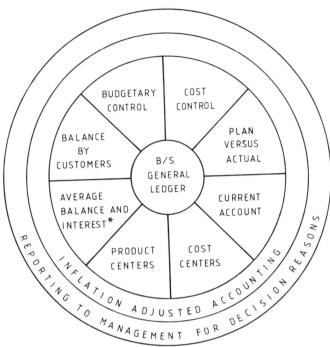

Figure 3.4 The internal accounting management information system and its
components

Due to inflation, floating exchange rates, deregulation and the inter-
nationalization of business, it is no longer enough to have available static
accounting concepts which can be embedded into financial reporting. This
is still necessary and helps in many ways by providing guidance and norms
– but more is also needed in terms of sophistication and detail.

The financial and accounting standards which we adopt for management decision reasons must go beyond providing a basic frame of reference.
They must be dynamic in order to help in establishing reasonable bounds for
judgment in:

- Preparing financial information which is sound and useful, and
- Increasing the understanding of, as well as confidence in, the content of
  accounting information.

That is the general type model of which we spoke on p. 51, though the
example which we took on p. 56 did not come from accounting but from
macroeconomics. The general model, we often said, has its uses – but if left
alone it can become sterile or off-base. Hence it has to be enriched with
specialized artifacts.

Something similar can be stated in terms of business statistics. When value statistics are examined in *real terms*, the equity and bond markets look quite different than under classical accounting. *Real statistics* are based on the same raw financial data as *traditional statistics*, but the individual series such as:

- Corporate earnings,
- Dividends, and
- Net worth

are adjusted as dictated by economic theory rather than current accounting practices. Economic (or real) profits are a superior measure to nominal profits because they more accurately measure the stockholder's payoff from owning equity in a corporation.

Payoff may take the form of dividends or reinvestment of earnings to expand a business. During periods of high inflation, nominal earnings do not accurately measure this payoff, for two main reasons:

- The cost of goods sold is calculated using historical inventory prices. This expense category may be dramatically understated when replacement costs of inventory are rising rapidly.
- While revenues and most expenses will increase in proportion to the inflation rate, depreciation, or capital consumption remains constant.

Both reasons lead to an imbalance in financial reporting practices, with the result that management decisions are taken on the basis of false facts. This is brought to attention because it is an issue of both *policies* and *models* – which the process of modeling alone cannot correct. Other similar issues pertinent to the *modeling domain* are deferred costs and accounting for reserves.

4 Organizational Prerequisites for Financial Models

INTRODUCTION

As we saw in the preceding chapters, the financial *model* is a computer program based on mathematical equations which *simulate* procedural issues, decision making processes, trading operations or accounting policies. As stated in Chapter 1, simulation is a working analogy which permits us to study how another system works, and how its component parts behave, by means of experimentation and measurements done on the better known structures, for instance, the mathematical models we have seen in Chapter 3.

- When analogous systems are found to exist, then the analysis of the behavior of one of them can lead to an understanding of the behavior of the other.
- By simulating the operation of a company's financial system, we project on oncoming activities and therefore on financial performance.

As working analogies, simulators are constructed on the basis of a relative simplification of real life situations and conditions. Typically, we employ the major factors affecting the process under study, and also map into the model their interrelationships.

- Every time we can construct such analogy by means of mathematical equations we make available to ourselves a powerful tool for representation and experimentation.
- This frame of reference conforms to the concept of *analogical reasoning* which has been one of the processes underpinning financial transactions of any type, for any reason, anywhere in the world.

The financial model we construct may be made for planning, operations, or control purposes. It may be algorithmic or heuristic; linear or nonlinear and use production rules or possibility theory. In most cases, it will map the market into the computer and focus on approaches supportive of interactive computational finance.

Whatever the specific objectives may be, the purpose of financial models is to facilitate understanding, allow for experimentation and enhance prediction. At times, simplicity and clarity must be emphasized more than mathematical sophistication. In other cases, complexity is unavoidable given the nature of real world conditions.

All cases of experimentation and evaluation have organizational prerequisites. It is simply not enough to have only mathematical expertise, though this is also necessary. In Chapter 3, we saw a number of cases where policy and procedural issues were involved. This brought into the picture organizational perspectives.

PRACTICAL OBJECTIVES WITH FINANCIAL MODELS

The first essential rule in developing successful financial models is that we should aim for *accuracy* rather than precision. This is the first practical goal. Much more important than the 6th or 9th significant digit in a model's results is the accuracy of the first two or three orders of magnitude – because that is what gives the trend and the direction.

- Accuracy is obtainable if we get our priorities right, set our goals and use the best brains to be found in the company.
- This statement is valid for knowledge acquisition, knowledge representation and any other modeling goal.

The second basic principle is that financial modeling does not need to be done at any cost and certainly it should not be done at any level of triviality. If it is done at all, it must be done right – appropriately choosing both the domain and the method.

Provided they are developed in an effective manner, financial models can be seen as one of the great advances in the art of management. Their potential applications are significant, particularly in view of the rapid changes which are taking place in every aspect of modern business and the complexities to be tackled when economic and financial issues are involved.

Promoting the art of management is the second practical goal. One of the reasons why an increasing number of companies develop and apply financial models is the realization that we must provide our managers and professionals with the best possible tools. This statement, however, does not only concern the end product but also the development process. Subgoals connected to the end product are:

- Reducing the time required to react to change,
- Taking a longer, more careful look into the future,
- Evaluating alternatives with full knowledge of all pertinent factors,
- Calculating profits and risks prior to making commitments.

Rapid development and implementation is the third practical goal. As the sophistication of business increases, it is becoming necessary to accelerate model making activities to meet planned objectives. Hence the need for advanced technology offering management a means of coping with new and challenging problems,

- Providing a fast, reliable method for forecasting the financial performance of the company.
- Ensuring a platform which makes experimentation and optimization feasible under criteria defined in a flexible manner.
- Basing decisions on a documented set of anticipated conditions, rather than recapitulating the past.

An easy to follow example is provided in Figure 4.1. Market inputs point towards the need for new investments. These are translated into R&D for new products, production facilities, inventory build-up (or reduction), sales forecasts and after sales service. Administrative expenses should also be accounted for.

A model for income estimates will include a tax module and profit modules (before and after taxes). These essentially emulate mental computational procedures by the chief financial officer and other members of the board, by means of analogical reasoning.

- Even if we start with a simple construct, the possibility that the financial model can become more sophisticated should be present.
- The model should be designed in such a way that its equations can be expanded to provide any required degree of detail.

As we saw in Chapter 3, equipment necessary for the processing of financial models can range all the way from personal workstations to supercomputers, exceeding mainframe power by two orders of magnitude. Other critical support issues are networks to bring a steady stream of current data, large distributed databases with historical information, and online data feeds with current market data. The provision of adequate supports is another practical goal.

The point has as well been made that the best-tuned financial models are focused; hence, they have locality. They are designed in full consideration of the operating procedures and management information requirements of the particular institution to which they belong.

Therefore, financial models made for Bank *A* and Project *B* are not necessarily suitable for use by another institution whose conditions are different – not even by a different project within the same organization. By contrast, the development procedures and methodology underpinning the construction of artifacts may be more generally applicable.

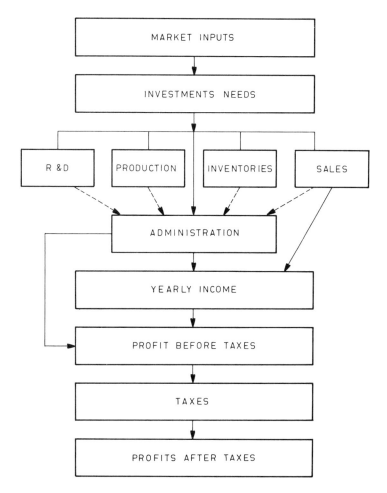

Figure 4.1 Forecasting the financial performance of the company

ORGANIZATIONAL ADVANTAGES OF HAVING A FINANCIAL MODEL

Once developed and fed with appropriate information, the right financial model can provide accurate projections – doing so rapidly and, depending on the equipment used, in a fairly inexpensive manner. Design should see to it that the artifact is comprehensible to its user because it follows a documented procedure, with experimentation assuring meaningful, action oriented results.

In an organizational sense, a basic reason for using models is to describe an operation, predict a likely outcome, and/or make feasible a comparison of alternatives. For all of these aims, as underlined in the Introduction, *accuracy* is crucial:

- Unlike the goal we follow with general accounting, in simulation we are much more interested in accuracy than in precision.
- It is the *order of magnitude* that we are after. This fits well with the objectives of management accounting.

An example from strategic planning helps to demonstrate that a financial model is particularly well suited to help in the determination of corporate goals, if it is accurate. The planning process basically consists of answering two questions:

- Where do we want to go? and
- How are we going to get there?

The first question concerns the goal, and has to be established by top management. Most of the effort in terms of modeling, to date, has been directed towards responding to the second question: having decided upon an objective, how is it to be achieved?

Tier 1 organizations have however found that the financial model could also help management with the first strategic question. It can do so by collecting pertinent information from each department of the company, then consolidating and massaging such information, therefore permitting them to focus on key issues.

- The sense of experimentation can be expressed in these simple, management oriented terms which are found in everyday practice.
- Managers and professionals need the financial model to make revised projections whenever a significant change occurs in anticipated events.

Experimentation through modeling permits us to concentrate on objectives and on resources, making feasible a documented answer to the query: Where does our company really want to go? Or even: What is the most likely outcome of a planned commitment?

Organizationally speaking, information introduced into the financial model must produce the same effect as if it applied to the real life situation. In accordance with this principle, a great deal of effort in the development of simulators is devoted to testing and modifying, assuring that the model will authentically emulate actual conditions.

In a wider sense than the enduser level, the benefits to the organization from a well-made financial model derive from *the industrialization of knowledge*. Once the computer-based solution is operational, very little manpower is required to obtain steady results. This:

- Encourages management to experiment, as well as to ask critical queries and get realtime responses, and
- Permits us to directly consider the effects of various interrelated actions whose outcome gets modified automatically during an evaluation.

Accuracy is conditioned by the detailed examination and understanding of all operations and accounting procedures, followed by their correct mapping into the simulator. The prerequisite analysis requires an implicit statement of assumptions which are reflected in the model. For instance:

- The available operating or policy alternatives, and
- Their impact in terms of revenues, expenses, and investments.

Such benefits, however, do not come to the organization as a matter of course. It is hard to make significant gains in performance without pain. As many companies have discovered, a cultural change which reaches all the way down to the fundamentals of how the daily business is being done is particularly important.

THE NEED FOR INTERACTIVE MODEL HANDLING

A financial model is for the enduser and it should be exploited interactively. This requires systems with communications links connecting any-to-any all the units of the company. Whether we talk of *concurrent engineering* or *concurrent banking*, this practice constitutes a major change to the classical approach where:

- Reports prepared in one area pass up and down through several management levels in a linear and detached manner, and
- The person preparing a report does not necessarily appreciate how his activity fits into the overall organization – or affects its user(s).

In contrast to this classical practice, a computer-based system emulating the whole enterprise or any one of its units permits both the retrieval of detailed data and the construction of consolidated statements capitalizing on embedded knowledge.

This simultaneous reference to *consolidation* and to *details* must be supported through a concurrent access to databases. One of the most basic organizational prerequisites to be fulfilled relates to the need for *interactively* handling the model in realtime.

The model's ability to predict is conditioned by the synergy it can establish with its user(s). Obtaining such synergy poses a number of conditions. One of the most basic is uninterrupted service based on dynamic interactivity between:

- The incoming datastream,
- The artifact itself, and
- The professional whom it assists.

That's why the batch handling of financial models is an aberration, even if some mainframers advise it as double. Those who give such advice are in total conflict of interest – whether they know it or not. Those who accept it condemn themselves to a protracted lack of competitiveness.

Next to prediction purposes, interactive model handling is necessary in budgeting and in cost control, as we will see in detail in Part Two. A realtime financial model enables the budget to be developed with proper recognition of the longer-run impact of short-term budgeting decisions.

- Since the simulator can operate on a multiyear basis, it is possible to estimate the effect of budgetary decreases or increases in one year as they may affect the level of operations in succeeding years.
- Interactivity makes it possible to constantly evaluate the short-term versus long-term consequences of different decisions, doing so in a cross-departmental sense.

Another financial model required for interactivity is the one focusing on the evaluation of information regarding ongoing transactions. For better control, this should be done not only when a period ends but also at any time during the operating timeframe – through ad hoc queries.

For instance, the user may elect to generate financial reports based on information in the database to be modeled according to his own set of rules. These reports may include the evaluation of:

- Trial Balance
- Income and Expense
- Revenue Trends
- Sales Forecasts or Quotas
- Actual Expenses versus Budget, and so on

Both the content and the level of detail to be followed by interactive reporting must be user-controlled. As Figure 4.2 indicates, text and data will typically come from a common database, but system design should permit maximum reporting flexibility with a minimum of user specifications.

The enduser should be in control of the interactive model handling and reporting procedures, including content, graphical presentation and actual positioning of report cycles. All this can nicely be achieved through a solution which presents the user with options and/or prompts him to select presentation procedures of his choice, through expert system supports.

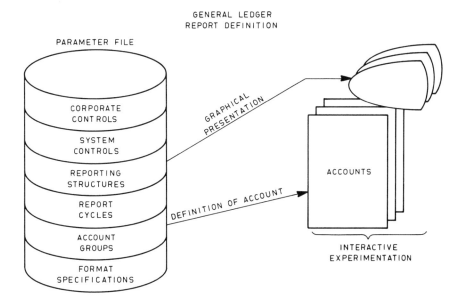

Figure 4.2 General ledger reporting in a flexible, interactive manner

This is a good example of how financial models can be made extremely valuable in comparing and in evaluating alternative courses of action that might be followed. By compiling the results of alternative plans, models provide information for determining realistic financial objectives and for controlling the outcome.

OBJECTIVES TO BE REACHED THROUGH CONCURRENT BANKING

Talking of strategic issues and organizational perspectives, the point was made that the first crucial question top management must answer is: 'Where do we want to go?' It has also been stated that financial models can be of assistance providing a sound basis for experimentation and the evaluation of alternatives, in answering this query.

Experimentation based on interactive financial models can lead to independent and/or interdependent estimates of net income, product profitability, fee structure, commitments in fixed and variable costs – permitting management to gauge how well current operations meet targets. For instance, in regard to:

- Market share,
- Growth potential,

- Profit and loss, and
- Cost control objectives.

Financial models are an efficient means for developing revised estimates of income and expenses when projected circumstances have changed or are expected to change. This helps to explain why financial models are sought after by companies which plan on a formal basis.

Examining the future is an integral part of the planning process. Strategic planners and financial executives want the advantages of speed, flexibility, and accuracy. Interactive experimentation provides many opportunities, for example in determining how closely operating plans meet management targets:

- Considering a base set of forecasts and their projected aftermaths,
- Examining several outlooks in terms of economic developments and financial performance,
- Determining their impact in both a detailed manner and an integrative sense.

These processes become relatively simple procedures once a valid framework has been established and enriched with models. Intelligent software can also compile and summarize the results of special studies conducted for a number of different purposes, providing the ground for experiments on improvement programs and associated investment requirements.

An example of these notions is given in Figure 4.3 which outlines a procedural approach permitting us to integrate into one computer-based, corporate planning model different sources of information which today are indispensable to top management decisions.

- The corporate planning model being proposed is seen as an interactive structure which covers all areas of activity.
- The concept underpinning this approach is that of concurrent banking – involving any product, in any location, at any time.

Seven inputs contribute to the corporate planning model of which the financial simulator is a vital part. The experimental process begins with introducing objectives, policies, forecasts, and other factors – every one of them contributing to the end results.

While this example focuses on the corporate level, other more detailed, operationally oriented models can serve each divisional manager in much the same way as the corporate model aids top management. A concurrent approach to planning, directing and controlling should again underpin this solution.

Divisional models will typically produce operating plans which are fed into a budget preparation program. The first approximation of this program may be a computer-based version of the formerly manual budgetary procedure (see also Chapter 5). The same is true of:

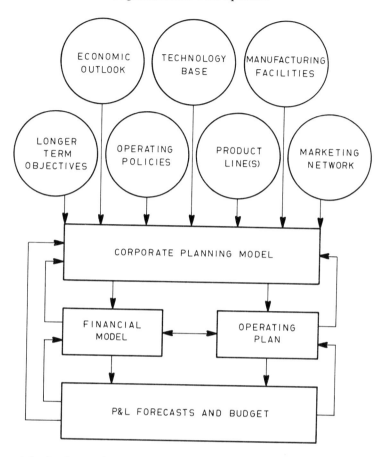

Figure 4.3 An integrative approach to financial modeling

- Profit and loss estimates, and
- The management of assets and liabilities.

Feedbacks can take place at many levels. For example, the budget program may extract information needed to prepare inputs for the corporate planning process, generalizing activity forecasts which it feeds into the financial model. Then comes the task of day-to-day allocations and reallocations, followed by the most important Plan versus Actual evaluation – to ensure that operations conform to plans.

PROVIDING THE APPROPRIATE TESTING PROCEDURES

While an increasing number of organizations are getting oriented towards the need of developing and using financial models, few companies have the experience to test the hypotheses which have been made as well as the artifact as a whole. Yet,

- Model testing is like the brakes in an automobile.
- Lack of testing (or of brakes) can be disastrous when things go downhill.

By *testing* for realism, consistency, omissions, and the achievement of functional objectives, the most important differences between real life and model-based results can be effectively analyzed. Some of the differences so defined may require a pruning of the simulator(s) in reference or the adjustment of one or more of its (their) components.

- Though testing any single component of a model is a necessary procedure, it is not in itself enough.
- Not only will different models be used concurrently, but they may also be combined among themselves in an ad hoc way.

Plenty of examples can be taken from concurrent engineering or concurrent banking to prove this point. The crucial issue is that of synergy. Synergy is, for example, very important in investigating sales objectives, resource requirements, costs and total impact. An interactive financial model can indicate the effect of a range of:

- Management policies,
- Investment allocations, and
- Operating programs.

For instance, when considering capital investments, institutions usually measure profitability as the rate of return or the present worth of the project. But this is only a partial approach as different departments, branch offices or other units also have their own criteria.

In many cases, each of these criteria yields a single number used to summarize the profitability over the life of a product or project – but the effect on annual financial performance is not indicated. By contrast, with a computer-based interactive financial model it is possible to add a new dimension to investment analysis – doing so through detailed cross-departmental *evaluations* and *tests*.

This leads to a different sense of the word 'testing', addressing not only the simulator itself but also its results. Many companies fail to appreciate that computer-based concurrent operations make this new dimension feasible and permit us to display the entire financial situation on an individual and on a consolidated basis. The result may, for instance, be a direct comparison of:

- Sales targets
- Product performance
- Profitability index
- Earnings per share (EPS)
- Return on equity (ROE)
- Risk by client, product and market.

By manipulating the critical variables affecting corporate performance, and by comparing them against milestones, we can highlight those areas where the planning and control effort should be concentrated.

We can experiment on the effect on net income of, say, a change in unit price or sales volume. This makes the financial simulator most valuable in profit planning and budgeting. A similar procedure helps to detect omissions, inconsistencies, or a lack of realism in the budget. (See also the presentation of models addressed to budgetary planning and control, in Part Two.)

As these references help document, the able use of mathematical models demands a systematic approach for specifying and collecting all required input information. The entire data collection process must be coordinated to:

- Avoid the misrepresentation of critical factors or essential information, and
- Prevent two departments from unknowingly assuming different values for the same variable.

Concurrent engineering and concurrent banking mean computer-based coordination providing the infrastructure necessary for the generation of critical reports which affect the whole manufacturing company or financial institution. This does away with water-tight departments and secretly kept accounts – and it benefits the organization all the way, from input to processing and output.

ESTABLISHING AN ACCEPTABLE ERROR LEVEL IN MANAGEMENT ACCOUNTING

A system solution valid for the 1990s should not only collect and store data but also process and present digested information, making available to senior management a polyvalent experimental tool. The mere collection of huge amounts of data is of little value if this information cannot be effectively analyzed, controlled, massaged and visualized in a comprehensible form.

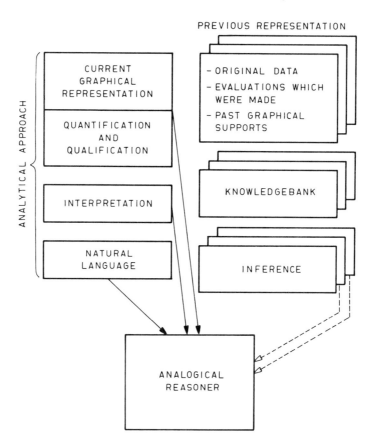

Figure 4.4   A graph analysis system using knowledge engineering

In every case, preference should be given to interactive visualization which can be assisted through a graph analysis system, as demonstrated in Figure 4.4. Its function should go beyond supporting current types of presentation (and hence what is already available) and include:

- Interpretation of multimedia information as well as natural language facilities and inference capabilities, and
- The ability to identify the level of confidence, from data streams to analogical reasoning.

Validated through rigorous testing procedures, modeling for senior management purposes should be able not only to present a one-tantum financial picture but also to produce online revised projections of net income, cash flow, balance sheet and off-balance sheet accounts (for the meaning of off-balance sheet financing, and the processes it involves, see Chapter 10) – doing so:

- In connection with queries which are both ad hoc and on a planned timeframe, and
- Through exception reporting and prompts, whenever significant changes occur in key variables.

Testing should not be rigid. The financial model must help to prepare budget guidelines which are consistent with the corporate objectives, integrating long-range planning studies, and ensuring that, when the *inputs* are correct, the output can be estimated within, say, 1 or 2 percent error for management accounting purposes.

Since accuracy rather than precision is important in management accounting, it is indeed curious that only a few, clear-eyed companies have established, and follow, the concept that a low error level can be acceptable:

- In order to close the month's books for a rapid report to management, the 'morning after' the 30th or 31st of the month, and not two months down the line as is the usual practice.
- To optimize budgetary allocations in a comprehensive manner, and provide for corrective action when it is still possible to reach results.

For instance, for management accounting reasons – but *not* for general accounting purposes – an acceptable error level may be the forementioned ± 1 percent from the true value. The true value and its precision are very important in general accounting but not in management accounting, where the crucial factors are:

- Order of magnitude, and
- Speed of presentation of the results.

This policy of an admissible error level is followed in other professions, for instance engineering. Engineering projects are calculated to admit a 4 percent or 5 percent error rate, yet produce valid results. That error rate is accurate enough for the projects to proceed.

There is also a philosophical side to this argument. Errors, Dr John von Neumann once said, are not that unwanted. They are the means which provide the feedback and therefore lead to corrective action. This fits well with the goals of management.

This notion of ± 1 percent can very nicely be used in a number of management accounting cases, including budgetary control. As the year progresses, more precise data will be collected and processed through a budget comparison program and an annual projection procedure.

- The budget comparison program calculates the variance between budgeted and actual results on a year-to-date and a current month basis.

This should be done very rapidly, not after months have gone by. Hence the wisdom of accepting a 1 or 2 percent error in exchange for realtime response.

- The annual projection procedure forecasts the anticipated value for each major account for the year, based on past relationships and possible variations.

An analysis of the results of these programs determines if the year is proceeding as planned. Another model should be available to handle deviations, indicating when revised inputs are necessary for each key factor or forecast.

The series of interrelated programs which have just been described constitutes a *technology-based* management accounting system. As it will be appreciated, this goes well beyond typical cases available today which simply concern procedures for collecting, storing, retrieving, and disseminating data with no or little regard to accuracy and to deadlines.

ENSURING ACCURACY AND QUALITY OF INPUTS

The message the previous section has conveyed is that, up to a point, compensating errors may be acceptable in the overall processing of management accounting information. This statement, however, is not valid for the *inputs* which should be both accurate and precise. Inputs may consist of such items as:

- Securities prices
- Product prices and volumes,
- Raw material costs,
- Labor costs,
- Capital investments,
- Subsidiary company incomes, or
- Discretionary expense items.

Rigorous methods for assuring the accuracy and precision of inputs are more important when there is the possibility that gross errors may exist in the data being collected. Many situations require a steady assessment of *data quality* well beyond the possibility of transcription errors.

One of the evaluations which has to be done concerns the appropriateness of the data for their use in the modeling effort – and its counterpart, the fit of the model to the data. It is most important to know:

- Where things can go terribly wrong and affect the results an evaluation or experimentation provides, and
- If and where we can get more information about a given piece of data to strengthen our estimate of accuracy.

To do this job in an effective manner, the financial analyst needs a set of tools which helps in understanding the nuts and bolts of data collection. A large batch of numbers is not necessarily helpful. It has to be *filtered*, then processed to produce estimates of deviations and *visualization* aids such as graphs, charts, patterns and other diagrams.

To exemplify the concept of market data filtering, Figure 4.5 presents a bird's eye view of the steps which it involves. These include the proper definition of the information source, followed by the establishment of enduser profiles, and leading to the structure of the data filter itself. An effective execution of this job requires that:

- The support services are properly detailed,
- Powerful filtering tools are made available, and
- Interactive query capabilities are guaranteed for all users.

Since the accuracy of inputs is so vital, we should never underemphasize the procedures necessary for data quality assessment, and focus only on the mathematics of modeling. If modeling is inseparable from data analysis, data collection is also indivisible from the overall modeling effort.

It is a sound policy to examine closely the data sources and their output in order to locate anomalies and/or atypical measurements which often exist. Data validation should take a systematic approach:

- First establishing the definition of the necessary data.
- Then identifying sources, timing, rates, and possible errors.
- Finally, proceeding with quality assessment of the obtained data volumes and their pertinence to the goal(s).

When this is appropriately done, various types of incompatibilities may be discovered. Some are straightforward, easily found and rather simple to correct. Others are more subtle, such as the discovery of the source of small biases in certain derived quantitative estimates – which itself requires exploratory data analysis as well as considerable work regarding data collection methods.

A rather expensive, in-depth analysis of data quality and of the properties of the information sources is often indispensable. Sometimes recommendations regarding the use of a particular time series have to be made. In other cases it may be concluded that:

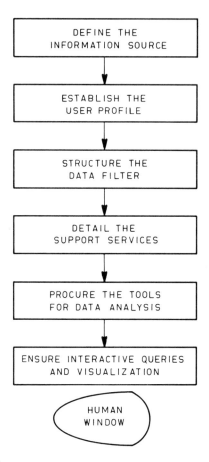

Figure 4.5   Basic steps in market data filtering

- There is insufficient data available to model the process, or
- The time series features too much noise to permit an efficient modeling process.

In conclusion, model development and the identification of *data sources* should go hand-in-hand, as the one can greatly influence the other. In the process of modeling, data stream should be regarded as essential and the appropriate methodology should be adopted to assure input accuracy.

Residual analysis, for instance, can often lead to a better model fit since patterns found in the residuals can be included in the model specification. Data smoothing is often used in residual analysis since it helps to spot patterns more quickly, as the following section documents.

THE CONCEPTS OF DATA SMOOTHING AND DATA FILTERING

Data quality is a basic organizational requirement, and it can be served through filtering procedures. The concept of *data smoothing* is derived from the fact that a time series can usually be thought of as having two components. The one is *smooth* or nearly so; the other is *rough*. Both require attention.

* The smooth part of a time series often represents the underlying *structural pattern*, or curvature of the data.
* The rough is the *residual*, anything which is not in the smooth part of the data streams, and usually is characterized by noise (noise is any unwanted input).

Through various numerical techniques we try to distinguish the smooth and rough parts of a data stream. We are interested in separating smooth from rough data, as we know that a smooth curve often gives a better idea of how life really looks without random noise – and there are also available mathematical equations to represent it.

One of the background reasons for manipulating time series in this manner lies in the fact that a statistical model is more robust when it is less sensitive to extreme points. Hence, there is true interest in looking more directly at smooth data, getting it into a form more convenient for analysis.

Establishing the consistency and reliability of data sources, as well as the error-free characteristic of the data stream, is a necessary procedure but it is not enough. In the drive to diversify the data sources, we often end with a glut of information which must be filtered in accordance with the specifications of the job to be done. That much was said in preceding sections when we spoke of the need to ensure data quality.

Contrary to the criteria used for data source dependability which are more general in character, screening must be tailored to the job. Hence, it requires an intimate knowledge of the process under study.

* One application's filter may not be that useful in the context of another job.
* Customization is reflected in Figure 4.5, which focused on the methodology of how to proceed with market data filtering.

Say, for instance, that we wish to map the foreign exchange market into the computer and that we should address the issue of appropriate page selection for currency rates. One of the first tasks is selecting the service vendor (information provider), after examining what he has to offer in terms of forex pages.

Then comes the problem of *value differentiation*. Foreign currency data can be used by traders in native form, but competitive advantages require that decision support packages (and hence, models) aid in trading currencies. An example on raw data is given by:

• Reuters' WRLD page.

This widely used and frequently updated WRLD page lists spot prices for foreign currencies in different markets. It is timestamped in a HHMM format which represents the time the data was reported to Reuters (Eastern Standard Time).

The WRLD page contains a code for the reporting organization and a *high* and *low* price for the market currently open. In a number of applications, the WRLD page data to be selected follows the pattern:

• Time (HHMM)
• Currency code
• Market (location) code
• Currency spot rate (bid–ask).

Updates are processed by appending new currency, market and time–price records to the database. Typically, timestamp–price data pairs are overwritten if a capacity limit defined by the market data filter is exceeded. The time–price file will include the market code, currency code, as well as associated price and timestamp pairs.

All this is fine except that the facility described is available to every subscriber. What will value-differentiate one organization from another is the models it will internally develop to manage the seamless cross-database access it will provide to itself.

A sound database organization sees to it that all incoming pages are stored in the market database. The selection of data from this database is done interactively through the user interface allowing for operations such as:

• Select all markets
• Select all currencies
• Select a market and a currency
• Select a date/time range given a market
• Select a date/time range given a currency,
• Evaluate date/time–price, and so on.

Once the model has been established, we can address possible problems connected with data sourcing. For instance adding other information providers to Reuters, such as: Telerate, Quotron, Telekurs and filtering all information as to maxima and minima. Filtering may be done, for instance, with the objective of establishing the widest reported range for the same date/time stamp or, more likely of establishing a window of trading opportunity.

These are but a few examples of goals to be reached by means of market data filtering. As incoming information has become a torrent, the emphasis has shifted from *data feed* to *data filters*. But apart from the necessary algorithms and heuristics, a good data filter requires high performance computing in order to be successfully done at subsecond speed – that is, without becoming a bottleneck.

HOW CAN WE FILTER THE INFORMATION WE RECEIVE?

One of the implications of the data filtering references made in the previous section is that model designers need to merge their requirements for data streams with the facilities supported by information providers, as well as the accesses to distributed databases. As we will also see in Chapter 15, interactive reporting plays a growing role in the financial industry, impacting on profitability through the nature of information which it provides.

The information elements we receive from clients, suppliers and other companies need to be filtered in a careful manner. Only vital data applicable to our job (past, present and future) should be retained for management reporting reasons. This can be nicely accomplished through an expert system which embeds the filtering rules.

Figure 4.6 presents the block diagram of an expert system built for filtering purposes. The application concerns investments in securities and, as the flowchart shows, the first filter works on two criteria:

- Markets, and
- Currencies

It does so for all references to securities which are of interest to the user organization. Since the realtime input is employed for operational reasons, timestamping has been added to the filtering chores. Filtering is a service which must be *personalized*.

- Only the enduser knows in detail his requirements, and
- These are dynamically changing.

Furthermore, the enduser accesses many databases, often ad hoc, and he also receives an input from a number of sources who are selling general-type services in large numbers. This means that there is a large variety of characteristics which need selection and homogenization.

The customization of data filters has become possible thanks to knowledge engineering. The use of expert systems capitalizes on widespread usage of personal computers. Today more than 75 percent of Dun and Bradstreet's credit reports are sent via PCs, fax, or voice mail. Subscription to Dun and

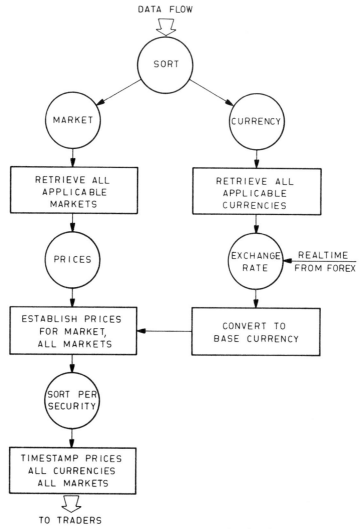

Figure 4.6 Block diagram of an expert system for filtering purposes

Bradstreet, which alone has over 100 credit products, will be more valuable if it is focused:

- If the user can screen and correlate the information which he receives, and
- If he can do so without devoting a significant portion of his time to such a job.

The basic Dun and Bradstreet report is an accounting of a company's business, its recent financial activities, its number of employees, and its dealings with other companies. There is plenty of work to be done in grinding this data. In fact, some massaging has already been done as Dun's Financial Profiles compare a company's balance sheet with others in the same industry.

This is the type of information to be fed into a financial model able to generate, for example, factual and documented comparisons between two crucial variables. The same can be said about internal accounting data. In the better organized companies, such

- Internal accounting information is subjected to a great deal of analytical treatment,
- This is instrumental in providing management with meaningful results.

Since the filtering of both internal and external information needs to be *personalized*, and there are a number of managers and professionals who would like the personalization to be done according to *their own* criteria, it is wise to store data in raw form – as it comes. Subsequently, it will be *interactively*:

- Screened,
- Processed, and
- Visualized.

Ideally, this must be executed on a person-by-person basis, as the need arises. This is the sense of an ad hoc, realtime assistance to enduser requirements which naive languages, like SQL, cannot support – and mainframes cannot manage to do at an affordable cost.

In conclusion, there is need for added value to the data input and to the databased information, by means of custom-made knowledge-enriched *filters*. This reference is written in the dual sense of:

1. *Screening* and retaining only the information which is pertinent to specific applications on a user-per-user basis, and
2. *Filtering* proper for smoothing reasons, where, for instance, minor fluctuations are mostly ignored as noise, or other criteria are employed.

Both references are important in applications such as *pattern recognition*, where we aim to detect and identify a limited number of patterns such as: up and down trends, support and resistance levels, peaks, troughs, heads and shoulders, anomalies and crashes. Or we target fewer but more complex patterns where only the truly essential information elements should be reflected.

USING THE INPUT FOR INTERNAL AND EXTERNAL EVALUATION

In a manner fairly similar to the filtering example on market data, the inputs for a planning and budgeting system can be used for evaluating how well the model fits the real world. We can capitalize on the fact that the model makes a projection based on certain assumptions which must be properly sorted out and examined in terms of fitness.

Inputs and outputs have values which may include a wide range of data from operating expenses to investments; but still fit within certain specifications. Some of these inputs, for example general economic conditions, represent constraints. Others, like tax rates in a multinational model, can be optimized.

If the finance model is built, say, for an oil company, then mineral depletion and other allowances are subject to optimization. By contrast, the permitted levels of crude oil production set by state regulatory agencies constitute a restriction.

- Inputs will provide values reflecting on allowances and restrictions.
- The model must see to it that individual decisions are taken within established constraints.

Because of this interplay between inputs and the mechanics of the simulator, any financial model should be subjected to two types of evaluations. One is internal, the other external.

An *internal* evaluation will typically consist of an assessment of how well the analytical reasoning mechanism which was chosen does its work. How well does the data fit the goals? Which advantages and disadvantages does the model/data synergy present? Many issues can serve to define the model's fitness.

An *external* evaluation triggered by the input will help to compare different inputs among themselves. The range of inputs, for example, may be extended to include an assessment of characteristics such as:

- Coverage,
- Detail,
- Timestamp,
- Minima and maxima.

The definition of proper input characteristics is always crucial. Inputs specified for income statements will indicate revenues, operating expenses, non-cash charges, foreign and home country taxes, net income after tax for parent firm and each of the subsidiary companies. The capital investment schedule will show capital expenditures made and to be made by each department.

Based on these inputs and the schedules to which they correspond, models will try to equilibrate cash flow in terms of source and use of funds. This is an important implementation field:

- Sources of cash consist of net income, recovery of capital, deferred taxes, borrowings, and reduction in working capital.
- Uses of cash entail funds required for capital expenditures, cash dividends, repayment of prior borrowing, or increases in working capital.

Based on the statement of earnings employed and stockholders' equity, a simple model can help to indicate the change in number of shares outstanding, stock, and the effect on cash flow of dividends payments. Other simple models will calculate earnings per share, return on equity, return on assets and capitalization for given market value, as we will see in Chapters 13 and 14, when we talk of ratio analysis. A tax model will:

- Detail the adjustments required to reconcile book income with taxable income, and
- Present special deductions, specific taxes, investment credit, and tax to be accrued.

The rate of return analysis will show return on both gross and net operating investment, and provide an evaluation in terms of profit margin and asset turnover. The financial and operating summary will highlight financial items such as net income, total assets, long-term debt, return on stockholders' equity, and return on total assets employed.

Part Three will outline how models can help in preparing balance sheets and why this requires that working capital is modeled in detail. The goal is to provide management with a comprehensive view of the company's operations.

All these references underline the overriding influence of organizational issues on input and output. Good ideas introduced by leading-edge firms should be studied and implemented quickly. Yet, in spite of the benefits this can provide, organizational issues are rarely looked at in this manner, especially if they require hard work and the cutting of red tape. Let's never forget that drive and determination are important factors in business success.

Part Two

Models for Budgeting and Budgetary Control

5 Financial Planning and Budgeting Procedures

INTRODUCTION

A budget is a formal written statement of management's plans for the future, expressed in quantitative terms. The financial allocations the budget makes, and the statistics being derived from them, chart the course of future action − provided the budget contains sound, attainable objectives rather than mere wishful thinking.

- The budget is a *planning model* and the means used for its development are planning instruments.
- These instruments work well when the company has the proper methodology and solid cost data.

The reason why a great deal of attention must be paid to costs is that the whole process of financial planning is based on them. Costing makes the budget an orderly presentation of projected activity for the next financial year, based on the amount of work to be done. Typically, the budget divides into four main chapters.

- Research and development
- Production schedules
- Marketing and sales
- Administrative activities.

Multiplied by the corresponding costs, each of these income and expense areas conditions the level of budgetary allocation in direct and indirect expenses. The budget also includes other chapters, such as capital investments.

The process of financial planning contributes directly to effective management, more than any other instrument. Each of the company's primary functions is directly served by budgeting − if and when careful study, investigation, and research have been undertaken in order to determine expected future operations and associated costs. Therefore a budget should contain sound, attainable goals.

The planning premises entering a budgetary process increase management's ability to rely on fact finding, lessening the role of hunches and intuition in running the enterprise. Because, as we will see in this chapter, the budget is quantitatively expressed, it makes possible effective management control, targeted through budgetary analysis and Plan versus Actual comparisons.

THE BUDGET AS A PLANNING MODEL

Organization-wide coordination through budgetary procedures is facilitated when each level of management participates in the preparation of the budget. Top management should be setting and explaining objectives, but each organizational level must establish its budget under these guidelines – subject to subsequent approval.

Modeling is important, but there also exist other prerequisites. One of the crucial issues with budgeting is the input of information to the database, necessary to permit realistic financial plans. The accuracy of both *unit costs* and *activity projections* must be fully appreciated. This input can come:

1. *Top down* from senior management to the divisions, departments, operating units and back to top management, or
2. *Bottom up*, elaborated at operating unit level, from there send to the department, the division and to top management where it gets approved and consolidated.

Alternative 2 is far preferable since it leads to a financial plan which has the salt of the earth. It starts close to the lower management level where the budget will have to be subsequently applied, and therefore it motivates the people who will later on have to work with that budget.

The problem is the amount of time required to prepare it. This amount of time can be long and the task may not be well coordinated unless it is executed interactively online through:

- Models, and
- Computers.

Various options have been provided to facilitate the budget input task, thereby enabling a manager to concentrate his efforts on those of his accounts that do warrant careful analysis. Short-cut methods include:

- An annual, quarterly and monthly amount to be prorated according to the actual number of days in each period.

The aim is to have projected amounts created automatically by the system, using forecasting techniques and standard costs.

- A percentage increase or decrease over the current year's actual and projected data to temper system-generated business forecasts.

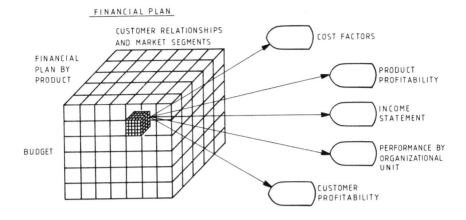

Figure 5.1 Profit and loss analysis in function of budgetary allocations

Such entries may be coarse and will need to be subsequently refined, but as they stand they do constitute starting points.

- Combination entries, with distributions resting on algorithms, wherever marked variations or seasonal fluctuations exist.

The models used to produce this information are typically run by computer. They work interactively and provide results in realtime. They also help to control Plan versus Actual results.

Computer models can be instrumental in the preparation of financial plans all the way to subsequent analysis for control reasons. Figure 5.1 presents the case of a profit and loss evaluation based on information derived from the financial plan and operating statistics – producing ad hoc interactive reports from cost factors to customer profitability.

As a result of this budgetary process, the activities of each department are integrated with those of related departments in the same area, nationwide and internationally. But as the Introduction has underlined, though managerial planning and coordination are important, they must be accompanied by control.

- Budgeting contributes to effective management control by providing the standard against which actual performance will be evaluated and variances revealed.
- This needs to be done both for each operating unit and for the company as a whole – and hence in both a detailed and a consolidated way.

The examples which we have seen help document that as financial plans budgets can significantly benefit from models and computers. They are quantitative, permit us to learn from past experiences, can be made flexible therefore adjustable to changing conditions, and help to gain management's confidence when they are well done.

THE INTEGRATION OF FINANCIAL INFORMATION AND ITS ANALYSIS

In terms of financial information, no divisional accounting system is an island. To function properly, all units and their budgets have to work in synergy. The model which we develop should pay due attention to this fact. For instance, the purchase order subsystem works in conjunction with the inventory management, production planning and accounts payable subsystems.

An integrative view of accounts is necessary, starting at the system design level. The budgetary methodology which we establish must be mapped through software into computers in a way which ensures that the different financial subsystems interact and relate among themselves.

- A flexible but integrated budgetary application is of critical importance to the profits and competitiveness of the company.
- The solution we adopt must be able to smoothly transfer the most up-to-date information from module to module, to the enduser.

Provided we have properly elaborated the model which we employ, budgeting helps to establish a series of relationships between activities across the enterprise. In a financial planning sense, the actual relationships or linkages between individual elements determine the structure of the model. Approaches to budgeting tend to share two basic characteristics:

- A definition or statement of which elements connect to one another, and
- An explanation of the manner in which the elements comprising the model are related.

Not all budgeting solutions are the same. Differences exist particularly in the flexibility with which budget updates and modifications can be made, as well as the accuracy characterizing the financial plans. With greater flexibility, it is possible to customize budgetary information by linking together a series of selected accounts in an ad hoc manner. This can be done for a:

- Specific enduser,
- Profit center or cost center, or
- Locality of operations.

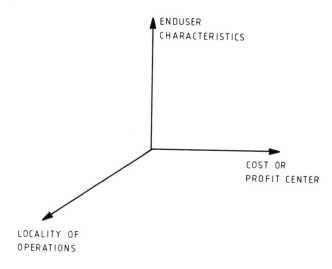

Figure 5.2 A frame of reference is very helpful both for financial planning and for control

Figure 5.2 suggests that a frame of reference can be followed for the analysis of financial data which maps itself into the space defined by these three key factors. Both the development of the financial plan and its evaluation should be done interactively online, preferably using color and 3-dimensional graphics for visualization.

This approach to online analysis procedures is no different than the one advised on p. 90 in connection with the preparation of budgets. Computer programs help in tearing apart the annual, monthly or other financial plans, line item by line item. They also assist in the parallel maintenance of different budgeting versions providing online services for simulation.

- Recorded in cash-flow accounting, the actual financial budget transactions can be used as a basis for Plan versus Actual comparison.
- Critical evaluations can be made along the line of profitability, cost overruns and other budgetary evaluation criteria.

The outcome of analytical procedures enables us not only to control current expenditures but also to prepare more accurately the new budget which can be checked through *variance analysis*. This leads to the issue of both algorithmic and heuristic support for budgets as well as that of the flexible procedural solutions to be adopted.

INTEREST BUDGET AND NONINTEREST BUDGET

We consider here an example from banking; pp. 98–9 presents an example from manufacturing.

Examined in a macroscopic sense, procedural solutions help to establish the major categories in budgeting. Every industry, and within the same industrial sector every organization, has budgetary procedures of its own. No two approaches are exactly the same, though during the last fifteen years the use of commodity software for financial planning has introduced a kind of common denominator.

In the financial industry, for instance, a major distinction is made between the *interest* and the *noninterest* budget. They share expenditures at the approximate ratio of 2:1; about 66 percent of a bank's annual expenses go to the interest budget and 34 percent to the noninterest budget. These are two clearly different classes of items, each requiring an appropriate model of its own.

- The interest budget covers the money paid to depositors, other banks (bought money), the national bank and other sources – that is, the *cost of money.*
- The noninterest budget addresses *all other expenditures.* This is the closest to the budgetary notion which prevails in the manufacturing industry.

For instance, in a financial institution significant noninterest expenses are salaries and wage benefits, investments in high technology (communications, computers, software), real estate and occupancy costs, utilities, and so on.

There is no standardization regarding the items which come under interest and noninterest expenses, but from one to another financial institution there are no major differences either. In terminology, the differences are rather trivial. Some banks use Net Interest Income. Others favor Net Interest Revenue, or Net Interest Earned.

Some banks use the term Net Interest Margin; others prefer Net Interest Spread; Net Margin; Interest Differential, or Effective Interest Differential. Nor are there standards about the monitoring of net interest margins and other variables.

- In the banking industry, the typical margin reports are for periods covering six months to a year.
- But leading financial institutions suggest that waiting so long for the evaluation of such vital information does not show quality of management.

This explains the attention paid in the implementation of fully online interactive information systems whereby net interest margin can be steadily monitored. That type of information, as well as all other budgetary issues should be interactively available through networked workstations, enabling management to quickly make decisions.

In managing the exposure which the bank is taking in the side of the interest budget, the executives and professionals of the financial institution should *at any time* be in a position to reach online into databases in order to:

- Critically evaluate conditions of imbalance, and
- Judge the volatility in interest spreads.

Provided the database is properly designed and available online, expert systems can be used in an effective manner to help the management of the bank in its mission to control margin imbalance and volatility. Knowledge engineering artifacts can focus the executive's attention:

- On deviations from standards (and/or trends), and
- The reasons for such deviations.

Interactively available on request, analytical reports should rapidly pinpoint change as well as exceptions. In this way, management can act while there is still time to favorably affect the profit and loss statement. This is true both of the interest and of the noninterest budgets, as well as of any commitment the bank has made.

DETAILED PROCEDURES FOR THE ELABORATION OF BUDGETS

The establishment of detailed procedures should account for the fact that a budget is a *short-term* financial plan, typically applicable to one year, a rolling year (eighteen months) or two years. Outlays and schedules advanced by the budget have definite functions and meaning for the purpose of planning and controlling expenditures.

What is presented by a budget is a formal plan of all the operations of the business for a defined future period. Although some of the aspects of preparing and stating the plan's details vary from one company to another, the overall process can be described simply as:

- A forecast of all the transactions that are expected, as well as their costs, and
- An estimate of all fixed costs and overheads, after having cut out the fat.

Well-managed organizations appreciate that the proper preparation of a projected financial statement is made in an iterative way. Subsequent to an initial tentative schedule, the different entries are evaluated, altered if necessary and accepted as the financial plan of the work to be done in a specific time period.

In banking, for example, this statement is just as valid of the interest budget as it is of the noninterest budget. In fact, both of them share some major issues in regard to the forthcoming transactions. For instance,

1. Net Interest Margin
2. Total Earning Assets
3. Loan Portfolio
4. Investment Portfolio
5. Other Assets.

The interest budget will be particularly affected by the cost of funds and their origins: NOW, Super NOW and other deposit accounts; savings and time deposits; money market funds and funds purchased from other sources including the reserve bank.

Because interest rates fluctuate, the cost of funds varies so significantly that no deterministic standards procedure can be followed. By contrast, a very good tool is *fuzzy engineering* which permits us to handle the vagueness and uncertainty of interest rates in an effective manner.

- The solution to be adopted should see to it that interactive screens present both summary and detailed information on each component of earning assets, nonearning assets, liabilities and other categories.
- If a 24-hour update policy is adopted, then enriched with expert systems support the computer should show rates for the current day, week, month and year-to-date compared with the same period last year.

Changes in margin from the previous period must not only be included but also explained. This is a good example of Plan versus Actual evaluation in a financial environment which includes significant uncertainties.

A similar statement can be made about marginal interest spread; including recording of the rates for the major groupings that are used in determining net interest margin. This information allows management to quickly monitor changes, subsequently taking corrective action.

The message these paragraphs convey is that the budgetary process is not a one-way street just piling up expense after expense and asking for its funding. By contrast, it is a two-way *creative process* which can be only then executed when there is a total view of both:

- Planning premises, and
- Control procedures.

A comprehensive solution to budgeting means a valid approach to plan-

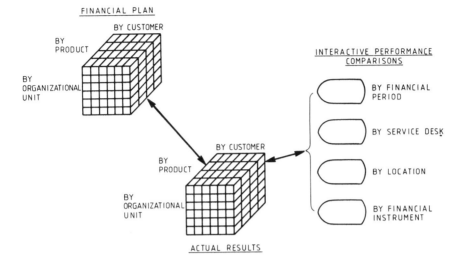

Figure 5.3 The elaboration of budgets and analytical studies have many issues in common

ning and control in a distributed, complex business environment. Hence the need for detail. A sound way to look at requirements is to examine them in a multidimensional way by:

- Organizational unit
- Product or service
- Customer relationship.

Monthly, quarterly, yearly, multiyear, and variable intervals must be examined, aligning the plan with the way actual results are reported (and vice versa). Wisely set procedures will be focusing on *value creation*, not on mechanics.

- As Figure 5.3 suggests, the elaboration of budgets and the making of analytical studies have many issues in common.
- The aim is to provide factual and documented evidence on the transition which has taken place from the financial plan to actual results – by customer, product and by organizational unit.
- Their synergy permits us to streamline the planning process, improve the credibility of the financial procedures and help to reduce costs.

Whether for planning purposes or for management control reasons, the online interactive presentation of budget information should be *future oriented*. The knowledge artifacts developed to fit this purpose should include a learning component which, based on states and values from past experience, can evaluate the outcome of financial allocation and therefore foretell coming events.

A SHORT-TERM BUDGET FOR SALES AND PRODUCTION

In a manufacturing organization, the purpose of the short-term budget is to integrate the forecasts of total sales by product and by marketing territory; estimate the effect of economic conditions on the cost of materials, labor and overhead; and determine the best measures to guarantee satisfactory net results. By indicating financial and market developments, the budget permits us to:

- Elaborate an organization-wide cost distribution,
- Show how variances in sales and costs influence net results,
- Study the impact on the general economic situation,
- Help to control expenses which cannot be easily regulated, and
- Set targets for all persons working in the company, in any capacity.

The goal is to provide management with an overall control of activities. In drawing up a master budget, the majority of companies find that the best procedure is to start with separate budgets for purchasing, production, distribution, and overhead, finally reaching results which reflect on profit and loss.

Taking as a background reference the sales budget, production budget, purchasing budget, overhead, and profit and loss from business and industry, the following is a brief description of what each involves.

Sales Budget

The best way is to budget the quantity and not the value of the goods to be sold in view of the effect of possible price fluctuations. Projected sales figures should be calculated by single product and for groups of products; also by territory in which the company operates.

Grouping should be based on similarities in *product description* and *selling channel*, and can vary according to the firm's line of business. One overriding factor in budgeting the sales quantity is to be very detailed as well as objective, based on sales forecasts validated through appropriate studies.

Production Budget

Classically, production costs are made up of the outlay spent on materials, labor and overhead. The materials estimate can be obtained by taking the quantity already decided upon when drawing up production schedules, and transforming it into costs by using standard cost figures.

A similar consideration is valid regarding the budget for manpower, multiplying projected time by standard wage rates to produce the direct labor costs. Efficiency studies should steadily strive to keep labor costs to a minimum.

The production budget should use standard costs and production figures commensurate with the sales forecast, plus or minus wanted inventory changes. The need for new facilities, if necessary, will be reflected in the semi-variable or fixed costs, depending on the case.

Purchasing Budget

The purchasing budget is based on the quantity necessary for production plus a small allowance for losses, scrap, substandard goods, and so on. Estimates should take into consideration the stocks of raw materials expected at the beginning of the period and at the end of it, using mathematical models to minimize investments in inventories.

Overheads

Overheads should be determined with the aid of the rule that administrative costs must rise much slower than production and be absorbed by the cost center to which they belong. Each department must prepare a budget of the nonrecoverable expenses which it will incur in the form of costs connected to trivia and administration.

Profit and Loss

On the basis of the above mentioned budgetary calculations, a profit and loss forecast can be prepared and submitted for senior management's approval. The statement should be composed according to the equations:

$$\text{Gross Margin} = \text{Net sales} - \text{Cost of goods sold} \tag{1}$$

$$\text{Net Result} = \text{Gross margin} - \text{Nonrecoverable expenses} \\ - \text{Administrative expenses} \tag{2}$$

Net Sales represents the revenue expected on sales. That is the gross sales amount minus all discounts and price reductions. *Cost of goods sold* is based on current standard costs and takes into account all the expected variances in the costs of materials, labor and overhead, but not variances due to capacity losses, or what is termed nonrecoverable expenses. The latter, as well as the administrative expenses, are subtracted from gross margin.

CASH FORECASTS AND CASH OUTLAYS*

The preparation of a budget is based upon the notion that the transactions which will be executed within its context represent the company's way of doing business. Financial transactions and business performance are inter-related.

- *If* some part of the financial plan can be taken as a starting point,
- *Then*, the rest of it may be established with fair degree of certainty.

This allows a better documentation for managerial decisions regarding issues involved in the allocation of funds. It also makes feasible a factual level of experimentation in regard to a number of queries which invariably arise with all issues connected with financial allocation. For instance:

- What will be the outcome of a deliberate action taken by management to open (or close) a new sales office? or a factory?
- What change in the company's management efforts may give an increase in the diversity of products?
- What if funds are immediately reinvested, thus reducing cash availability?

Spreadsheets have been used since the early 1980s in providing an inter-active means for answering *What-if* queries. The challenge now is to include more computer intelligence. This has to be done in a focused manner which can best be explained by return to the fundamentals.

The first major contribution of a budget is that it requires making financial forecasts for the organization as a whole, as well as for each of its departments, factories, sales offices, foreign operations and so on. These are expressed through means which can greatly be assisted by knowledge artifacts.

1. *The cash budget* forecasts direct and indirect cost outlays, balancing them against receipts or other sources of funds.

Before the estimated income statement and the future balance sheet can be prepared, account must be taken of the effects of operations upon the cash position of the organization. This is necessary for two reasons:

- The timing of cash receipts and disbursements will have an important bearing on the amounts of receivables and payables in the projected balance sheet.
- The amounts of money needed to execute transactions, and for financing costs, must be determined if the estimated income account is to be complete.

---

* See also Chapter 11 on cash flow and its management.

The cash budget is usually prepared by first noting the effects on the cash position of operating expenses and costs. Coupled with data from the capital expenditures budget, it will indicate the disbursements for the budgeted period.

2. The *capital outlays budget* defines the investments the organization plans to make during the coming financial period.

It is possible to forecast such disbursements by estimating projected investments as well as accrued direct and indirect costs at the end of each month of the budgeted period.

In the general case, it is expected that only slight differences will exist between the budgetary estimates (at the end of the various months) and the different disbursements. If only minor differences exist between the successive accruals, disbursements will tend to equal the budgeted labor, materials, and other costs.

The need for cash forecasts and cash outlays is one of the key references which help document that the process of budget preparation entails the making of many analytical decisions with respect to the relationships and the functions which should be maintained in the operations of any company – whether a financial institution or a manufacturing firm.

- This is as true of direct costs as it is of overhead and of investments – the principle being that only productive items should be budgeted.
- Therefore, budget preparation and administration must steadily maintain accounting and statistical records – to evaluate profitability post-mortem.

Followed by leading-edge organizations, this procedure is critical to the establishment of a system of internal controls, enriched with financial analyses which highlight *high performers* and *low performers*.

In conclusion, if the financial plans and the accounting system have both been established on sound principles, the budget estimates and the account classifications will provide a sound basis for evaluation. For each department, section and project, there should be available:

- Projected budget figures,
- Authorizations to spend money, and
- Actual results for the given period.

These three sets of figures can form the basis of comparative analysis in *performance reporting*, all the way from cash estimates to expenses. Budgetary authorization does not mean the automatic right to spend money. Therefore, comparisons have to be made at both regular and ad .hoc intervals: Clearly stated policies serving this purpose are required.

THE MASTER BUDGET AND FINANCIAL RESPONSIBILITY

One of the basic policies regarding budgetary practice is connected with the unification process which should bring together the different departmental budgetary estimates. It has already been stated that no divisional accounting system is an island. Therefore, there must be a *master budget* which:

- Summarizes all estimates for all departments,
- Portrays the anticipated result of all forecasts,
- Leads to a projected profit and loss statement, and
- Establishes a balance sheet which will result from the fulfillment of those estimates.

This master budget will be transmitted to the financial department and from there to the senior executives who constitute the budget committee, for their consideration. The budget committee may approve the estimates as made, or *optimize* expenditures in connection to expected results.

Let us however repeat the principle that a budget is no authorization to spend money. As a financial plan it provides *guidelines*, but money-spending has to be authorized by specific management decisions.

- In direct labor and direct material, this comes as a result of the production processes whose output is controllable.
- In capital expenditures, specific management actions are required which abide by a set of by-laws.

For instance, by-laws specifying how procurement should be made. Any procurement must be subject to written competition between suppliers in response to a request for information and request for offers.

From initial financial planning estimates to consolidation into a master budget, the processes which come into play involve *management's responsibility*. From lower level to higher level management, personal accountability has to be engaged, as already noted in preceding sections.

It is also a matter of managerial responsibility that budgetary estimates are completed at the time desired and in proper fashion. Also, that they adhere to proper financial principles. Key among the latter are the terms characterizing *cost/effectiveness*. Attention should be paid to the fact that many costs tend to get out of control, as they accrue continuously and have to be settled by cash payments.

- It is a rare case where bureaucracy and its out-of-control expenditures are deliberately planned.
- Typically, bureaucratic costs grow up and, if they are not curtailed, they run out of control.

Not only do expenditures for sundries and administrative items have to be tightly controlled, but forecasting disbursements on account of production costs and distribution costs must also be done very carefully. A good policy is separating all items in the operating schedules into classes to increase their visibility – particularly those which:

- Require recurring cash payments, and
- Will recur from month to month, or day to day.

The managerial responsibility involved in the preparation of budgets requires not only estimates of expenditures but also fairly accurate cash forecasts. As noted, cash forecasts are more difficult than projections on expenditures particularly for some classes of items.

All these reasons demand that even if a budget is prepared with the greatest amount of care it should be subject to critical financial analysis, both at the approval stage and post-mortem. One element all rigorous evaluations have in common is the need of a conceptual view of how to derive added value from raw data reflected in a budget. Figure 5.4 presents a layered approach to interactive mining of computer-based information:

- From a database of raw data,
- To profit and loss information.

Though the focal point of the flowchart in Figure 5.4 is an information system tooled around the *customer relationship*, the schema is valid for the implementation of other financial planning criteria, for instance, cash forecasts or Plan versus Actual comparisons, as well as the development of a composite picture of profit and loss.

FINANCIAL AFTERMATHS OF BUDGETARY PROCESSES

The elaboration of a master budget may involve a compensation process, as many industries follow the fairly bad practice of one division selling internally to another division before the product reaches the market. Hence, both for profit and loss and for cash-flow reasons, it is wise to proceed with a thorough study of financial aftermaths which may be hidden by the budgetary process.

The purpose of an *a priori* financial analysis of aftermaths is to provide a critical view of expenditures in a *detailed* and *consolidated* way. The capital and credit required to put the various operational budgets into effect should be carefully examined – along with the expected benefits from carrying out some of the budgeted business transactions.

Another domain where *a priori* financial analysis on aftermaths can be

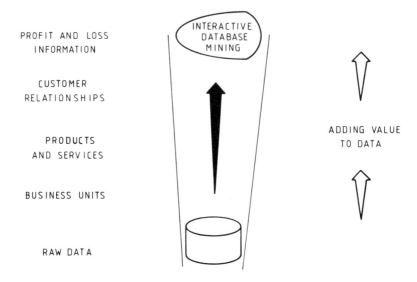

PROFIT AND LOSS
INFORMATION

CUSTOMER
RELATIONSHIPS

PRODUCTS
AND SERVICES

BUSINESS UNITS

RAW DATA

INTERACTIVE
DATABASE
MINING

ADDING VALUE
TO DATA

Figure 5.4   Conceptual view of how to derive added value from data

helpful is to ensure the coordination of three budgets, each dealing with one separate aspect of finances:

- Cash Budget,
- Investment Budget, and
- Capital Budget.

As we have seen on p. 100, the *cash budget* is concerned with current operations and is normally drawn up by the chief accountant. He will obtain his data from the budgets for sales, production, and so on, as well as from statistics on the length of credit periods for:

- Accounts receivable, and
- Accounts payable.

In terms of receipts the expected income will be derived from cash sales and time payments, as well as sale of disposable machinery, furniture, land, securities and other assets – also interest or dividends received on bonds and stocks. (Time payments are budgeted on the length of credit at various periods of the year, and on the credit period stipulated in the contracts.)

The monthly and total figures of disbursements are calculated from payment for raw materials and other purchased goods, direct factory labor (salaries and wages), sales and administration expenses as well as other periodic payments, for instance, rent, utilities, bonuses, taxes, dividends, patent licenses and redemption of loans.

The *investment budget* is a forecast of requirements to open new sales offices, expand production, replace machinery and so on. Typically, this will be the combined responsibility of departmental managers and should contain:

- A description of the projects,
- An estimate of the sums involved,
- Information regarding long-run prospects, and
- A forecast of the profits likely to be yielded.

The development of an investment budget is probably best explained by describing the problems connected with investments at the start of a new production program, including all changes in cash that new investments will involve as well as those brought about by the start-up of operations on new equipment.

- In this sense, the investment budget may be regarded as a supplement to the cash budget.
- Other companies, however, look at it as part of the capital budget.

In the most accepted form, the *capital budget* defines how the money needed for current operations and for investment plans will be procured. If a shortage of funds appears likely, such possibilities as a bank loan, a reduction of stocks, or the issuance of shares, are typically considered.

Should the reverse situation arise, where the firm has a surplus of cash, the capital budget may be used for buying securities or repurchasing the company's stock. In either case, the capital budget must thoroughly reflect itself in management accounting, and the same is true of the investment budget.

One of the basic reasons for the systems and procedures set for management accounting purposes is to provide the means by which executives can consider developments in the firm's activities on their own merits and in relation to the economy as a whole. In this connection, financial analysis can provide a valuable reference when taking day-to-day decisions.

Many companies have found that good results are obtained in conjunction with a *breakeven* analysis. As we will see in Chapter 6, a breakeven chart shows fixed costs and variable costs, the latter connected to varying quantities of output. The breakeven reflects:

- Total revenue from sales, and
- Total cost

as the intersection of these two lines. Profit and loss in regard to a given output, sales volume, product prices, costs incurred in connection with the different transactions, all influence the *Costs* and *Revenues* lines. When some basic factor in the budget is changed, the position of these two lines is altered, causing the breakeven point to move.

FLEXIBLE AND MULTIPLE BUDGETS

Flexible or *variable budgets* consist of a series of separate financial plans geared to different rates of activity. For instance, production costs may be estimated at several possible levels of output and operating expenses may be budgeted at various amounts of sales.

- In preparing alternative budgets, careful consideration must be given to the effect of changes in volume on each budgeted chapter.
- The process of flexible budgeting should also ensure that in all cases overhead is kept in control.

Flexible financial plans are geared to changing levels of activity. They contrast with inflexible plans which are typically the best guesses of financial planners, statisticians or operating departments during the budgeting cycle. Flexible budgets permit us to create a more accurate structure, based upon real operating conditions.

The process of flexible budgeting has however prerequisites. Its implementation requires the correct identification of the activity basis which will be applicable to each of the alternative financial plans:

- Hours of work,
- Standard costs,
- Units of production,
- Financial accounts, and so on.

When this work is well done, the resulting flexibility is enhanced through the ability to extract basic amounts from either posting level accounts or from any level of information databased in the general ledger. It is however necessary to specify the range of accounts which constitute the framework of variable budget calculations.

Another strategy is the *zero budget*. Popularized during the years of the US Carter Administration it supposes that the different chapters of the budget regarding the current year are zeroed out. Each department, down to the smallest unit, has to rejustify its existence otherwise it will receive no funding in the next financial plan.

As a variation of flexible budgeting, some organizations follow the policy of maintaining and reporting on multiple budgets. Zero budgets and multiple budgets should not be confused. For multiple budgeting purposes companies prepare:

- A *historical budget* established on the basis of last year's performance adjusted to accommodate new forecasts.
- A flexible *current operating plan*, which reflects the major revisions on the original 'historical budget'.
- A budget focusing on variances between Plan and Actual data from the last three years, as a projection on possible new deviations.
- Budgets prepared on the hypothesis of *major exogenous events* which radically alter budgetary allocations.

During the Cold War years, for example, several American companies had ready alternative budgets and – if there had been an outbreak of war – the corresponding financial plan was ready to be applied.

Similarly, alternative scenarios can be built for major economic events such as inflation, deflation and stagflation. Once the budgetary process has been modeled and mapped into the computer, there is a wealth of experimentation which can be done practically at no extra cost, to permit the evaluation of different scenarios and their aftermaths.

In conclusion, a great deal of financial analysis can effectively be done by means of models and computers. Technology helps in making interactively available copies of all versions of the current year's budget. That is:

- The original budget and all revised plans, whether they are updated quarterly or more frequently,
- The variances from the original budget and the proposed or preliminary new operating plans.

This approach can also be taken in terms of projections for one or more future years, just as it is sometimes done in retrospect for past years. On a forecasting basis, emphasis is not placed on hard data but on *soft data*, including hypotheses and the calculation of the probability of different events taking place.

THE GENERAL ELECTRIC EXPERIENCE IN SETTING A BUDGET

We have seen the reasons why before a budget is set up, facts and figures must be thoroughly checked and confirmed. Too many people in management are too much inclined to overlook details or to accept a rather low degree of accuracy. Because of expediency, managers often fail to scrutinize the background reasons for costs.

- Some budgetary calculations are taken for granted or reckoned on assumptions of little value to the end result.
- Even if the reasoning behind other spending assumptions is logical, there is the risk that it is based on wrong facts.

A financial plan requires not only correct facts and carefully normalized costs, but also a well-tuned underlying system of values. Pragmatism should dominate. There should be no excessive optimism if sales are booming, whereas if sales are low the sort of pessimism which brings disinclination to take on new commitments is to be avoided.

No reasonable financial plan can be based on this type of unstable attitude. Only by objectively considering each and every important factor liable to affect future activities can a satisfactory picture be formed of the problems lying ahead.

- The budget system should be built to a pattern which puts every fact and figure in its proper perspective, according to its true worth.
- But relations between the various levels of management should instill a dynamic rather than a formal, moribund approach.

This is the right strategy and it can be significantly assisted through mathematical modeling. The knowledge artifacts at workstation level, the seamless access to distributed databases, and an interactive visualization can be instrumental in setting up and controlling budgets.

Budgeting is both a systematic and a flexible study of costs, facts and figures. The many factors influencing a company's future development must be accounted for with due consideration to vagueness and uncertainty – and hence the multiple financial plans of which we have spoken and the use of fuzzy engineering models.

A steady interactivity with databases is important because, among other key reasons, by reflecting the results of past decisions accounting figures can help management to avoid repeating past mistakes. Taken together,

- Budgeting,
- Accounting, and
- Statistics

help provide the major part of the background information needed for formulating policy and reaching decisions. This is the sense of using a corporate memory facility prior to making financial commitments (see also Chorafas, 1990a).

One of the best known approaches to risk analysis with overall fallouts to the conduct of the business was implemented many years ago by General Electric. It led to abandoning the single-option deterministic system and replacing it by estimates of a range, or *bandwidth*.

This approach does not lead to a single result but to a spectrum of results with different probabilities. Its first implementation was made in the GE budget for 1970 and contained three parts:

- Risk analysis

- Results probability
- Budget partition.

The risk analysis module serves in determining the bandwidths of factors influencing profits. Not only does it register the expected value but also the limit values which can be *exceeded* or *fall short* at the 90 percent level of confidence.

In the longer run, in one out of ten cases the estimated value can exceed the higher limit or fall short of the lower limit values. This is part of management by exception. Fluctuations can always happen, but the stated example:

- Does not mean that budgetary costs altogether rise or fall by 10 percent. Not even the out-of-control chapters vary by such a huge amount.
- What it means is that one out of ten budgeted items can present a variation outside its limits due to uncertainties.

Influencing factors are political and economic sensitivities, price-and-standard of living indices, market volume, the company's own market share, variations in sales price, cost of material, wages, salaries and other important issues.

At each departmental and divisional level, management must specify how much percent a given higher or lower value can deviate from the expected value, and what would be changed by such variation in regard to profits and losses. GE uses *residual income* as reference of profits.

- Tribute is calculated from the rate of interest multiplied by the average capital requirement of a given project.
- Results indicate how much the net profit, decreased by the capital interest, is influenced through deviations from *expected value*.

The second part of the planning formula contains a probability analysis of turnover, highlighting costs and revenues. Besides the most probable result, the highest and lowest limits are indicated within a 90 percent probability range.

- Probabilistic examination at 90 percent might show that the profit can change to a loss
- This immediately leads to scrutinizing much more closely this particular item of business.

A third part of the formula specifies the suppositions behind the budget and the degree of probability which they have. The vice-president responsible for a product line must decide on the values he should select and integrate them into his budget plans for the next year. He must specify not only the most probable values but also the expected range. This is a refined form of the flexible budgeting of which we spoke on p. 106 above.

6 Developing and Using a Budget Analyzer

INTRODUCTION

Whether or not in a conscious manner, management uses an income statement and a budget for the same purpose aeronautical engineers employ physical models and digital simulators of aircraft. The budget predicts the anticipated outcome of a business strategy, and if the projected results are unsatisfactory, management can alter some of the variables and the financial allocation made to them.

Corporate financial models are instrumental in predicting the economic performance of a company. They accomplish this by translating the budget process into a series of algorithms to be solved with the aid of computers.

- Assumptions made about the future, and expressed in an algorithmic form, are executed step-by-step through computers.
- The results obtained can be interactively investigated so that corrective action is taken in time to bring the budgetary process under control.

The purpose of any organization is to achieve output, says Intel's Chairman Dr Andrew S. Grove, whether it is widgets being manufactured, bills mailed out, visas processed, or insurance policies sold. 'Yet in one way or another we have all been seduced by tangents and by the appearance of output,' Grove suggests.

To separate the real output from the imaginary, we need measurements and metrics. This is precisely the function to be played by a *budget analyzer*, as this chapter will demonstrate. This will be done by using as a background the basic financial concepts which have been introduced in Chapter 5.

The more classical and less sophisticated types of budget analyzers are simple quantitative models. Because quantification is important with any financial plan, more recent approaches introduce a certain amount of judgmental factors, including the possibility of vagueness and uncertainty. Fuzzy engineering sees to it that this is done in a way which significantly improves financial planning and control (see also Chorafas, 1994c).

QUANTIFICATION IS A FORM OF PROTECTION

Many people work very hard to get something accomplished, and then are frustrated by others who are preoccupied with irrelevant aspects of this or that task. There is a lot of this kind of pettiness going on and, therefore, the clear statement of objectives, as well as their quantification and metrication, is a form of personal assurance.

A manager's output is the output of the various organizational units under his control and influence. Since managers cannot be at every place at the same time, they must have a system that gives them leverage. Planning and control is done not only by establishing a budget but also by properly analyzing it in conjunction with goals and results obtained.

No detail should be missed from this evaluation. Imparting knowledge, skills, or values to a group of subordinates represents a geared activity *if* and *only if* the members of the group carry what they learn to many others.

- Whenever a manager is performing tasks that rightfully could be delegated to a subordinate, his leverage is kept low.
- By contrast, a wider span of control as well as delegation are examples of higher leverage.

But delegation without corresponding accountability, and therefore without following through, is abdication. No manager can ever wash his hands of a task for which he is responsible, even after he delegates it.

We are still responsible for the accomplishment of every mission under our authority and monitoring the delegated task is the only practical way to assure results. Queries to be answered in an effective manner in this connection include:

- How much to monitor, so as not to abdicate responsibility for completion of a mission,
- How to judge whether our subordinates are performing the delegated task in an effective manner, and
- How to increase or decrease our frequency of monitoring, depending on the quality of results.

We can answer these queries if we are capable of both *quantifying* and *qualifying* the tasks under our control. That is precisely the area where financial algorithms and heuristics come into the picture.

Both for planning and for control, over the last twenty years the managerial profession has been enriched with mathematical tools which proved to be of significant assistance in the process of quantification – in fact of *numeracy* the way it was defined in Chapter 1. A very simple example of a corporate financial algorithm is:

Income equals *Revenues* minus *Expenses*

which for any practical purposes we can write as:

Income = Revenue − Expenses, or $I = R - E$ (1)

Revenue is a generic term for the amount of assets received or liabilities liquidated in the sale of our products and services. The same term denotes the gain from sales or exchange of assets, other than stock, as well as the gain from advantageous settlements of liabilities. Revenue does not arise from a gift.

Revenue is recognized upon the transfer of an asset or the performance of a service, accompanied by a concurrent acquisition of an asset or a reduction of a liability. The usual criteria for the recognition of revenue are always subject to modification according to new legislation or income directives.

Costs are incurred along the lines discussed in Chapter 5 (cost control is discussed in Chapter 7). The cost structure changes with the level of operations. Productive costs are connected to the creation of revenues. The component parts of (1) can be expanded:

Revenue equals the *Sales Volume* (SV) times the *Unit Price* (UP)

$R = SV \times UP$ (2)

Similarly, we can write:

Expenses equal *Fixed Costs* (FC) plus *Variable Costs* (VC)

$E = FC + VC$ (3)

(1), (2) and (3) can be combined into slightly more complex, personalized algorithms which satisfy the computational requirements of *Income* and *Expense* statements. Still, such algorithms will not say much about judgmental aspects relating to budgetary issues.

This is the qualitative part of analytical processes in finance, and can best be handled through knowledge engineering.

IMPROVEMENTS THROUGH THE INTRODUCTION OF KNOWLEDGE ENGINEERING

For budgetary control reasons, an improvement over simpler methods is obtained through variance analysis. A simple model is shown in Table 6.1. This table uses the concept of *Actual* versus *Plan* (budget), identifying the variance. *Variance analysis* is significant when we deal with a large number of chapters which can be much more detailed than the example in Table 6.1 shows (see also Chorafas, 1960).

The evaluation of variances can be made through the skill of financial analysts or, even better, by means of an expert system which has the ex-

Table 6.1 Variance analysis for budgetary control, example from a financial institution

	actual	*budget*	*variance*
Total income			
Total expenses			
Gross result			
Total costs			
Net result			
Taxes			
Net result after taxes			
Projected transactions			
Projected income			
Actual transactions			
Total income from transactions			
Projected cost per transaction			
Budgeted expenses (plan)			
Actual cost per transaction			
Actual expenses			
Projected transactions/Employee			
Actual transactions/Employee			

pert's knowhow coded into its rules (practical examples are given in Chorafas and Steinmann, 1991). The new generation of realtime expert systems is composed of five main component parts:

1. A knowledge definition facility enabling financial analysis through rules,
2. The inference engine which applies each rule to the problem under investigation,
3. A knowledge verification section which tests the validity of each rule against historical data,
4. A cross-database access facility for information mining purposes, and
5. An agile user interface for visualization and the invocation of other facilities.

In the more classical decision support systems retrieve, calculate or display data through manual action by endusers. This may be better than the obsolete batch-type routines mainframes are using, but it is not efficient either. The modern, competitive way is to work through *agents*.

• Agents are knowledge artifacts which reside at the user's workstation.
• They prompt the user and execute increasingly sophisticated chores.

Among other advantages, agents permit knowhow regarding data interpretation to be interactively defined, applied and verified. This process is dynamic and therefore provides more leverage than the now classical types of decisions support.

Whether through agents or by means of rules in its knowledgebank, a properly designed and implemented *budget analyzer* expert system can help managers in significant ways, for instance by highlighting unusual expenses. It can also permit us to automate detailed investigations:

- Collecting information elements from the databases, where they have been stored by legacy (as in old data processing) financial programs, and
- Analyzing this information to identify variances that exceed established limits, or criteria of chance deviation.

In one of the leading financial institutions, an expert system written along this line of reference parses report files and generates graphical presentation, with details available at the user's choice. Digital Equipment Corporation has a budget analyzer which automatically controls expense accounts submitted by staff members, establishing deviations and pointing to corrective actions.

An agile, interactive enduser interface (human window) allows the user to investigate each account, but the expert system can also provide prompts and alarm signals. With state of the art computer gear and flexible programming languages, this job is doable – thanks to the cutting edge of technology.

THE USE OF GRAPHS IN FINANCIAL ANALYSIS AND ACCOUNTING

In finance and accounting many people seem to be locked into traditional, tabular forms and formats. Yet not long ago a study of financial reporting demonstrated that graphics greatly assist in comprehension of budgetary contents. One of the best examples has been a trend-spotting experiment which showed that users of graphs thought the task was less difficult than their counterparts who used tables.

- In this and other activities relating to financial analysis, the group using graphs had significantly better performance.
- Novel formats, such as a graphical balance sheet shown in Figure 6.1, effectively convey a message of inbalances difficult to spot through tables.

On several occasions, the practice of using a graphics presentation for financial reporting, as well as for forecasts, leads to improvements in the quality of decisions. The comprehension of forecasts and associated deci-

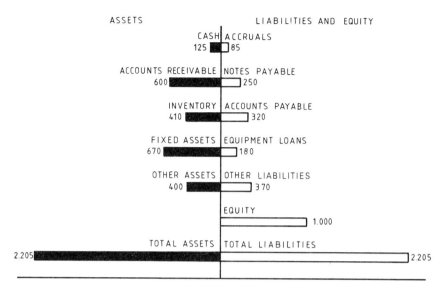

Figure 6.1 Graphical presentation of a balance sheet ($ thousand)

sion accuracy is steadily found to be significantly better with graphs than with tables. There is, however, a learning effect with graphs.

The way they are implemented in a financial environment, interactive graphics are a very effective medium for expressing the output of a given analysis, other evaluation or experiment. The principle is that:

• Computer output must be presented interactively in a way that is easily understood by its users – not just by computer professionals.
• The actual execution of algorithms and heuristics by the machine is merely an upstream process that implements the method for arriving at the solution to a problem.
• The human window has two critical requirements: easy input and comprehensible output of the results.

Tier 1 financial institutions are now moving further than the improved output which can be be achieved through graphics. They have found that an animation language can provide an agile interface. It supports expressions used in computing or found through database access, and assists in modeling and command chores.

Through an agile, user oriented computer programming, graphical language can access with significant ease information channels, mathematical models and business functions – as well as *time-and-space* variables. Programs can be user-written at visual programming level, *then* enriched through generators and compiled by the machine.

Instead of focusing on the details of a specific programming language or algorithm, the user ports his attention on problem design techniques. This can be achieved through a diversity of programming paradigms, including data abstraction, object oriented approaches, rule-based expert systems, fuzzy engineering artifacts, functional icons, and generally:

- Constructs familiar to the enduser,
- Which will be handled by embedded interpreters.

Under this strategy, it is most essential for the enduser to learn about the technology of implementing friendly languages and linguistic supports for programming paradigms. If nothing else, the user should be able to define the characteristics of the visual output he wants.

A computer literate financial analyst is not one prepared to use a specific language, but a person able to work through language metaphors for solving his specific problem. We will speak about the need of *computer literacy* – and why such knowhow must be steadily updated.

- In a nutshell, this is the sense of *advanced technology*, and
- As such, it goes a long way beyond classical data processing.

Until the late 1970s, and even today among retrograde industrial companies and financial institutions, technology was applied in a *defensive mode*. The main emphasis was (or still is) on cost reduction. But since the early 1980s we have seen the use of technology as an *offensive weapon* for the purpose of:

- Generating revenues in the market, and
- Placing barriers for slower moving competitors.

Cutting-edge banks and other financial companies have been able to appreciate that the sudden explosion in volumes and proliferation of ever more exotic financial instruments (such as some of the options, futures, forwards and swaps, discussed in Chapter 10) has generated a new set of challenges for the applications of technology in finance, particularly in terms of:

- Designing, marketing and trading new products, and
- Bringing the associated amount of risk under control.

It is important to appreciate that even if the computing programs are sophisticated, a retrograde output such as character user interfaces (CUI) and tabular presentation cancels most of the benefits to be obtained by on-line computing. Interactive 3-dimensional graphics is the way to look at output.

Will the laggards always stay behind? A reasonable bet is that, as competition intensifies, those industrial companies and financial institutions ahead of the pack will apply pressure on the rest to catch up. But until they do, the leading organizations will be able to reap the benefits of an increased sophistication in their technology, their products and their markets.

PREREQUISITES FOR THE USE OF A BUDGETARY MODEL

To handle the budgetary process in a successful manner, we should start modeling from a top management viewpoint so that a grand design can be made. Under this perspective, all areas of operations have to be considered even though some of them may be viewed in relatively little detail the first time around.

In case this process is being done for the first time, it is wise to develop a simulation which addresses the grand design but also includes specific implementation examples. If the simulation focuses on the financial system, then the experimenter needs to know:

- Where the company is in a financial sense, and
- How to reach the goals in the best possible manner.

The simulator will permit us to evaluate alternative courses of action, but experimentation calls for knowledge of market potential and strength of competition; for expertise in connection to the internal costs of our enterprise; as well as for confidence in the human and financial resources of our organization.

Budgeting is a financial business, but this being said it is correct to emphasize that both for its design and for its evaluation, strategic, marketing, product and manufacturing engineering factors must be given due weight – as Figure 6.2 shows. *If* these requirements are not properly analyzed, *then* they cannot be satisfied. As a result,

- The budget becomes just a numerical expression of wishful thinking, and
- The setting of objectives is limited to a projection into the future of previous years' figures without appropriate qualification.

Due attention should also be paid to the influence of factors *beyond control* which, as far as possible, should be limited to exogenous variables. Otherwise, management should be in control of its own business.

Within the budgetary perspective, constant attention should be given to predicting developments and trends, taking the necessary action to protect or to change budgetary objectives. The latter however should not be altered unless exogenous factors beyond *our* control make the current budgetary

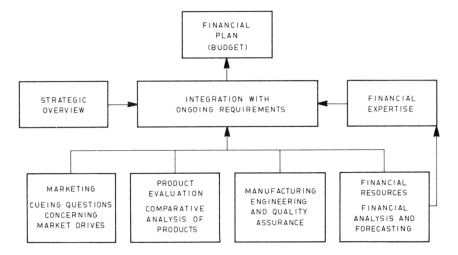

Figure 6.2 A disciplined financial planning process

allocations unrealistic – as discussed in Chapter 5 in connection with flexible budgets.

- The mathematical model which we build should carefully reflect not only budget construction but also the generation of alternatives and their evaluation against one another.
- The first effort should be kept along relatively simple lines aimed at gaining experience. More sophisticated versions should come later.

This, too, is part of the job a budget analyzer should fulfill. For reasons of credibility as well as of efficiency, I would highly recommend maintaining strict scheduling deadlines so that model development proceeds at rapid pace – but making haste carefully.

Efforts should also be invested in training and familiarizing management with the operation of the model. Equally important is the strategy of soliciting comments for improvement and incorporating these suggestions into the budget analyzer.

A rapid development timetable can be effectively maintained leading to a compressed implementation timeframe, if we use rapid prototyping. Subsequently, after the model has been tested and found valid, we may wish to compile it in an assembler language for reasons of accelerating the response time.

Documentation is particularly important in system development as it is in budgeting. All documentation objectives should be fully computer-supported. This will significantly improve over current practice where:

- Often the first budget submitted to management is fully documented.
- But as successive revisions are made in the budget, the backup becomes progressively poorer.
- As a consequence, the approved budget may lack adequate documentation and explanation facilities.

A computer-based financial model helps in correcting this state of affairs since all forecasts and expense chapters are stored in the database. They are changed as the budgetary process progresses, automatically updating all items concerned.

Having outlined these background factors, we will in the next section see how the familiar budget schedules of a company can be translated into equations, providing the basis for a corporate model. The case to be shown in this procedure is kept purposely simple to demonstrate the methodology: without appropriate methodology even the best algorithms will give substandard results.

THE BUDGET EXPRESSED IN ALGORITHMIC FORM

A budget analyzer will be written in algorithms or in heuristics. If we are focusing on the procedure of the sales budget, we can easily appreciate that it can be expressed in terms of equations. Say that our first aim is that of providing a model of *sales revenue* for the first quarter and let

$R1$ = Revenue for the First Quarter
RJ = Revenue for January
RF = Revenue for February, and
RM = Revenue for March

These four variables can be combined by means of a very simple equation of the form:

$$R1 = RJ + RF + RM \tag{4}$$

where the revenue for each month is equal to the quantity (Q) sold times the price (p). Thus, the January revenue can be written:

$$RJ = QJ \times pJ \tag{5}$$

The same relationship applies for February, March and every other month of the year. Models for sales forecasting will provide reasonable estimates for Q (see also Chorafas, 1990b).

This simple example might be easily converted to represent quarterly revenue.

	January	February	March	First Quarter
Desired reduction in inventory	50,000	30,000	20,000	100,000
Sales for the period	280,000	340,000	380,000	1,000,000
To be produced this period	230,000	310,000	360,000	900,000

Table 6.2 Developing the production budget

This, however, would not be true if to promote sales in the winter – as auto manufacturers do – we were offering a discount during, say, February. Then, instead of *p* we should introduce the discount price.

We must also algorithmically express the different expenses. As we have seen on p. 112, the income equation is:

$$I = R - E$$

Table 6.2 shows a simplified approach to the development of a *production budget* based on the sales budget and desired inventory levels. The production for the quarter is the total of the amount produced in each month. Let

$P1$ = Production for the Quarter
PJ = Production for January
PF = Production for February, and
PM = Production for March

With the relation between $P1$, PJ, PF, PM being:

$$P1 = PJ + PF + PM$$

Normally, the production level required in a month equals the desired ending inventory for the month plus the sales for the month less the beginning inventory.

Say that there is available a simulator which optimizes inventory level. Given the projected demand for sales, this simulator has already advised an inventory reduction of 50,000 units for January, 30,000 for February, and 20,000 for March – to a total of 100,000 units for the first quarter. A simplified production equation which accounts for inventory changes is:

$$PJ = QJ - VJR + VJI \tag{6}$$

where *VJR* stands for Inventory reduction in January (by the stated quantity 50,000 units); and *VJI* for a possible increase in January inventory. In this particular case, for planning purposes, the value of *VJI* is zero.

Since our hypothetical company has only one product, either *VJR* or *VJI*, or both, had to be zero – which is a constraint to be imposed on the system. *Constraints* are very important in modeling. They express, so to speak, the soul of the financial model.

If however our hypothetical company had more than one product, then for some of them *VJR* could be zero and for others *VJI* could be zero. Also,

• These two factors may vary by day, week, or month.
• They may vary per product as well from product to product.

In the case of a lamp manufacturing company for instance, since lamps are made of glass and glass has a large amount of breakage at setup time, such variations are quite usual. They are expressed production-lot-per-production lot.

Experience with financial modeling demonstrates that it is always preferable to have a more general equation and set constraints than to write very situational (hence limited perspective) algorithms and have to change them every time a situation changes – or from one product to another. Once a general model has been developed, we can adjust it *parametrically* – thus converting it from general purpose to special purpose.

BENEFITS FROM A PARAMETRIC DESIGN

As a financial plan, the budget can play a much more dynamic role than the one it is usually allocated in business and industry. For instance, the sales budget provides the basis for a polyvalent projection of income by forecasting:

• The physical quantity of units expected to be sold over a given period.
• A projected analysis of these units by market and type of money (in case of multinational operations).
• Market risk, country risk, currency risk and associated hedging possibilities regarding income.

The sales forecasting model can be made parametric, using the parameters to specialize it by market. This process can become so much more accurate if we have been instrumental in building a simulator which extrapolates on historical data by market (within a given margin of error) and the most likely future demand.

Other parameters may address issues of seasonality. In Chorafas (1990b) I have described a fairly accurate forecasting model I helped make at Osram, the German lamp manufacturer. Lamps are a highly seasonal product and this makes the construction of prediction algorithms so much more challenging.

In a production planning model, too, parametric design requires a considerable level of sophistication which will alter the characteristics of the simple approach we followed in the previous section. Proceeding step-by-step, after having calculated a month's production, the first quarter's production will be:

$$P1 = PJ + PF + PM \tag{7}$$

where *PF* and *PM* are the production levels for February and March. These can be obtained in a similar way to that of January (*PJ*). The production for the quarter equals the sales for the quarter plus (or, in this case, minus) the change in inventory.

The incorporation of *parameters* makes the model more specific, transiting from a generalized to a custom-made version. Through parameters, the experimenter can force changes that affect the system's behavior.

- The simulator's input corresponds to the set of states provided by its parameters.
- The experimenter will observe the effected changes through the model's output.

We have seen an example on p. 120 with *VJR* and *VJI* in (6). This and similar algorithms can be converted to fit any particular product in the planning phase, through the appropriate use of parameters.

Every product has its own characteristics and therefore its own parametric requirements. For instance, in scheduling the production of lamps breakage can be a parameter. Not all types of glass have the same breakage rate, hence if the scheduling algorithm includes breakage (as it should) then the multiplier of this factor will vary by specific lamp type.

- The use of parameters can also permit the combination of transformations making feasible coupling different schedules together.
- Any one production system can be regarded as the coupling of its parts – and the same is true of a financial system.

Whether parametrically or otherwise, having set the production levels we are well positioned to develop the labor and materials budget, a capital expenditures budget, and a sales budget. These are the issues we will consider in subsequent sections.

To avoid the budget work being a cumbersome and time-consuming process, it is wise to establish a planning model with auxiliary programs for the various areas of activity. The human resources should primarily be used for qualified planning work and practical use of the budget – not as number crunchers. The latter is the work computers can do more effectively.

This advice will be best appreciated if we keep in mind that the budget is a management tool. Once the computer-based model has been done, all managers can participate in the decision process regarding budgetary planning and control. Performance should be compared with plans – not just with historical figures.

- Management oriented financial reports should give the financial highlights, but provide for access to detail.
- These reports should be short, descriptive, graphical and delivered on time.
- We can in fact give *too little* information by supplying *too much, too late*.

If many products were to be considered and several time periods were involved, the computer program would be more complex, but in its fundamentals the methodology would not change in a significant way. In fact, in subsequent sections we will elaborate on how to make the budget model more sophisticated, both through algorithms and by means of heuristics.

In conclusion, the success of a budget system is a function of the detail and accuracy with which its component parts have been built. Success also depends on quantification, qualification and *participation* by all players in the budget system.

Great attention should be given to the human factor, because the budget itself as a system does not automatically result in better management. A budget is made by people and for people; hence the response of people – and their accountability – makes the difference.

ACCOUNTING FOR LABOR AND MATERIAL COSTS

Starting in the mid- to late 1960s, several of the financial planning models, developed by business and industrial organizations, offered valuable assistance in budgeting (see also Chorafas, 1965). More than a quarter century down the line, many companies have a library of computer-based models which can determine expenses and investment requirements in marketing and production. We will consider manufacturing as an example.

Let's start with a warning: every company has its own principles and its own approach to financial analysis and capital budgeting. The algorithms many companies use are often esoteric, as we will see in the discussion which follows. Sometimes this is even true within the same firm, where different factories follow their own budgetary procedures rather than a company-wide normalization.

Typically, a factory prepares a budget proposal and sends it to headquarters. Several leading manufacturers today have operating available expert systems which, at the corporate levels:

- Screen these budgetary proposals,
- Verify their chapters, one-by-one,

- Integrate the financial plans into one company-wide schema,
- Suggest corrections and adjustments, and
- After management authorization of the different expense items, create a corporate model of allocated funds (see also Chorafas, 1991b).

A similar practice is followed by financial organizations regarding budgets submitted by their branches. In Tokyo, the Dai-Ichi Kangyo Bank has such an expert system by means of which all budgetary proposals, and their credentials, are evaluated – using different criteria by branch, rather than a monolithic approach.

This solution is followed within a set of management standards providing for a homogeneous evaluation of budgetary proposals, but within a policy of customization. When algorithmic and heuristic solutions are followed in tandem,

- The algorithmic part will typically address the more deterministic aspects of the job such as the calculation of depreciation.
- By contrast, judgmental-type evaluations will be done by the heuristic rules of expert systems, which can help to personalize financial allocations.

Computing the cost of labor will be algorithmic. In our manufacturing example, the algorithm for the labor budget starts with the specifications for the product which, say, calls for 0.10 hour of unskilled labor at \$10.00/hour and 0.05 hour of semi-skilled labor at \$20.00/hour. Hence, the direct labor is:

$$L = 0.1\ UL + 0.05\ SL \tag{8}$$

where:

L = Labor cost per unit
UL = Cost of unskilled labor per hour
SL = Cost of skilled labor per hour

Labor cost per unit changes over time and as a function of investments in automation. Gains in productivity, for instance, are keeping a lid on unit labor costs in the industrial sector with productivity growth often tending to offset wage inflation. In addition, strong productivity gains can reduce a company's need for additional workers – therefore affecting the linear relationship which traditionally existed between labor input and the output of goods.

Gains in productivity mean that manufacturers are able to produce more without the help of much additional labor, giving management the upper hand in labor negotiations. Not surprisingly, therefore, hourly compensation gains at factories have moderated significantly since the early 1980s. In stark contrast to manufacturing, however, productivity improvements in service industries have been very low.

- One lesson this reference teaches is that budgetary models are not transferable from one industry to another – and quite often not from one company to another within the same industry.
- Contrary to classical data processing routines which can be bought (and should be bought) in packages, algorithmic and, most particularly, heuristic solutions should be self-made.

The system also has to be upkept. As every industry knowns, hourly labor costs change with time due to inflation, contracts signed with labor unions, the minimum wage level set by government and other factors.

The labor cost algorithm will typically find these changed values in a table which is dynamically updated. However, since for simplicity I have given the values in reference to our basic model, we can write:

$$L = 0.1 \times 10 + 0.05 \times 20 = \$2 \tag{9}$$

Accordingly, the established production schedule will tell how many pieces will be manufactured, and therefore what the labor content is. On a monthly basis, the labor cost will be:

$$LJ = PJ \times L$$
$$LF = PF \times L$$
$$LM = PM \times L$$

It is relatively easy to calculate the *direct labor* budget, which is part of the variable cost of production. Another part of variable cost is *direct materials*. Different approaches are taken regarding their valuation, and they relate to the way we value inventories:

- First-in, first-out (FIFO),
- Last-in, first-out (LIFO),
- Weighted average, and so on.

A computational algorithm can be developed for overhead as well as for depreciation of buildings and equipment which constitute the fixed costs. Fixed and variable expenses can be plotted in a graph as in Figure 6.3, which shows the total manufacturing cost: direct labor plus direct material (variable cost), semivariable cost and fixed cost.

This is a summary approach which is found in most books. In practice, if we wish to really control expenditures in a dependable manner, then things are different. We should establish detailed breakeven charts:

- By product, and
- By cost center.

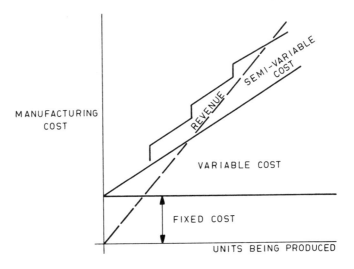

Figure 6.3   Fixed, variable and semi-variable costs in a breakeven chart

If the cost center is a major organizational unit, then we should bring the breakeven analysis down to much finer detail. Summaries never provide the basis for insight, yet insight which is factual and documented is what we need in order to control costs.

THE CONCEPT AND PRACTICE OF BREAKEVEN

A chart like the one shown in Figure 6.3 is important as our cost evaluation will be accurate only when we establish the profile of each source of expenditure, controlling its variation. Companies that do not know their costs, for each product or service, are taking unwarranted risks. By and large, these costs will fall into three classes:

- *Fixed* costs do not change as the rate of output varies. An often quoted but imprecise example is *overhead*.
- *Semi-variable* costs do change with the rate of output but by big steps, as for instance happens with *capital investments*. Then, they hold steady over a range of output.
- *Variable* costs vary with the changes in the rate of output, being a *direct function* of the latter.

Fixed costs might not actually be fixed and the reference to semi-variable costs is made with this in mind. A sound policy will see to it that at low volume levels it is better to bet on semi-variable costs – while fixed costs must be avoided. Much of the concept behind the *virtual corporation* lies in this reference.

Theoretically, a rapid expansion of activities sees to it that fixed costs can be more easily absorbed. In reality, this does not happen that easily, while semi-variable costs will also be incurred due to necessary growth of facilities to meet demand.

• The concept of *breakeven* is essentially an attempt to balance costs of all types against the revenue to be obtained from the goods produced.
• This is no idle exercise but a practical approach which can be algorithmically described, with the results presented in a graphical form.

Figure 6.3 has been shown an example. The breakeven point is where the rising revenue line intercepts from under the curve of semi-variable costs. What is not shown in a static figure, however, is that breakeven is a moving target.

The reason why the breakeven point is dynamic and steadily changes is found in the fact that both costs and revenues change with time. As changes are made in any or all of the primary determinants of income and expense, the breakeven point shifts up or down.

The breakeven is practically affected by every major decision management makes. It does not change only as a function of market response. In an algorithmic sense, the breakeven point is calculated by means of the following equation:

$$p \times Q = v \times Q + F \tag{11}$$

where:

p = Selling price per unit
v = Variable cost per unit
Q = Number of units that must be sold to breakeven, and
F = Fixed costs (semi-variable costs have not been considered in this equation)

On the basis of this simple equation, we can compute the number of units which must be sold to breakeven:

$$Q = \frac{F}{p - v} \tag{12}$$

And we can calculate total profit (*TP*) before tax through the algorithm:

$$TP = (p \times Q) - (v \times Q + F) \tag{13}$$

However, as we saw in Figure 6.3, there is also a step-wise increase due to semi-variable costs, for instance, for new investments necessary for a contained increase in buildings and machinery due to the need for further production capacity. A more sophisticated algorithm than the one in (13) will reflect this reference:

$$P \times Q = c \times Q + s\,(Q_n - Q_{n-1}) + F \tag{14}$$

where $Q_n - Q_{n-1}$ identifies the quantity range for which a semi-variable expenditure needs to be incurred, and s the unit cost equivalent in the $Q_n - Q_{n-1}$ range. For output below Q_{n-1} we do not need to add semi-variable costs; while beyond Q_n new semi-variable cost expenditures will be necessary.

Let's now look into the income side of the breakeven equation. Say that the item which we have considered sells on the price list at $10, but this is not what the factory makes. Typically the transfer price from manufacturing to sales is at 50 percent (or less) of the price list. In a graphical form, Figure 6.4 explains why it is so important to hold overhead (part of fixed cost) low, so as to breakeven with the lower number of units possible.

In Figure 6.4a, fixed costs are much lower than in Figure 6.4b. Therefore, an amount of sales *A* is enough to help breakeven; while in Figure 6.4b a much larger amount *B* is necessary.

When in the early 1980s Lee Iaccoca turned around Chrysler and saved the company from bankruptcy, he did so by using a sharp knife to cut overhead and other fixed costs. By reducing Chrysler's breakeven from 2 million cars to 1.2 million, the new chief executive was able to make a profitable company out of one which was heading for receivership.

PAYING ATTENTION TO DIRECT LABOR AND DIRECT MATERIAL

Not only the fixed costs but also the variable costs should be thoroughly controlled. This means paying significant attention to the costs incurred in connection with direct labor and direct materials – and hence, to the direct costs.

We can reduce the labor content through automation, keeping well in mind that this will correspondingly increase the investments – and the subsequent depreciation. A sense of balance is therefore advisable. Similarly, we can reduce the material costs through substitute materials and redesign.

A good rule for testing how efficient we are in controlling direct expenses in manufacturing is what IBM calls *capitalization*. This is not the classical use of the word. In IBM jargon it essentially means:

Direct labor + Direct material
= 15% or less of list price

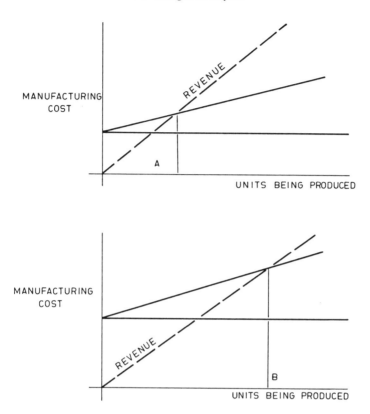

Figure 6.4 Production needed to breakeven: production level *A* is less than *B* because fixed costs are lower

This is an easy algorithm which can be implemented for cost control purposes but also for *value analysis*. The latter is an effort to focus on imbedded value in a product, comparing costs to those of the competition and coming up with proposals for substitutes to bring unit costs down.

While many companies consider overhead an evil (which it is), few managements appreciate the importance of controlling direct labor and direct materials. Those organizations which do so gain significant market advantages over their competitors.

* Every manufacturing operation includes a good many service functions – from sales to after sales services, and
* Nowhere is the watch over direct labor cost more important than in the service industry.

Sales costs can be expressed algorithmically in a way similar to the example we saw in production. Often, about one third of the list price is allocated to

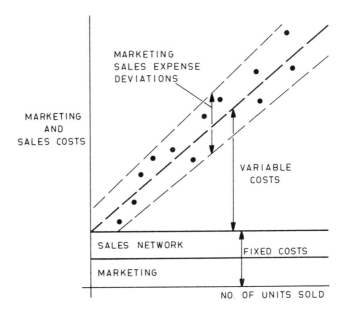

Figure 6.5 A chart for sales expenses needed with breakeven studies

marketing and sales. The difference between list price and transfer price (from engineering) is typically going to R&D, general management and profit margins.

In a way similar to that of any other financial plan, the marketing and sales budget will have fixed and variable expenses. Both have to be watched very carefully:

- The fixed costs concern marketing administration and the costs incurred by the network of sales offices.
- Variable costs represent sales per item – such as salaries, commission to the salesmen or other modes of compensation.

Even a fixed salary for the direct labor contributed by the salesforce is amenable to a variable unit price cost of sales, if the salesman works on a quota basis – as he should. It is always advisable to have quantitative sales targets and judge sales performance against them.

Since salesman productivity often varies widely, even if a normalization effort is made, sales expenses are not exactly linear as in the case of the breakeven charts which we saw in manufacturing.

- This is particularly true in the sense of variable sales costs per unit.
- By contrast, fixed sales costs follow a simpler pattern as Figure 6.5 suggests.

Precisely because of variations in direct sales costs, multiple regression analysis has proved to be a very useful tool. In Figure 6.5, the different dots represent results normalized on units sold, by level of sales, with statistics collected over several years through the network. Hence, they are based on historical records.

In this particular case, simple regression analysis was tried as a first approximation. To improve the accuracy, multiple regression analysis was then used. The results obtained indicated that the relationship between the variables being considered was essentially nonlinear:

- One reason for nonlinearities in sales costs is that performance by individual salesmen varies much more widely than by individual factory workers.
- Another reason lies in the fact that though sales quotas are necessary, a points system in sales is often heterogeneous and in other cases it tends to reflect the goods to be promoted rather than their intrinsic value.

These guidelines are as valid in the marketing efforts associated with manufacturing industry as they are in banking. The quantitative expressions which we are considering are applicable in a broad sense. But it is no less true that every industry has its own approaches to production and sales costing.

For example, in banking it is advisable to convert the quantitatively constructed budget to a budget which connects with production and sales volumes. This operation is rewarding in terms of financial planning and control. It is not complex, and basically comprises:

- Relationship banking policies with client identification
- Number and kind of customer accounts
- Properly identified account oriented transactions
- Nonaccount oriented support activities such as general expenses.

After providing the necessary infrastructure, if we multiply the number of transactions by cost standards, the result will be a transaction oriented cost budget. Costing details by customer, service center and transaction permit us to obtain a properly laid total cost budget which can be controlled for variance, as we saw at the beginning of this chapter. But attention! The cost budget should be a consequence of the business activity budget – not vice versa.

7 Building Models to Control Costs

INTRODUCTION

Chapter 6 has explained why the control of costs is so important, a fact easily dramatized through the disappearance of companies unable or unwilling to control their costs. No matter their exact nature or to which category they belong, the notion of costs both precedes and underpins any budgetary process. All expenditures should be subjected to rigorous analysis, answering the questions:

- *What?*
- *How Much?* and
- *Why?*

All answers should be factual and documented. Many quantitative estimates can be effectively provided through modeling. The use of algorithmic approaches, and hence mathematical statements, does not necessarily require an understanding of calculus to grasp their significance – or to appreciate the type of the control operations taking place.

Semantic meaning, causal explanations as well as questions of origin(s) and destination(s) of costs, play a very important role in management control. A valid explanation typically proceeds from the more abstract to the more concrete, covering both the main theme and related issues.

- An analytical response to the queries: What? Why? and How? provides a basis for observation and analysis of actions in what may loosely be termed the 'Black Box' approach.
- But higher intelligence investigations go beyond What? and How?, to answer the question: Why? Many things which are done don't need to be done at all. They are part of the procedure because of a historical accident and inertia.

The term Black Box, which originated in the Second World War, was applied to the procedure followed when examining captured electronic equipment (typically enclosed in a square box which was painted black) that could not be opened because of the possibility that there existed destruction charges inside.

- In these cases the investigators simply applied various forms of input to the box and measured its output.
- While this was done, they addressed the appropriate protocol whose contents were analyzed through educated guesses.

Keeping a protocol of results during this input/output analysis made it possible to find out *what* this piece of equipment was doing without necessarily establishing *why*. In finance, too, up to a point *why* takes the back seat in favor of the question *what*. But in reality we are interested to see that all three questions: What, How Much and Why are being answered in an effective manner.

COST CONTROL AS MANAGEMENT STRATEGY

Cost is an expenditure or outlay of cash, other property, capital stock, or services. Alternatively, it is the incurring of a liability identified with goods or services purchased – or representing any loss which has been incurred, during a given period of time usually corresponding to a budgetary timeframe.

Costs are measured in terms of the amount of cash paid (or payable) or the market value of the property, capital stock, or services given in exchange. But costs can vary widely:

- *Controllable costs* are those which are properly studied, then directly authorized and regulated at a specific level of management authority within a given time period.

Many people advocate that a manager should be held accountable only for controllable costs. This approach misses the point, because in real life the distinction between *controllable* and *noncontrollable* costs is often blurred – whether by accident on or purpose.

- *Noncontrollable costs* are those which have not been properly studied in terms of their need and their limits – hence expenditures can be carried way off target.

A thorough management investigation on costs sources and destinations must proceed with an objective evaluation of reasons and returns. When this is done in an efficient manner, the findings typically uncover areas which require immmediate management control. This leads to a number of questions:

- What criteria should be used in highlighting the out-of-control expenses, where a deep analysis must be carried out?

- What specific evidence is there that the criteria which are used are the most appropriate?
- What are the characteristics which a statement of objectives should include in order to guide the hand of cost control?

In the background of these queries is a concern about the completeness of analytical specifications regarding the management of costs. Background reasons regarding the lack of appropriate control often revolve around two factors: *personnel* and *financial issues* – from the utilization of appropriate skills, to unwarranted debt, the payment of high premiums and so on.

- Often, for instance, there is no motivation in regard to containing costs for the people who carry out a given business activity or manage a project.
- Systems and procedures regarding the evaluation of results versus what the budget has outlined is defective – leading to run-away costs.

As we have seen in Chapter 6, budgets are built around certain basic estimates, but not all estimates are valid. A great deal has been said about the need for forecasting strategic elements in a business context, such as sales levels – which have subsequently to be proved. A similar statement can be made about the estimates of costs.

To help in the control of all costs incurred in the enterprise, accountants have long established the practice of dividing them into some relatively homogeneous classes. This is, for example, the sense of differentiating between:

- Fixed Costs and variable costs,
- Direct costs and indirect costs, and so on (indirect costs are discussed on p. 137 below).

But to be of any use in the sense of a management planning and control, costs must be both *meaningful* and *credible*. Also the database containing cost elements must be accessible by all managers and professionals concerned by projection regarding costs and benefits – as well as the control of expenditures.

- Meaningful costs means consistent definitions in an enterprise-wide sense, relevant to the business and at the appropriate level of detail.
- Costs are credible if they are realistic, understandable, and recordable – also controllable in the way the Introduction has outlined.

All cost elements must be accessible on demand through multiple tools, and they must be stored in distributed networked databases. Access to cost elements should be timely, ad hoc, flexible and proven in terms of reliability.

THE PRINCIPLE OF THE LEAN ORGANIZATION

The application of the concept of controllable costs is key to the strategy of keeping our company lean. The *lean organization* is not just a tactic to squeeze costs out. Rather, it is *a business philosophy* which dramatically improves results by capitalizing on the changes which take place in the market.

- The lean organization is prepared to spring at a moment's notice, exploring business opportunities.
- It is constantly on the lookout for new ways to do business, and always ready to shred what does not work.
- It takes advantage of its lack of bureaucratic fat to make quick decisions and put them into action.

As Figure 7.1 shows, the planning, usage and control of costs is essentially a data staging operation. Its efficient handling requires a policy of cost standards, cross-company cost relationships, the gathering of raw data and their reconciliation, as well as editing, translating and balancing cost accounts. It also requires sophisticated software for applications reasons and services – but charges have to be reasonable in respect to competition, and the quality of the output has to be high.

In Figure 7.1, direct labor, direct materials and other costs are allocated by product lines *A*, *B*, and *C*. Then they find their way into the accounts of clients who purchase the company's products.

Definitions and relationships, including the impact of costs, must account for organizational units, products, customers, market segmentation and other dimensions. Linkages must be established with regard to relationships and roles, observing flexible reporting hierarchies, with plenty of information databased and accessible on demand.

At Wall Street, and in all major financial centers, one of the key roles of the *financial analysts* is precisely that of identifying the *lean* and the *fat* organizations for investment and other reasons.

- Investors like the lean companies because they have the future ahead of them,
- While they move away from fat companies, their unwarranted expenses and bureaucratic budgets.

The role of financial analysts is to contribute *insight* and *foresight* regarding this segregation. That is how experts try to predict a company's future. Financial analysts do so through inspection, assisted by mathematical tools and computers. But it is company management which should take the initiative to trim the budgets and the costs.

At Travellers, Sanford I. Weill obsessively eschews such bureaucratic hallmarks as organization charts and memos. Unlike many financial-services

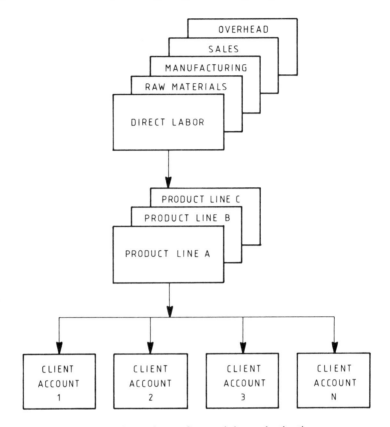

Figure 7.1   A cost allocation scheme from origin to destination

monoliths, Weill runs his sprawling conglomerate as if it were a small family business with the owners' money on the line.

'We are all refugees from larger, more traditional institutions,' says long-time Weill lieutenant Robert I. Lipp, who spent 23 years at Chemical Banking. 'A large, publicly owned company can be run like a privately owned company.' In spite of being a billionaire, Sanford Weill is ruthless in paring expenses.

- He sets up precise reporting systems so he can calculate profitability down to the level of individual offices, and
- Roots out extravagance, having designed a system that will measure productivity only on the basis of factors that line managers can control.

It is not just Travellers which follows this policy. Any well-managed firm does so. Quoting from Sam Walton, who is one of the most successful businessmen of the post-Second World War years:

It goes back to what I said about *learning to value a dollar*. It is great to have the money to fall back on. But if you get too caught up in that good life, it is probably time to move on – simply because you lose touch with what your mind is supposed to be concentrating on: Serving the customer (1992).

Commenting on how and why companies fail Walton suggested: '*Their customers were the ones who shut them down*. They voted with their feet.' All this is very relevant to the preparation of the proper financial plan – whether we talk of companies or other organizations. The root of many failures is in the costs, and they have to be controlled.

CONTROLLING DIRECT AND INDIRECT COSTS

Chapter 6 has outlined the difference between fixed, variable and semi-variable costs, also giving the advice that fixed costs have to be kept low, and variable costs must be carefully controlled. This can be more effective if we establish a distinction between direct and indirect costs, as well as other dichotomies which assist in understanding the profile of a cost structure.

The bulk of the costs of carrying on the business are known as operating charges or the *cost of doing business*. A good many of these costs arise from materials and labor, and hence they are variable costs – to a large extent of a direct costing nature – but there exist as well other expenses.

Because the weight of depreciation expenses is increasingly being felt, many companies add it to the direct costs while, as we have seen in Chapter 6, in terms of classification it belongs to the fixed costs category. Other cost chapters also exhibit a similar behavior.

A good example is Research and Development (R&D) costs whose importance in an age of rapid technological progress should never be underestimated, not only in manufacturing but also in banking.

- R&D expenditures are a *cost of staying in business*.
- As such they contrast to fabrication and sales, which are costs of doing business.

R&D costs are partly direct and partly indirect. Pure research and much of applied research represents indirect costs. By contrast, development projects are largely direct costs relating to a given product or service.

Many companies split the R&D organization into two parts: the research laboratories which are centralized, and the developments units attached to each product division. General Electric's labs in Schenectady are an example of the research line of reference. By contrast, the dividing line between:

- Bellcore, the jointly owned research affiliate of the Baby Bells, and

- The R&D labs maintained by each of the operating companies of the Bell System, is less clear.

One element the costs of doing business and staying in business have in common is personnel expenses. The importance of the payroll as a major cost factor underlines the need for internal control to ensure it does not become disproportionally large.

As the name implies, *direct labor* is a personnel cost directly applied to a given line job, while *overhead* is an indirect personnel cost. One way to control indirect personnel expenses is through a management policy which sees to it that:

- The growth in business is much faster than the growth in overhead, and
- Critical ratios are established to see such a policy through.

The need for control of personnel expenses is further reinforced by the fact that payments for indirect personal services are seldom accompanied by physical evidence that can be related to the disbursement for them, as is the case with costs of materials and supplies. Cost control should keep in perspective that while materials and supplies can be warehoused this is not true of personnel expenditures.

- The services paid in connection to the payroll often disappear from view as soon as they are rendered, even if at least some of their effects can be seen.
- It is therefore necessary to establish safeguards against error, waste and fraud, and this must be done at the point where these costs are incurred.

Efficiency in personnel administration requires that the person who carries on recruitment and placement of employees in jobs should not be the one who supervises their work. There should as well be available metrics, such as standard times, for work being rendered.

Such metrics can be productive when they integrate into a properly established accounting model like the one shown in Figure 7.2. This presentation differentiates personnel costs into direct and indirect (overhead) expenses. Then it combines these expenses to present a pattern of plant efficiency as well as an interactive report on labor content, of products and services.

The attention which we pay to personnel costs should take account of the fact that salaries and wages are only one chapter of personnel expenditures. But there are also other operating charges which can be linked to personnel, arising from sources such as:

- Rental costs,
- Services, including maintenance,
- Fringe benefits,

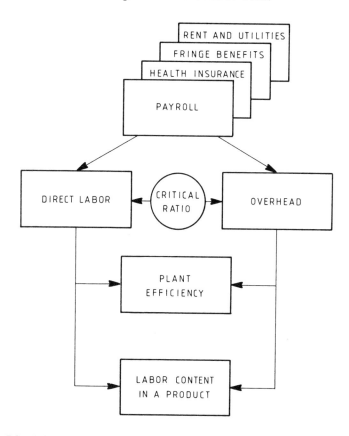

Figure 7.2 All personnel expenditures must be watched very carefully, with metrics able to calculate efficiency and labor content

- Insurance, and
- Social Security taxes.

Metrics are necessary for each and every expense item. The standards we have should be steadily updated as new contracts are signed, commitments made, the law changes and new regulations show up. For instance, the 80 percent of health insurance charges advanced by the Clinton Administration, and planned to be charged to the employer, dramatically changes the equation of the cost of labor.

OVERHEAD EXPENSES AND BUREAUCRACY

In former times, when personnel costs were more linear, accountants were advised that the disbursements for such items must be controlled through a disbursement voucher. Today, while this is still necessary it is by no means enough. A disbursement voucher is an after-the-fact document, while emphasis must be placed at the origin of costs.

Due to the fact that many personnel expenditures are a dead weight, attention should be given not only to the accounting documents used to record each personnel transaction but also to a complete model of direct and indirect costing:

- All personnel costs should be tracked very carefully, using appropriate technology.
- Direct costs can be squeezed by means of automation at the workplace.
- Being more perverse, indirect costs should be swamped through top management decisions.

This statement is important in connection to all indirect costs, but the specific target area is *overhead* – which is a different way of saying: *bureaucracy* and its perks.

At Safeway, cutting costs has been the top priority of Henry Kravis and George Roberts. They slashed executive perks, taking away 350 company cars. They also cut headquarters staff by 25 percent, to 850, saving $15 million–$20 million a year.

In 1993, Safeway required the company's top five executives to give up the bonuses they had already earned for 1992, when profits fell 20 percent. 'When shareholders lose, managers should lose,' stated Steve Burd, Safeway's new Chief Executive Officer who instituted a bonus plan tightly tied to performance (*Business Week*, October 18, 1993).

Such cost cuts at the top, Burd acknowledges, are largely symbolic. But symbolic sacrifice is often crucial in wresting concessions from labor. In February 1993, Steve Burd threatened to close all 84 Safeway operated stores in Alberta, Canada, unless the union agreed to concessions. The union accepted:

- Longer hours, and
- Lower pay.

A cashier who earned $638 for a 37-hour workweek now earns $608 working 40 hours. Those wage rollbacks added up to an annual saving of $40 million. This is the way to cut the fat out of an organization and keep it lean. The operation is necessary at both the managerial and the workers' level.

Overhead does not mean fixed costs, but rather expenditures which are indirectly chargeable to the units of production. Usually, operating charges are set so that they can result in approximate absorption of the indirect costs of labor.

In most cases the calculation of overhead is an approximation which leads to the question of overapplied or underapplied overhead balances. To right these balances, the amount of overapplied or underapplied indirect cost ought to be traced through the accounts. This can permit us to establish whatever corrections are necessary in a way similar to the one which was shown in Figure 7.2.

Errors made in posting a cost item can be corrected only by tracing it through the accounts affected. To correct discrepancies it is important that the handling of costs of completed work is quite clear to everyone concerned – including the procedures by means of which costs are posted to record:

- Direct labor,
- Direct material,
- Indirect labor,
- Depreciation, and
- Other expenses.

The emphasis placed on the trimming of indirect costs, and most particularly of bureaucracy, should not lead to the assumption that other sources of costs are unimportant. The rationale behind every single expenditure should be reevaluated with imaginative methods and systems improvements aimed at cutting costs.

A good example on how much *imagination* and moving away from the beaten path can help in business efficiency is offered by Hewlett-Packard. Contrary to its competitors the company which grew to become the No. 2 computer manufacturer in America, Hewlett-Packard:

- No longer stockpiles countless versions of printers and PCs in warehouses, as the old practice demanded.
- Instead, it stocks components and software at distribution centers and combines them at the last minute to match each customer's order.

By such changes, Hewlett-Packard has driven operating expenses from 41 percent of sales in 1988 to 30 percent today. This is an excellent example of what can be achieved in cost reduction by a management willing and able to take the necessary steps.

Through well-defined channels of accounting, we can follow, record and evaluate incurred costs. All expenditures must be recorded on product and service cost files in the database, making it feasible to follow in an analytical way:

- Inventories,
- Work in process,
- Finished goods, and
- Goods sold.

For management accounting purposes such information should be available interactively, with expert systems exploiting discrepancies for exception reporting. The output of an ingenious exploitation of cost files will impact on budgetary procedures, as we have seen in Chapter 6. It also facilitates and documents auditing.

THE PROCESS OF ESTABLISHING STANDARD COSTS

Under a standard cost system, accounting procedures are basically the same as under any other kind of costing arrangements, except that normalized metrics are being readily applied. Proper standards permit refinements of the basic control procedures, leading to an accounting system which serves management purposes in an effective manner:

- The establishment and use of standard cost is the basis for setting unit costs for product accounting purposes.
- It is also the first step in an attempt to understand the procedural aspects of how norms should be established and implemented.

A standard is *a unit of measurement* which can serve as a level of reference. The meaning of variations from standards obviously depends on the reasons for deviations, which we aim to uncover and control. The amount of variation indicates the type of control action necessary.

The nature and scope of standard unit costs may be approached from several points of view, one basic way being the historical frame of reference. Another is making appropriate measurements, for instance through Method and Time studies or Work Sampling, which lead toward norms (see Chorafas, 1989a).

With the *historical* approach to cost standards, we attempt to establish what it ought to cost to perform a given operation, produce a product, or render a service. One way of tackling this is to base the standard on past performance:

- The unit costs actually experienced in a past accounting period are taken as being the standard cost – eventually upgraded for inflation.
- This has the merit of being realistic, in the sense that the figures thus developed are actual data based upon real events that have transpired.
- The negative aspect is that the activity for which a standard unit cost is sought may be something which has been done in an inefficient way or has never happened before.

If a standard unit cost for a new product or operation cannot be set directly from experience, there is always the possibility that the new activity (in some respects at least) is similar to something that has been done in the past. It is rare, indeed, that an entirely new process is developed from scratch.

The real risk with the historical approach is that a job too costly for the benefits which it is providing might become a standard. For this reason, historical cost data must be carefully audited prior to being accepted as frame of reference.

In other words, while there may be ample information to establish what the precise operation or product cost has been, there is doubt as to what level of efficiency is implicit, say, in last year's cost. This is the same objection that can be raised to the historical basis for budgeting.

Work Sampling is a better method because it permits us to visually inspect the work done, for instance, in an office. It makes it feasible to separate productive time from idle time and also to distinguish among the consistent elements of productive time.

- The method is easy to implement and is not costly, hence it can be repeated following the automation of some productive time elements.
- Costing becomes more accurate as idle time is weeded out, and with it unnecessary jobs – if management has the guts to do it.

Not only costing but also budgeting needs a steady upkeep. Because of taking last year's figures as the standard for this year's performance means perpetuating the inefficiency levels of last year, other ways have been devised to overcome the problem, for instance, the *zero budgeting* procedure. Whether we talk of costs or of whole budgets, the principle is that:

- Past practices typically hide many inefficiencies, while our strategy should be to reevaluate all cost chapters.
- In many cases, it may be difficult to fill the gap between what has been done and what is rational. Hence, it is simpler to start from scratch.

For all new cases and for all old cases which are doubtful, setting a level of efficiency from which to measure deviations is best done by viewing the problem from a fresh viewpoint, focusing attention on how the job *ought to be done*. This means norms without too much dependence on what has already become a habit. Innovation and imagination can always be of help.

WHAT IS MEANT BY PROSPECTIVE COST STANDARDS?

The real advantage of *prospective* or computed cost standards is that they are independent of habitual forms of operation or thought. This approach is frequently found to be the most effective solution to the cost control problem, because it is making a fresh start. The principle is to analyze the situation independently of prior experience.

- This does not mean that historical cost or other data are of no relevance whatever for management planning and control purposes.
- But it implies that existing cost data should be reviewed in the light of an independent study which leads to normalization.

This is the background reason for practical, analytical cost studies from which cost standards can be set. For instance, the motion and time analysis of a task or operation as well as work sampling methods can give an independent basis for forecasting costs, as suggested on p. 135. (This analysis is not necessarily stopwatch studies but method/time/measurement, work sampling and other approaches.)

Test runs of certain operations over limited periods of time with appropriate analysis and interpretation can yield important information as to how a given activity *ought to* be performed. Such studies provide not only a basis for setting a cost standard for a given operation, but also ensure valuable data for checking other similar or related activities.

The case for calculated standards is based on the prospective evaluation of a job subjected to measurement procedures. It is a proactive approach characterizing a management oriented towards obtaining tangible results.

- The constant search for improvement is a reflection of dissatisfaction with mere mediocrity in measuring management operations.
- What happened last year is of main consequence only as a guide, in the sense that it may have taught us something about what should be avoided.

The emphasis on improvement and the use of the prospective view to establish standard costs, does not necessarily mean that they must represent ideal performance under perfect conditions. Managers must meet situations as they occur, and they must work with the materials and facilities that are available – often far from being optimal.

Therefore, it is always good to keep in mind that the establishment of standard costs does not represent a search for ideal performance, nor does it aim at reaching a theoretical minimum unit cost.

- The realistic view is to set the standard cost in terms of what may reasonably be expected from existing personnel skills, methods, materials, and equipment – after weeding out inefficiencies and undesirable features.
- Taking the problem for what it is and recognizing that the aim is to achieve reasonably attainable results means that the standard cost is a forecast of what can be, should be, and probably will be the experience of the future.

This has significant impact in terms of the plans that are made to effectively use available resources. Due to these factors, standard costs are closely related to the process of budgeting and of management control. Like the budget, they are a means of establishing what will be regarded as *satisfactory* rather than exceptional or ideal.

In conclusion, cost standards assist in producing a comprehensive solution to profitability measurement and reporting. Their effective exploitation helps to provide management with multidimensional views in terms of:

- The organization as a whole,
- The products and services,
- The customer relationships.

They permit us to do sophisticated funds allocations and transfers; they can be instrumental in product pricing; and they make feasible better control over operations. They are also a proven solution since they have been employed in the manufacturing industry for 80 years – though their usage in banking dates back only to the late 1960s.

PROFIT CENTERS AND THE CONCEPT OF ACTUAL COSTING

While past costs do not necessarily make good standards, the usual practice is that actual costs are evaluated by comparison with past figures and very seldom with standard figures. Yet, the latter approach forms a fairer basis for determining whether or not a good job has been done. As we have seen in the preceding sections, one of the key reasons for the normalization of costs is to:

- Permit foreseeing oncoming cost items, and
- Make corrective steps feasible ahead of time.

Reasons of optimization as well as of better management dictate that models are necessary to allocate not only costs but also revenues, assets and liabilities. Once developed, these models are very easy to handle since all information is databased and the algorithms themselves are processed by computer.

The majority of models available today for this purpose exploit a family of ratios and massage statistics from the organizational centers (see also the discussion on critical ratios in Part Four). Particularly important are those centers which have been identified for responsibility and control purposes:

- A *profit center* generates revenue against which it balances the costs incurred, with (hopefully) a difference remaining as profit.

A sales office, for example, is a profit center. It addresses itself to the market and generates an income from the sale of products and services. By contrast:

- Units which are limited to internal billing constitute *cost centers*, whose budget is either part of the overhead or the expenses incurred are billed to profit centers.

In accounting jargon, the way to distribute cost center charges is known as *absorption costing*. This is a traditional costing approach, such as overhead allocations. In this connection, the term *direct costing* is often used to imply that overhead amounts are excluded, though this term has different interpretations in different companies.

- Both approaches – absorption costing or direct costing – have been used in *standard costing* or *actual costing.*
- Therefore the model to be established must be precise and properly reflect prevailing organizational practices.

Absorption costing is more widely used but the utility of direct costing has been enhanced by means of more sophisticated methods regarding *performance evaluation*. A great deal of restructuring in industry today is done for performance reasons.

A more sophisticated implementation of direct costing is based on a matrix distribution of costs. This is also known as the *simultaneous approach*, because it takes into consideration the interactions of various departments. The method is quick to set up and maintain, from a computer processing standpoint.

- An algorithm for allocating the costs of each department, product, or service to each specific area of operations is established.
- The resulting cost equations are solved simultaneously, as the method implies, making feasible the effective distribution of costs.

One of the problems is overhead, and it results from the difficulty in distributing it in an equitable way. As a rule, no method is really that efficient, and some of the approaches to implementing actual costing of overhead are controversial. For instance, it is unfair to base the distribution of general management overhead on the amount of profits made by a division, because:

- This penalizes the more successful and more efficient operations,
- It obliges them to absorb other people's inefficiencies.

Neither is the amount of business, and hence of annual revenues, a good measure for overhead distribution – or for that matter, an algorithm which

TYPICAL
SITUATION

DESIRED
CONDITION

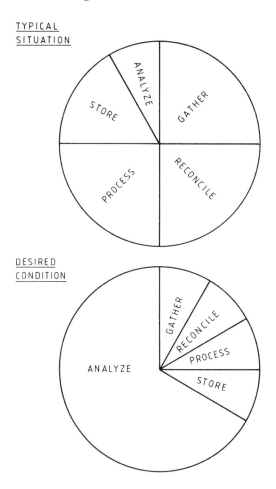

Figure 7.3 The need to cut the fat in overhead can be facilitated by proper analysis

allocates the same amount of overhead to all operations independent of other criteria.

Given that there exist no ideal solutions, the best approach with overhead is a thorough analysis of its reasons and a sharp knife to cut the fat. Figure 7.3 contrasts the typical situation in handling overhead with a better organized, and therefore desirable condition. As such, it provides food for thought.

- In the typical situation, the company spends most of its time in gathering and aimlessly processing overhead information.
- By contrast, the emphasis should be on the analysis of the reasons and the control of the overhead.

It is silly to spend a large chunk of time in gathering, reconciling, processing and sorting out overhead costs. These activities should be automated, with emphasis placed on the critical analysis of personnel and other overhead expenditures. Each unit incurring overhead should pay for it out of its profit figures, or show it as a loss.

METHODS OF ACCOUNTING FOR DEFERRED COSTS

The question of whether or not to defer certain costs from one time period to another is one of the biggest puzzles which exists in accounting. Behind this decision often lie some controversial management rules which tend to manipulate the profit and loss statements as well as the balance sheet.

As a general rule, a sound approach is to avoid capitalizing costs, writing them off in the year they occur. The exception is that companies can capitalize costs only when these provide benefits beyond the current year, but this exception rests on doubtful grounds and is misused.

- It is not that easy, in fact often difficult, to determine if work done today will bring future revenue, how and when.
- Such decisions tend to be fuzzy, and hence the concept of deferred costs is often practiced for the wrong reasons.

For instance, some companies defer R&D expenditures – which is a bad practice since it loads the balance sheet of the following years. A better approach is to make the R&D lab an independent business unit which charges the parent company a royalty for the patents which it uses. Morgan Stanley did this with its Advanced Systems Group (ASG).

In a similar manner, it is quite difficult to determine how much of the legal and public relations costs are attributable to future developments, for instance relating to patents or marketing. Hence, accountants are well advised to write every expense in the accounts of the year when it has incurred.

- Because the capitalization rules quite often are not well defined, financial analysts and investors get nervous when companies seem to be aggressively capitalizing costs.
- Even when a company has written specific rules on capitalization of costs, these rules may be followed in a variety of ways or leave huge loopholes in their application.

Software development is an example. The rules may say that a company can start capitalizing the cost of developing a product when it has reached the point of technological feasibility. But given the complexity of software, when does this milestone *really* come?

- Due to such ambiguities, some companies like Microsoft do not capitalize any development costs.
- But other software firms do capitalize between 10 percent–20 percent of their total R&D budget – a bad practice.

How can investors be protected against unexpected writeoffs that can send a stock plunging? One way is to look at spelled out policies, or at least at what a company includes in the *other assets* category on the balance sheet. That is where most firms tend to dump a lot of deferred costs.

These are some of the challenges facing cost management systems. Problems arise every day due to the heterogeneity of rules and regulations in a cross-border manner. For instance, there exist many legal ambiguities within the European Union – from one country to another. Accounting laws have locality, which does not help the need to support increasingly complex cross-border deals.

- These problems are not unavoidable, if legislation gets homogeneous and compatible.
- But as the case is now, they stand in the way of normalization and competitiveness.

Once this message has been understood, the effectiveness of accounting rules and regulations must be considered both in a national and in a cross-border sense, with a consistent effort invested towards problem solution.

As with other implementation domains, a sound way to proceed involves prototyping and knowledge engineering. It is always wise to evaluate the impact of current accounting rules, not just on the current bottom line but also on the longer term – including the reaction of investors as well as the work done by financial analysts.

Accounting procedures should be organized to give a comprehensive view both of the work currently in process, and of the staying power of the firm: financial, technological and in marketing. Business and industry are confronted today with major changes in the way management accounting reports are projected, implemented and maintained. The norms must be flexible, but they should be there.

The changes necessary to capitalize from the environment which develops are not just technical. They are primarily managerial and financial. Much depends on whether or not we have the intellectual vitality to face the new challenges. Also, on our ability to inspire confidence in our financial reports.

CURRENT ASSETS, SHORT- AND LONG-TERM COSTS

As we will see in Part Three, the balance sheet separates *short-term* from *long-term* items by calling the first group (including cash balances and customer receivables) *current assets*. Expenditures associated to merchandising, renting, insurance, and the like represent short-term items.

• Merchandising costs are essentially current assets which are *turned over*, that is, expensed and replaced.
• This circulating nature of assets is more rapid than investments in tools, equipment, buildings, and other longer-term items.

A similar sense of short-term and long-term distinctions applies to equities. More or less in a universal manner, the criterion used to separate current from fixed equities is the due date of the obligation.

• Short-term debt is labeled current, to distinguish it from long-term or permanent debt.
• The amounts charged to long-term asset accounts are costs applicable to future periods.

Usually, however, more than a couple of years are involved in the case of fixed assets. The cost of an investment is simply carried forward on the balance sheet until the investment is sold or liquidated. The gain or loss from holding that investment may be deferred until it is disposed of.

In this sense, the statement sent by brokers to their customers talks of *unrealized* or *paper* profits and losses. These will become actual when the customer sells, for example the futures contract(s), with the corresponding credit or debit written to the customer's account.

• Quite different from investments are the costs of buildings and equipment necessary to regular operations.
• Some part of these operating assets must be charged to each fiscal period if the flow of expenses is to be measured properly.

There are also other aspects of cost accounting to be brought into perspective. It frequently happens that a firm pays in advance for services to be received. For instance, for rent of office space.

• Strict cash-basis accounting would show such a payment charged to a Rent account, which presumably would represent expense.
• But a trial balance taken one month after a quarterly rent payment would not show the correct expense for this item.

Such assets are in the nature of *prepayments* to the extent that the services they represent are applicable to future accounting periods. An ingenious way of looking at the difference between *expenses* and *assets* is through the concept that:

- *Expenses* are costs applicable to current period operations, and
- *Assets* are costs, or potential costs, applicable to the future.

Inversely, if the period of time taken is short enough, all costs are assets at the time of incurral. They become expenses through operating transactions which convert and deliver those services to the market.

Hence, prepaid rent is an asset, and as such appears in the balance sheet at the close of the fiscal period. Rent expenses arise from the amortization of the cost, relating the proper amount to the current operating period. Correspondingly, the cost of depreciable assets may be:

- Charged as expense to the period in which these assets have been initially acquired.
- Carried as assets until retirement occurs, at which time the cost is transferred to expenses,
- Carried as assets indefinitely, but *replacements* charged to expense when they occur, or
- Amortized over the periods in which each asset is used in the business.

Such approaches to the problem of allocating long-term costs are conditioned by management policy, organizational culture, and the law of the land. Since there exist variations, particularly for management accounting purposes, it is appropriate to clearly define the chosen option, ensure that it can be legally supported, and stick to it after its definition.

8 Methods and Procedures for Better Control Over Costs and Budgets

INTRODUCTION

In Chapters 6 and 7 we spoke of fixed and variable costs, direct and indirect costs, short-term and long-term costs. It is the duty of management to control all of them, not after the fact but at the very beginning of an accounting period, starting with the forecasting and planning phase.

- From financial forecasts are developed schedules of operating charges and revenues.
- From these spring plans for the procurement of resources needed to carry on the projected operations.

Summarized and combined with income and charge items, these schedules are used to prepare evalutions of disbursements in regard to projected income. Management control over costs should see to it that expenditures rise much slower than income projections.

This is an important mission of management facilitated by the fact that the financial plan is a combination of all types of estimates. In its details, it is providing a complete set of cost and revenue projections which account for all other company plans.

One of the best ways to control costs and budgets is to have them expressed in terms of the *transactions* to be executed and the *aims* to be attained. These have to be studied analytically, both:

- *A priori*, that is prior to being finalized, and
- *Post-mortem* in a critical Plan versus Actual sense.

Plan/Actual evaluations permit the enforcement of budgetary standards in an execution sense. They also make feasible the subsequent analysis of deviations, all the way to their origin. Management should be keen to highlight deviations as well as to identify exceptions. This is a comprehensive way to assuring whether or not the managerial plans are effectively being followed. It is also a means of determining:

- What kind of corrective action is necessary,
- On which issues of accountability it should focus,
- How it should be carried out, and when.

Business is no club where old chaps are welcome to do as they please. There are responsibilities to fulfill and everyone, from the president to the foreman and the workers, should be accountable for them. Nobody should ever be permitted to lose sight of targets, revenue objectives, costs and the satisfaction of the needs of the company's customers.

QUALITATIVE AND QUANTITATIVE MANAGEMENT REPORTS

Appropriate reports must be prepared to establish factual and documented comparisons between planned and actual performance. Plan/Actual results must be analyzed promptly, at regular intervals as well as by exception. Financial analysis should be done in a form permitting a comprehensible interpretation.

- The efficiency and adequacy with which managerial decisions are carried out can be improved by means of interactive Plan/Actual reporting.
- Both *quantitative* and *qualitative* evaluations give clues to the way in which related activities are being performed and how they can be brought under control.

Based on the policies followed by a leading financial institution, Figure 8.1 brings into perspective the fact that performance measurement can be effective only when management has taken care to ensure there is a formal system of control by which everybody and all organizational units abide. While the structure of this system varies from one company to another, its contents should cover all operations.

Management can use Plan/Actual results to keep well informed as to what is really happening in different parts of the business. This permits us to judge whether or not the outcome that is expected is in reality achieved:

- Without cost overruns, and
- At a high quality of output.

But while Plan/Actual cost evaluations are very important, they are not enough. The financial plan itself may be biased, including significant cost items which should not be there. This can happen not only in terms of minor articles but also of whole departments.

In 1958 I published a book on Operations Research (OR). Shortly thereafter IBM asked me to join its Applied Science division and the first mission

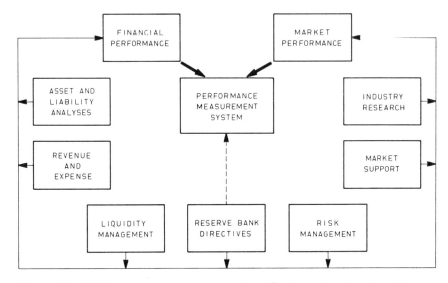

Figure 8.1 Performance measurements can be effective only when there is a formal system of control

was to study how many departments in the corporation devoted their activities to OR. The findings were surprising:

- Eight (8) different IBM departments were identified spending time and money on the then novel operations research activities.
- Many of these departments did not even know about each other – and when they knew, they did not necessarily care.

This is an example which happens in many companies around the globe. It is amazing how many duplicates and triplicates of the same function hide behind a stone. Once a department feeds on the budget it tends to stay there for very long.

For these reasons, management must examine cost centers from both a macroscopic and a microscopic viewpoint. All expense chapters require careful auditing and the understanding that the enforcement of approved financial plans may be effected in several ways, all of them requiring:

- Highlighting duplicate and triplicate costs,
- Keeping a close check on actual results, and
- Insisting on explanations for differences.

Such differences may show up in terms of real output and/or controllable charges in the specific budgetary chapters. A good way to account for them is to use breakeven analysis both for profit centers and for cost centers.

As Chapters 6 and 7 have shown, breakeven for profit centers is straightforward, since fixed and variable costs will be weighted against obtained revenues. The risk with cost centers is that because they feed on the company's budget, the growth in their fixed and variable costs risks not being visible. There are two ways to remedy this situation, and both involve qualitative as well as quantitative management reports.

1. *Internal billing* is quantitative, but it should be coupled with a qualitative audit of the need for the cost center's services and the quality of products it provides.

It should be appreciated that *qualitative* does not necessarily mean subjective. Though much of what this report includes is a matter of opinion, the findings have to be documented by comparisons with other similar services by external suppliers, their quality and their costs.

2. *Freedom of choice.* In no way should management oblige the company's profit centers (and other cost centers) to purchase the products and services of a given internal unit. This breeds inefficiency.

The market is the best criterion and every profit center should be allowed to buy the services it needs from the market, *in competition* with internal providers. Such a policy will make the internal departments run faster, seek to upgrade their quality and be careful over their costs.

Bankers Trust, for example, has instituted this policy in connection with the provision of information technology services. The result has been salutary – from cost reduction to a very competitive offering of IT services, which made Bankers Trust a Tier 1 bank in information technology.

USING BREAKEVEN ANALYSIS IN THE FINANCIAL INDUSTRY

The way it has been explained in Chapter 7, breakeven analysis provides a relatively simple and clear framework for profit planning. As will be shown in the following pages, a profit formula can be devised which is an easy and concise way to evaluate the effect of changes on the bottom line by:

• Analyzing each expense item all the way to its primary determinants, and
• Using analytical tools to improve productivity, and therefore profitability.

The banker's fixed costs include those associated with real estate, rental, utilities, office equipment, administration and data processing. The last two chapters are heavy in personnel expenditures. While computers came into the bank to reduce personnel expenses, they ended by significantly increasing them.

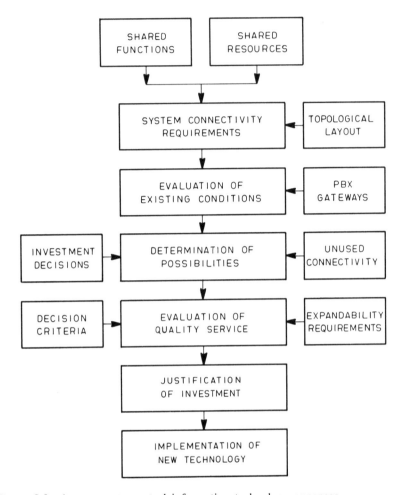

Figure 8.2   A strategy to control information technology expenses

There is another reason why administration and data processing constitute good examples of cost-cutting for lower breakeven. They are both cost center-type expenditures. They do not produce direct profits in a market oriented sense.

A sound policy would see to it that all expenditures in computers, communications and software are very tightly controlled. My forty years of experience in this domain documents that there is much fat to cut.

- Figure 8.2 suggests a strategy which I found very effective in controlling information technology expenditures.
- Since most expenses in computers, communications and software have curiously become fixed costs, *downsizing* is a wise policy.

In fact, downsizing is a good policy for all fixed costs. In implementing a valid costing procedure in service oriented situations, we must be able to integrate our knowledge of costs, and our metrics, into a series of straightforward steps.

Management which is seriously planning to lower the company's breakeven point, should be keen to learn lessons from companies that have done so already. These companies have carefully studied the cost structure of each organziational unit, as well as providing a basis of financial allocation based on results. Ongoing cost patterns must be detected and compared to the most efficient solutions which are known.

Provided that *standard costs* are properly established and implemented, the overall cost pattern which develops will show if our costs are under control. Leading-edge companies think that pattern analysis:

- Reflects rather accurately the *true cost* of providing our services to our customers, and
- Permits us to *price products* for a fair return on capital.

It also provides a common denominator; a *yardstick* by which productivity achievements, or lack of them, can be measured. The result is indices which point to *cost trends*, by showing when and where they are *out of line*.

As we have seen on several occasions, standards are a major part of a costing effort, and the same reference is valid regarding the choice of proper rules and formulas. The breakeven formulas we have seen in Chapters 6 and 7 can be further developed and customized to fit *banking* requirements. If:

- *p* equals the average *rate of return* on *earning assets* per dollar of *investible deposits*,
- *v* is the average *interest* rate paid per dollar of investible deposits,
- *F* stands for fixed costs, and
- *Q* is the number of dollars of average total investible deposits at breakeven point,

then the breakeven formula of a bank is:

$$Q = \frac{F}{p - v} \tag{1}$$

Notice the correspondence to the industrial formula, where *p* stood for selling price per unit and *v* for variable cost per unit. In the bank's case *v* is the variable cost calculated out of the cost of money of investible deposits – hence the bank's *interest budget*.

- Many banks do not add direct labor to the variable cost, because the payroll is part of the noninterest budget.
- Instead they talk of *overhead* as a cumulative term for all payroll costs, which is not an accurate way of looking at this subject.

In fact, it is a very bad policy which does not allow us to control the true overhead costs, which are by definition indirect. However, since such issues do not constitute the purpose of this book, we will not insist further on this point.

Assuming, then, that we will not include labor costs in our model, when values are determined for F, v and p and fit into this equation, Q will represent the level of investible deposits greater than that which will show a total profit (TP) expressed by the equation we saw in Chapter 6:

$$TP = (p \times Q) - (v \times Q + F)$$

Where Q now stands for actual investible deposits, not breakeven deposits. Furthermore, the quantity:

$$p - v$$

is often referred to as the *contribution margin*, for it contributes toward covering all fixed costs up to the breakeven point. Beyond that point, the contribution margin represents profits, assuming that fixed costs do not increase at some distant point either directly or through the introduction of semi-variable costs.

THE IMPACT OF THE BANK'S DEPOSIT MIX

It is important to appreciate the similarity which exists in algorithmic representation between the manufacturing and banking industries. In our example, any increase in handling a given financial product above the breakeven point will show a profit. The same is true regarding a breakeven analysis on deposits, provided that the marginal reinvestment rate exceeds the interest rate paid.

In principle, the breakeven point is a function of the bank's deposit mix, as reflected in the average interest rate paid on investible deposits. With any analytic accounting procedure, changing the mix has an immediate impact on financial results. In this case,

- It is a frequent and understandable management strategy to look for a change of the deposit mix in the direction of demand deposits,
- The effect is to decrease the value of v because a low interest is paid on demand deposits.

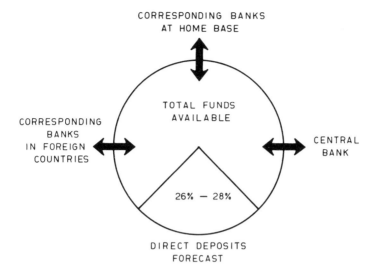

Figure 8.3 Developing the overall financial plan

Decreasing the value of v results in a higher contribution margin, $p - v$, and a lower breakeven point. Thus the value of demand deposits over time deposits is documented through such an approach, but neither management nor the financial analysts should forget that there are operating costs associated with demand deposits.

While the interest paid on bought money is significantly higher, the associated fixed and variable costs are lower. Few financial institutions have in place the sophisticated information systems necessary to capture and integrate these costs. Typically, banks 'hope' that their fixed costs will be covered faster and profit will be much greater, but they are not able to account for all of their cost aspects.

Figure 8.3 gives a hint in the direction of deposits analysis, based on the policy followed by a leading commercial bank. This policy differentiates the sources of funds, then integrates them into a consolidated budget. The process:

• Starts with a deposit forecast
• Involves a properly studied projection on loans
• Calculates the borrowing costs and interest from lending
• Evaluates the interest costs against the lending costs, thus projecting on profit margins.

In this particular example, based on market share, management calculates that 26–28 percent of needed funds will be made available through direct deposits. The balance will be bought money. The following references are applicable regarding deposits and loans:

- Deposit forecast based on market share: 26–28 percent of needed funds
- Projected cost of client deposits W percent (interest cost)
- Loan forecast: XXX based on market share and loan percentage
- Forecasted average interest rates Y percent for borrowing and Z percent for lending.

A differentiation is made between short-term borrowing, with Y' percent interest rate, and long-term borrowing with Y'' percent interest rate. The same is true regarding short-term and long-term lending, respectively with Z' percent and Z'' percent interest rates.

- Fixed interest rate long-term commitments are matched, and derivative financial instruments are used for hedging purposes (see also Chapter 10).
- Part of this hedging is internal, with other departments of the bank carrying the risk – which is being expressed in cost factors.

An increasing number of financial institutions adopt a strategy of risk-adjusted return on capital. Those which have done so comment that the experience is rewarding. Though it reduces profits, it does so because it accounts for risks being taken.

All cost factors need to be closely watched as a shift in the deposits, borrowing and lending mix impacts heavily on profits. No sound policy can rest on the hypothesis that bank deposits are relatively permanent and can be reinvested at the average rate of return on average earning assets. This is vanilla-icecream banking which has no place in today's world.

ARE SOME ASSUMPTIONS MADE BY THE FINANCIAL INDUSTRY REALLY SOUND?

As we have seen in the preceding sections, there exist many similarities between the financial algorithms used in the manufacturing industry and those in banking, the latter having been largely derived from the former. But not every concept or practice can be carried from manufacturing into banking. An example is *inventorying*.

In industrial operations as products are sold to the market the cost accountant watches for changes in inventory levels. Inventory changes are invisible in the banking industry where the product of many service industries is either consumed or is not.

- If not, it must be written off as a nonincome producing expense – or, simply, the benefit which might have been cannot be counted.
- This impossibility of inventorying, that is deferring to a later period, is typical of the service sector of the economy, banking and airlines being examples.

In other words, of the two pillars on which a good breakeven analysis rests, *costing* and *inventorying*, in the service industry the second is virtual and at times impossible. This places even more importance on costing – and the associated cost allocation, in all of its many ramifications. It is also a reason why many banks lump all personnel costs into overhead.

As alert bankers appreciate, this practice is not sound. At the same time they can see that there are no easy solutions, though the more cost-conscious banks try to make the models which they use both more realistic and more sophisticated.

For instance, in the examples which we have seen, by dropping the assumptions that average investible deposits equal average earning assets and that revenue not related to earning assets shall be ignored, total income (before income tax) will tie into the income statement, provided the break-even equation is modified accordingly. This modified breakeven formula is:

$(1 + D)(p \times Q) + S = v \times Q + F$, or

$$Q = \frac{F - S}{p(1 + D) - v} \qquad (2)$$

Comparing the breakeven equations (1) and (2) we observe two new terms in equation (2), which are:

D = Difference between average total earning assets and average total investible deposits, as a percent of average total investible deposits
S = Revenue not related to earning assets

Simplifications always exist. The way this equation is practiced in the banking industry, D and S are assumed to be constant relative to deposits. In reality, these quantities may not vary significantly as average investible deposits change, but they do vary.

Total profit income tax can also be calculated by an algorithm where Q represents actual average total investible deposits (not breakeven deposits). It can be shown that such a modified total profit formulation becomes a framework for profit planning. This is a rather straightforward way of evaluating the effect of changes in the fundamental determinants of profit figures.

Once the algorithmic expression has been established, the values of the elements which it includes may be varied, with the resulting effect upon profit shown in a quick and easy manner. This is why algorithmic approaches help so much in experimentation. For instance, through a financial model we can evaluate what will be the effect of:

- A change in the prime rate, or the general level of interest rates.
- Increasing service charges, trust department fees and so on – in conjunction with or independent from rate changes.

Whenever estimates for any of the elements of the formula are not fully certain, we can use probabilities – or even better fuzzy sets – to make explicit such uncertainty, applying a subjective possibility distribution to estimated outcomes (see Chorafas, 1992, 1994c).

Say, for example, that regarding the problem of the effects of a change in the interest rate on the volume of time deposits and ultimately upon profits, we are uncertain as to how far deposits will decline if the interest rate is reduced by a few basic points. Using expert opinion structured in a subjective possibility distribution, we can estimate the decline in the level of time deposits.

HOW TO DEVELOP COST ACCOUNTING MODELS

The polyvalence of pricing and cost control algorithms described in the foregoing sections suggests that a financial model must have access to all forms of data, including average balances, loans, interest rates, statistics on revenues, and evidently cost information. The primary purpose of many models currently in use is to evaluate incomes and costs as they apply to:

- Organizational units,
- Products and services,
- Customer relationships,
- Supplier relationships, and so on.

There is more than can be gained in terms of experimentation in terms of costs rather than fees or interest on loans, because interest and fees are subject to tough competition. Therefore they are steadily under pressure. By contrast, downsizing internal costs can be a rewarding enterprise.

But a sound cost analysis *has* its prerequisites, some of which are organizational and others are translated into information technology requirements. Figure 8.4 shows an example from a cost control project which focused on relationship banking. Notice that:

- At the core is the customer's basic code (*bc*) providing a unique identification, which is lacking from many banking systems.
- The next layers include customer information as well as the constraints on this specific relationship.

At the level of the constraints come risks associated with the account as well as costs. Both have to be watched. Costs are also connected with each

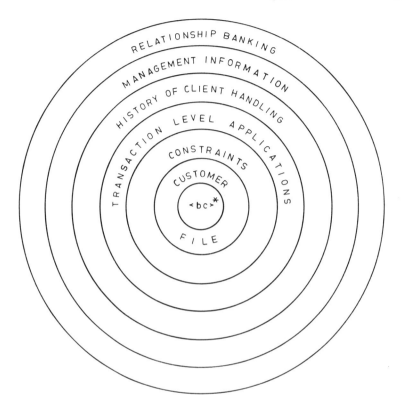

Figure 8.4 Design approach to the information system goals and priorities

and every transaction the customer makes. The management of the customer relationship itself also contributes to the expenditures.

This is a reference from banking which should be extended to any other sector of industry. The need for proper identification and classification of costs is present in every case. Every production activity involves expenditures – some of them are warranted but others are not.

Financial analysts should know the ramifications involved in costing, and they should watch out for evidence of an efficient control over expenditures. In recommending the shares of Placer Dome for investment in March 1994, Prudential Securities gave this reason:

Major Cost Reductions. Cash costs declined 23 percent since 1990 to $184 per ounce in 1993, mainly due to productivity gains.

To control the costs we have to know them. We also have to transfer them into an account which accepts them. The mechanics of transferring costs is no real problem, but organizational reactions and political infighting can be a roadblock.

- Transfer is typically accomplished by allocating direct costs or by generating standard costs and charging them.
- But the flow of costs, that is who allocates to whom and how much, is a problem – and the solution varies in every organization.

A valid cost accounting model will pay significant attention to the flow of costs; in other words, the path that *allocations* and *charges* take from the originating unit (the source) to an end receiver. This flow may be broken into phases or completed in one phase, according to organizational procedures.

Typically, general ledger costs are classified by *cost center* or *profit center*, and by *account number*. In cost accounting, the costs accumulated in a general ledger for a cost center, or those in selected accounts within a cost center, may be allocated by:

- Identification of the factors to be used in transferring expense items,
- Selection of clearly defined distributive operations to be performed, and
- A closeout sequence which permits us to empty the accounts into which costs have been temporarily parked.

The model will necessarily depend on organizational policies and procedures. These may, for instance, stipulate that costs can be distributed to products initially, and then to profit centers that manage each product.

Another choice is associating costs with detailed activities which are often referred to as *subprojects*. Examples of such activities from a banking environment are:

- Opening a new account,
- Making an installment loan,
- Processing cheques and the like.

One of the major contributions a good accounting model can make is to highlight incompatibilities which exist between organizational procedures and the way standard costs have been developed. *If* the two are incompatible, as is often the case because of miscoordination, *then* the close-out of intermediate accounts and subprojects will suffer because of missing or biased correspondences.

Even if these correspondences were right many years ago, when they were established, the chances are that they have become increasingly unrealistic as time passes by. Organizations are dynamic and change over time. Yet few accounting systems keep pace with this fact, with the result that accounting procedures are out of phase with regard to the structure which they address.

THE IMPORTANCE OF GETTING ACCEPTANCE

From internal accounting and cost charges to the pricing of products, the keyword is *acceptance*. Unless the clients to which our products are offered think that the price is appealing, they will not buy them. Similarly, if profit centers internal to the organization believe that the charges are unreasonable, they will react negatively.

It takes a significant amount of fairness and coordination to effectively transfer the cost of different activities to the profit centers for which they were performed. First, the profit centers must be in accord with the standard costs and the charging method. Second, the information should include:

- The unit cost of each activity, such as the cost of opening an account.
- Cost by activity and group of activities (products).
- Both the detailed and the total cost of the various activities.
- Product profitability reports and associated comparisons.

The model governing cost transfers from cost centers to profit centers must be well established and upkept, so that it can work automatically. Since the recipient departments will check on the charges, the content of these charges must be sound.

This is why performance against standards by activity, product, operating unit and the organization as a whole is so important. Sound concepts cannot be implemented overnight but neither should they take years:

- The activities of each department must be identified and weighted,
- Standard costs must be developed and incorporated into the system, and
- References external to the organization provided to enhance the standard job.

For instance, a leading financial institution debated what should be the cost of its private communications network to the operating departments. The latter felt that the charges were too high, while the people managing the network – that is, the service providers – had precisely the opposite opinion.

The solution adopted in this case was to take the rate applicable by five international public network providers and try to develop a frame of reference (see Chorafas and Steinmann, 1990). When this was done, it was found that the tariffs the five vendors advanced were so different among themselves in terms of:

- Structure,
- Discounts, and
- Exceptions

that it was not possible to linearly extrapolate averages. As a result, it was necessary to build a model which permitted to them apply a scenario of realistic network usage. Each scenario was priced according to each network provider's price structure, making it possible to develop a common cost denominator.

Developing cost/benefit scenarios and building models to implement them is a rewarding job for several reasons. First, it helps in clearing our mind about issues which can often be confusing. Second, it provides a basis for experimentation:

- Advancing hypotheses
- Testing them, and
- Obtaining documented results.

This analytical process increases the competitiveness of an organization and of its units. It provides relevant evidence of changes which are necessary in order to be on a par with the most efficient of our competitors. And it permits us to implement technology which is really state-of-the-art.

IMPROVING AND REFINING THE COST SYSTEM

Unless we proceed analytically and experiment through simulation, as the previous section has suggested, improving and refining the cost system may require an extended period of time before reliable data is produced. When a situation is complex, the model and the artifacts it requires must be implemented in phases.

- Some of the information may be developed immediately and applied right away.
- While other modules, the remainder, are being under development or are even in the process of being defined.

As we have seen through practical examples, cost accounting models are necessary because, among other advantages, they help to classify the issues on hand and better define the processes of setting standards. Once done, such models help in experimentation, and hence in improving current practices.

One of the more important areas in which cost account models can be used is in defining and developing fair allocation techniques. None of the existing approaches to the allocation of charges is ideal or can satisfy everybody. Compromises therefore need to be made. Among the better known approaches are:

- *Calculated percentages based on statistical data*, with the top management specifying which amounts are to be used in the allocation.
- *Calculated percentages based on multiple statistical data*, where the basis for allocation requires more than one statistic (for instance, both number of accounts and number of transactions).
- *Weighting factors* for each type of statistic affecting the recipient center, and based on some objective criteria.
- *Standard unit costs* to serve as a basis for calculating the actual amount transferred to the recipient center.
- *Direct money allocation*, essentially specifying an amount to be charged to a recipient center – something often done with general management overhead expenses.

If standard costs are the basis of the transfer, it is wise to calculate the *variance* between actual and standard, as we have seen in Chapter 8. It is also proper to maintain a *From – To* computer file which can serve as an audit trail, indicating what costs are allocated from a cost center to various recipient centers.

Another file, *To – From*, helps in providing a *reverse audit* trail for the recipient profit center receiving charges from multiple cost centers. The basis for each allocation, as well as the appropriate factors, must however be clearly identified to assist in answering recipient center questions.

In conclusion, whatever is decided in terms of costing and charging accounts should be fair to all concerned. This requires significant study and documentation, and therefore experimentation able to assure:

- Fairness in charges, in the sense that they are competitive industry-wide,
- A solid basis for productivity growth, assuring that costs diminish over time, and
- Going beyond cost/effectiveness in obtained results, to guarantee end-to-end quality.

A cost accounting system is put in place to meet management's expectations in all these factors. At the same time it helps provide the infrastructure for budgetary appropriations, as Chapters 6 and 7 have explained. From this comes the wisdom of assuming full responsibility for enhancing the value of the solutions which we provide, through appropriate modeling.

THE NATURE OF THE MODELING EFFORT

The use of quantitative and qualitative criteria in connection with financial planning should be done through prototyping. During the initial study, critical questions concern the type of model to be constructed, and its scope in terms of how much of the company's operations should be represented and the skills needed:

- In the background are the potential uses of the model's modules as they become available one by one.
- In the foreground is a rapid development timeframe and project organization as a whole.

As was explained in Part One, it is wise to start by drawing the largest system, and subsequently defining the modules it should contain. As we progress from grand design to detail, it becomes necessary to determine whether:

- Deterministic,
- Stochastic, or
- Heuristic approaches

will be chosen for the different modules – considering them on an individual basis as well as in terms of an aggregate. Just as important is to define the kind of user oriented output which should be built through a parametric, graphics oriented approach.

Part of the task will be to determine if the necessary data is available, define the shell which will be employed for prototyping, and assess computer capabilities necessary to handle the problem. These are some of the key issues to be considered when determining the type of model(s) we wish to develop.

Companies with experience in the development of financial models for all sectors of their operations comment that when they work to define the larger system they find themselves confronted with two conflicting procedures.

1. They must look at a single segment of the company in very fine detail, but
2. Consider the entire company as an operating entity, from a macroscopic viewpoint.

Precisely because of this apparent conflict of goals, my personal advice has been to gain perspective by initially developing a broad scope model. The aim of this coarse grain approach should be one of providing a consolidated outlook to be properly focused in the next phase.

After the overall framework of the aggregate model has been worked out, it is possible to elaborate on the factors which it includes in a detailed fashion – module by module – after establishing the right priorities. However, detailed work should not start prior to having obtained feedback from the potential users.

- Sometimes this is not that easy since few people know or appreciate what a corporate model is, or how it can be of value,
- Prototyping, however, helps to explain the goal as well as to show the deliverables, even if these are still coarse grain.

Knowledge engineers and systems analysts should clearly define potential uses for everything they construct, and present their work in a way comprehensible to endusers. Then, they should train the endusers and do so in a nontechnical manner, their presentation being enriched with:

- Demonstrations made on the prototype, and
- One-day to three-day seminars to be attended by users as well as by senior management.

Organizations which follow this approach should keep in mind that computer-literate senior management and the endusers appreciate *speed of development*, *quality of software*, and *sophistication of the solution*. Also the ability to swamp computer costs.

Systems specialists should be aware of the fact that the new programming style starts not in the computer room, but at the user's desk. Contrary to the obsolete approaches followed by mainframers:

- The enduser should be directly responsible for developing his software.
- The computer specialist must act as his consultant, not as his bottleneck.

While there are many prerequisites to a new and efficient software strategy, the foremost is that development time is *hours*, *days* or at maximum *weeks*. Not months and years – the way the slow-moving data processors as well as the unwilling and unnecessary mainframers work. Everybody should understand that speed means competitiveness.

SIZING UP THE JOB WHICH NEEDS TO BE DONE

When we talk of cost control systems and measures, it should be implicitly stated that these include communications, computers and software. There is no way and no reason that the careful watch over costs in profit centers and cost centers should exclude information technology.

The 1980s and early 1990s have seen a huge increase in expenditures connected with computers and software, yet there has been no improvement in the results. If anything, people and companies are suffering from information technology rather than benefitting from their investments. As a rule:

- The more money is thrown at a problem, the less will be the output.
- The more management abdicates its responsibilities, the more the process will get out of control.

There is absolutely no reason for projects to be undertaken in budgeting, costing, information technology or any other domain, if we are not sure about what we get out of them. No effort should start prior to sizing up costs and benefits.

What may be the size of an algorithmic and heuristic system covering budgetary requirements for a financial institution? For a manufacturing and sales organization? This question does not address itself to the simple examples we have seen in this chapter but to a complete financial model with many specialized modules.

A valid answer can be given through past experience. Taking three different references from practical applications examples into account, the answer is that it may feature:

1. In terms of *data streams* a level of 3,500 different input items (information elements) typically required to emulate a year of operations during which these inputs will be repeated many times over.

Though only an estimated 10 percent of these inputs will be of major importance in terms of the effect on net income, all of them have to be classified according to the area where they are applicable and their relative weight in terms of processing requirements – realtime or other. Also in order to facilitate data collection.

2. Regarding the *architecturing* of algorithms, simulators and expert systems necessary for the complete works, the best approach is to rely on modular constructs.

Again as an average, some 100 relatively simple models may be needed, or a smaller number of fairly complex simulators – the former approach being better than the latter. Again talking of the three projects as an average, the number of equations may tend to be at the 2,800 level, with a range between 1,600 and 3,700.

Within this same reference perspective, the number of expert systems of the IF ... THEN ... ELSE type completed or planned stood at about 50 –

with 20–1,000 rules each. An average of 150–200 rules can be taken as order of magnitude.

3. In connection with *development tools* and *database* management, the choice should be object frameworks and software-hardware codesign.

Object frameworks is the latest in applications development. The new generation of development tools is fully object oriented, operating at client – server level and supporting an increased diversity of applications.

Not only is the customization of the application(s) at a premium, but there also exists a fast growing requirement to decrease the costs of designing and testing new systems. Effective cost control, as well as overcoming time constraints, requires basic changes in the *style* and *environments* of information technology tasks.

The same principles which we have just seen call for a great deal of attention to be paid to system output. In terms of time and cost, the number of outputs is less of a constraint when we are able to handle flexible, ad hoc queries.

The three systems in the background of this case study featured among themselves between 100 and 400 output screens, the larger number representing the less elegant solution in terms of design. The most modern of the three integrated financial models provided for all queries to be flexibly structured by the enduser in an ad hoc manner.

WAYS AND MEANS FOR BUDGETARY ENFORCEMENT

It will come as no surprise that the soundest of the three solutions also took the least time and its cost was very reasonable. It was done on client–server, used knowledge engineering and was executed in five months – while the more cumbersome approach which was carried on mainframes required three years.

Whether in banking or in manufacturing, with information technology as with any other project, not only has the budget to be optimized, but its control should also be punctual. Therefore, in concluding Part Two, I have added the present section to focus on the most efficient ways and means for budgetary enforcement.

The best case study will be the one we have already considered with the General Electric experience. Since its first inception, the GE's financial planning program profited from *Monte Carlo* simulation. The simulator permitted a polyvalent analysis with change of hypotheses, repeating the number crunching afterwards.

In an operational sense, the determination of alternative budgets proved to be most useful in terms of management decisions. It provided an integrative environment for experimentation since the model could be used not only for budgeting, but also for long-term planning and strategic studies.

Closely related to the probabilistic budgetary process is a comparative planning and control approach. Management determines the *tolerances* in which the budget is registered. From this statement, for every month of the year, an artifact calculates the percentage from which the real results diverge from planning (Plan/Actual).

- *Tolerance limits* by department and budgetary chapter are transferred to an integrated output in which the cumulative budget statement represents the zero-line.
- From month-to-month, as actual results become known, the *percentage deviation* is drawn up and brought to the attention of management.

As long as the values are under the tolerance limits, it is assumed that the year's aim is in the way of being obtained. When an input drops out of tolerance, *an audit* is made. This control process is completed by a program which, from month to month, finds out the probability that a department or division has reached the year's budget or surpassed it.

Many financial institutions and manufacturing companies today have adopted similar interactive processes whereby online controls permit us to systematically evaluate *Plan versus Actual.*

- Pinpointing the origin of differences between projections and obtained results, and
- Computing the reasons for variations leading to corrective action.

Such dynamic approaches permit us to determine in a factual and documented manner the necessary controls. They make it possible to reach timely decisions which help avoid further deviations. This is the true sense of *budgetary enforcement.*

Another approach to budgetary enforcement is to place an absolute limit upon outlays. A definite amount is appropriated for each specific operation. When this is exhausted, expenditures for that operation *must cease*, unless management grants an additional authorization.

Budgetary enforcement counterweights the fact that, in the general case, business budgets are subject to many influences which may destroy the validity of original estimates. In other cases, a policy is implemented which obviates the need for frequent budget adjustments and revisions.

Absolute-limit features are followed, for instance, in retail merchandizing budgets, designed to limit the amount of expenditures and the level of inventory investment by department. For example:

- The buyer is not permitted to place orders for merchandize in excess of the amount calculated as *open-to-buy*.
- Open-to-buy is computed on the basis of retail prices, and adjusted to *cost*, applying initially planned mark-up figures.

Except where conditions have manifestly changed to such an extent that revisions of the budget are absolutely necessary, the procedural constraints are upheld and their observance is taken as criterion of performance.

Such procedures make it feasible that the chief executive uses the budget as *a performance standard*. He holds each of the major department heads (and project leaders) responsible for the fulfillment of his specific part of the short-term financial program.

Each department head may in turn uphold this responsibility record in connection with his subordinates for their specific performances, according to the budgetary appropriations for their sections. This means that each section head must definitely be aware of what *results* are expected of him – as well as being in a position to initiate his own plans for controlling the operations of his particular unit.

All this leads to a concept of *budgetary analysis* and requires powerful tools for a prompt and accurate evaluation. We have extensively spoken of this need. The wisdom of management co-involvement with the policies and procedures necessary for implementing budgetary control has also been underlined.

Part Three

Modeling Balance Sheet and Off-Balance Sheet Operations

9 Models for Balance Sheet Reporting

INTRODUCTION

According to the old organizational concepts, an organization should be viewed like a pyramid. The chief executive officer at the top of that pyramid would have staff and line executives reporting directly to him. Each of the senior vice presidents would be receiving information from factory or sales office managers, according to his function. Below that level would be departments, sections, projects, and so on.

- Through a model, we can build an image of that hierarchical organizational structure, as it is usually done by all firms.
- Figure 9.1 identifies three tiers of that pyramid and indicates the type of information technology (IT) support each one requires.

Typically, at the higher organizational layers information gets distilled and reported in summary and/or by exception. Emphasis is on accuracy rather than precision. By contrast, great detail and precision characterize the information requirements of the middle layer – but laws on how reporting should be done usually address themselves to issues connected to the bottom layer.

Though many of the IT supports are recent this organizational model has been good for more than a century but it is now in full evolution. The new model is a federation of independent business units.

- In a federation of independent units, the central authority comes through inverse delegation – from the periphery to the center.
- Therefore, the two modes: federation and decentralization are totally distinct – with federation being the preferred solution in the 1990s.

Federated solutions have evident aftermaths on the accounting structure of the company, including the general ledger, the balance sheet, and off-balance sheet operations. A federated organization is held together through realtime interactive reports, emphasizing pattern and substituting reduction through algorithmic approaches for the clerical effort.

In Part Two we have seen algorithms appropriate to budgetary procedures. In this chapter we will focus on balance sheet reporting, but we will also go beyond the strict quantitative presentation to underline the need for an infrastructure. The examples come from different companies; they have

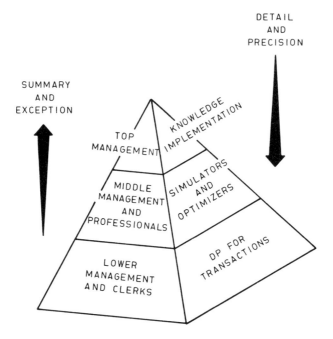

Figure 9.1   Reporting structure in a layered organization pyramid

been chosen by selecting the best elements which have been implemented so far.

INFORMATION TECHNOLOGY AND THE GENERAL LEDGER

In Chapter 1 we spoke of the origins of accounting and the contribution of Luca Paciolo. As it was explained, one of the three tools Paciolo normal-ized was the *memorial* whose functions, in present-day practice, are up to a point covered by the *general ledger.*

General ledger accounting is the cornerstone of any financial information and control system. The general ledger accumulates all of the financial and statistical information and provides the necessary support for controlling this data to ensure that it is valid and accurate.

General ledgers are an extended means of financial accounting and part of the information they contain is management oriented. Out of this information are produced valuable references about the company's financial position, voucher listings supporting ledger contents, as well as analytical reports such as:

- Profit and Loss statements, and
- Responsibility accounting documents.

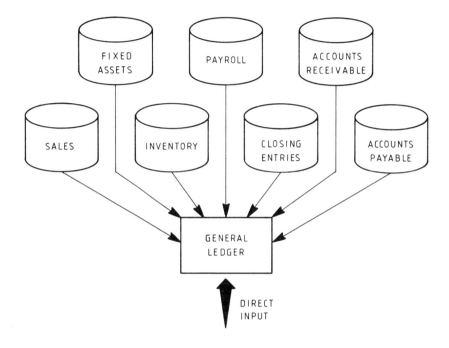

Figure 9.2   The general ledger is the storehouse of the company's accounting information elements

Responsibility accounting reports reflect current operating trends and are meaningful if they arrive on a timely basis. It seems strange that the majority of general ledger systems currently used continue to produce documentation in batch reports, rather than using interactive visualization.

Information streams into the general ledger from many sources, as shown in Figure 9.2. Most of the files to which this information is addressed is already databased, but disorganization prevailing in data processing sees to it that the same information elements are input many times, at great expense and with many errors.

Well-managed companies act differently, abiding by the principle: *one entry many uses*. This means one entry of each input data with the general ledger providing the framework for multiple distribution of the input.

Models are necessary to edit and prove transactions as well as validate general ledger account numbers and responsibility center codes. This is true of all entries including accounting, financial, statistical and other issues such as addition of a new account, profit center and cost center debits/credits, and the like.

• Entries should be online through direct input or generated from other systems and communicated database to database.

- Processing models – not manual intervention – must allow us to handle multiple edits, correct invalid entries and in general provide input filtering.

While some editing procedures are specific to the application, many are of a general nature and can be characterized as multi-phased edit aimed to provide the user with stringent control over input. Syntax checking, balancing, key checking and constraint evaluation are examples.

Syntax checking controls the transaction code associated with each journal entry, and needs to be validated. The presence of a numeric amount must also be verified. Balancing concerns the individual debits and credits. Key checking concerns, among other issues, general ledger account number and cost center identification. Entries bearing invalid codes must be listed so that they can be corrected before the ledger is posted. Constraint checks produce several sets of warning reports after the general books have been posted. For instance: transaction alert and account alert. An error alert permits us to substitute batch practices in editing with online approaches to the detection of invalid data.

The validation function of a general ledger greatly extends its classical range of features. The same is true of the incorporation of cross-referencing of general ledger fields, which makes it feasible to define comprehensive controls as well as to execute experimental tests, without the need for complex computer programs. A valid approach will see to it that:

- General ledger operations are executed in realtime.
- It is feasible to proceed with parallel update of several ledgers.
- Financial values can be expressed in different currencies, plus the primary currency of the firm.

Parametric solutions permit flexible transfer of information from and to various applications as well as ad hoc operations. For instance, conversion to local currencies, the change of allocation period and date-related operations.

High technology should be used as a competitive weapon, to promote the automation of general ledger operations. Manufacturing companies and financial institutions which stay with old technology are culturally gridlocked and just plain lost in a fast-changing marketplace – even in matters regarding accounting.

A modern organization cannot risk having low performance in its general ledger chores, neither can it afford the luxury of mediocre technology. By emphasizing not only the warehousing of accounting information but also database mining and the benefits to be obtained from fully interactive solutions, an able management provides itself with background information on how to develop and sustain successful business operations.

BALANCE SHEET IMPACT OF ORGANIZATION AND TECHNOLOGY

In Part Two we have focused on simple models, avoiding associating them with the different organizational levels. It was however underlined that the solution sought after should be highly modular. What we will now see is how some of these modules could be adjusted to a given organizational level of reporting.

When online access to databases substitutes paper-based documents the reporting channels of the organization will be typically served through algorithms and heuristics. The Introduction has given a reference to the type of models which will be most appropriate at each level of organization.

General ledger database mining is done for *balance sheet* and for *off-balance sheet* reporting reasons. For both purposes, the component parts of a financial model should be designed and implemented with the aim of bridging an important gap that often exists between:

- Those people whose job is to develop and supply knowledge in order to enhance the competitiveness of the firm, and
- Those who must manage output, assuring an uninterrupted flow of high quality financial information.

This is one of the key missions to be given to knowledge enriched approaches to balance sheet reporting. Such reference is not only valid by structural level but as well (if not primarily) regarding the managers and professionals who work at the same level, practically peer-to-peer. In traditional industries, the chain of command was more or less precisely defined; with a person making a certain kind of decision occupying a more or less stable position in the organization chart. However, in businesses that deal mostly with information and knowhow, and most particularly in a federated organization, a manager has to cope with a new phenomenon:

- A rapid divergence develops between power based on position and power based on knowledge.
- This occurs because the base of knowledge that constitutes the foundation of the business changes every day.

Enriched through the appropriate models, a dynamic financial reporting structure is necessary to assure that the enterprise does not get out of control. A significant part of *what-if* experimentation with balance sheets, of which we talk below, rests on this requirement.

- In the past, people holding old-fashioned position power made all of the

decisions, even if they were unfamiliar with some of the financial fundamentals.
- This has led to a number of blunders and prompted computer-based experimentation, to enhance managerial and professional accountability.

The more dynamic is a market, the faster the renewal of the knowhow on which *our* business depends. Markets are dynamic because of rapid changes in customer preferences, leading to a greater divergence between knowledge and position power – and hence the *status quo*. That is why an alert top management sees to it that:

- The physical barriers separating positional managers into watertight compartments are stripped away, while
- All cognizant executives and professionals are provided with up to the minute financial, market and product information.

This is also the reason why in Part Two I have so insisted on the need for having an open, polyvalent budgetary system which is interactively processed through computers. A similar reference is valid in terms of balance sheet reporting.

This requires not only computer-based models but also creativity and talent enhanced through lifelong learning. We spoke of this need for lifelong learning in Part One. One of the priorities is ensuring that the best talent is available and is supported by knowledge-enriched financial and accounting reports.

ANALYZING THE INCOME AND EXPENSE STATEMENT

From beginning balances to transactions and closing balances, algorithmic solutions help differentiate debits from credits, mapping their effects on the company's financial structure. Procedural programming has been classically used for balance sheets and income statements but batch procedures saw to it that:

- The *balance sheet* which should indicate an instantaneous financial picture came to management too late in order to take meaningful decisions.
- The *income and expense statement* (or *profit and loss* (P&L)), showed the flow of sales, cost, and revenue over too long accounting periods, inhibiting the management of change.

The classical, procedural programming featured by legacy systems does not interpret the aftermaths of a change in total *net worth* between the beginning and the end of a given period. Also, it only works over relatively long periods, which means that it averages out the financial results.

Yet, one of the requirements with dynamic markets is that of reporting at *higher frequencies*. This calls not only for faster input and output but also for the ability to compare the positions of balance sheets through expert systems, providing a basis for understanding and examining changes shown but not commented on by traditional income statements.

A similar reference can be made about expense statement. A company's P&L reports the benefits from and the costs of its operations. Depreciation of plant and equipment is one example of a cost of operations. Salaries and wages for employee services is another – as already discussed in Part Two.

Accounting recognizes expense for the incurred costs as use of assets. Companies generally acquire assets, some of which, such as employee services, may exist only momentarily. As we have seen on different occasions, through practical examples:

- Expenses are incurred as the benefits embodied in the assets are used up.
- Labor cannot be inventoried, but it must be reflected in the accounts.

Employees' services may be acquired in many ways. For instance, by paying wages using cash that may have come from operations, incurring debt, or issuing stock or warrants. Apart from salaries and wages there is also the expense of providing benefits such as health services, life insurance, a pension plan.

Employees' services are also acquired by issuing equity instruments such as restricted stock and fixed or variable stock options directly to employees. Whatever its nature may be, all compensation expense should be recognized regardless of how an employee's services are being paid for. Commitments made today even for future years have to be written down immediately as an expense. This is what Financial Accounting Standards Board (FASB) Statement 106 stipulates.

As employers pay compensation to employees, market forces are assumed to keep the value of these services more or less the same. However, it is difficult or outright impossible to directly *value* employee services, particularly at an executive level. As a result, compensation cost is measured based on the value of what is paid to the employee.

Measuring forms of compensation such as pensions and other postretirement benefits is more complex, but accounting requirements increasingly specify measurement methods. These are often normalized through government-set standards which more or less set how these expenses should be reported, as is the case with the FASB.

Normalization is necessary because there exist many ways both of acquiring assets and of reporting them in official statements. For instance, plant and equipment may be acquired in many ways, such as by:

- Paying cash which is the simpler, more linear but least used method.

- Incurring debt or issuing stock in exchange for the plant and equipment.
- Issuing stock to acquire another company, and thereby its assets including plant and equipment.

Such variations in method can be instrumental in dressing up an income and expense statement beyond recognition. I had a professor of accounting at UCLA who impressed upon his students that if a manager is allowed to choose his accounting method he can prove practically everything – making a money-losing enterprise profitable, and vice versa.

Governments are aware of this fact and, therefore, they established norms in P&L reporting. For instance, standards regarding how depreciation expense is recognized for plant and equipment, regardless of whether cash, debt, or stock is used to pay for it.

- An income statement would be seriously incomplete and earnings would be overstated if depreciation was not recognized.
- The recognition of depreciation expense reduces taxes but also the company's profits, or increases its losses.

Enterprises would be more profitable, on paper, if they discontinued the depreciation practice, but few people, if any, would recommend not recognizing depreciation to eliminate its adverse effect on the income statement.

A similar reasoning applies to stock options used to acquire employees' services. In America, the FASB correctly believes that the so-called adverse effect on the income statement due to options is no longer an effective argument for hiding a good deal of compensation settlements.

'WHAT-IF' EXPERIMENTATION WITH THE BALANCE SHEET

The user of a financial and accounting statement will typically ask a series of questions aimed at answering professional worries or providing insight in connection with important decisions. Meaningful questions will never be made in the abstract; they typically reflect a specific situation and the way in which it may evolve.

As an example of 'What-if' experimentation we will build a scenario based on the insurance industry. Legitimate questions in evaluating profitability are of the kind: What if inflation rises by 10 percent over the next two years but premiums only increase by 5 percent? What are the effects on the company if the interest rate:

- Increases by 10 percent?
- Decreases by 10 percent? or
- Remains the same as that of the last period?

Accurate answers to these queries provide a valuable aid to planning. They are also of help to financial analysts investigating P&L and cash flow or other critical issues which impact on the bottom line.

Effective answers to queries of this kind can be provided by information in the database which has been handled through a spreadsheet. More sophisticated replies will require mathematical models which map into the computer the range of operations of the company, the market and the way the company interacts with its market.

For instance, one of the modules of the artifact may simulate the money flows that arise as the result of risks taken in underwriting. These flows typically include:

- Premium receipts,
- Claims payments,
- Investment of funds,
- Investment income,
- Expenses,
- Taxes, and
- Dividends.

The net result of all money flows occurring in a given period of time is ultimately reflected in an insurance company's balance sheet. This statement is valid for any firm, though each has its own ways and means of proceeding for management accounting reasons.

The changes in balance sheet levels that result from money flows must be calculated according to general accounting rules. But for management accounting purposes there exist degrees of freedom, and interactive reports should preferably be structured in a way which permits us to change some of the parameters online and experiment with the obtained results.

Figure 9.3 presents an example from an insurance application which capitalized on networked databases to provide a rich environment for experimentation. Important elements in this process have been aggregate flows such as underwriting profits and total earnings.

- The primary flows, which together comprise the aggregate flows, are generally calculated from simple basic equations and numerical parameters specified by the user.
- This contrasts to econometric models which attempt to forecast the values of such items as gross profits, by relating them directly to important economic indicators and their own past values.

A similar approach to that shown in Figure 9.3 can be used in connection with loans given to different companies as well as underwriting issues. Japan's Mitsui Bank has built an expert system for *scoring* company loans which

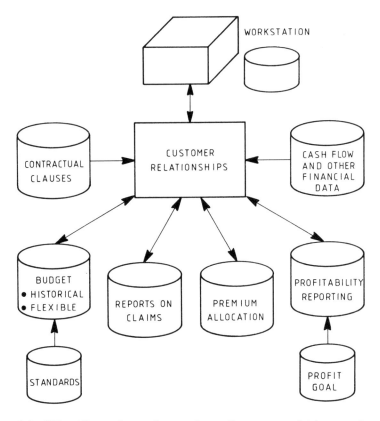

Figure 9.3 'What-if' experimentation requires online access to databases and
artifacts which simulate or optimize business conditions

significantly improves upon past practices. Since 1986, it *analyzes* balance
sheets, using *public databases* and Mitsui's own databases, to companies
applying for loans. This model reflects on:

- Company profits,
- Acid test (current assets over current liabilities) (see also the use of ratios
  in Chapter 13),
- Liquidity and cash flow,
- Long-term assets,
- Capital ratio, and
- Future business perspectives.

Other critical variables, or sensitivities, used by the Mitsui model include
company size, annual growth, productivity, and the quality of management.
There are success factors that banks can learn from insurance companies, as
insurance companies can from banks.

For instance, one of the premier insurance firms has designed a model for senior management experimentation which involves different balance sheets as levels of reference, with *what-if* queries posed at the simulated end of each year, semester, quarter, or month. This can be done for as many time periods as required. A simulated year may be divided into periods of equal or unequal lengths if the user so wishes.

ROLE AND FUNCTIONS OF A DESCRIPTIVE MODEL AND OF AN OPTIMIZER

A *descriptive* model written for experimentation purposes should be neutral with regard to the decisions specified by the user, simply calculating the *what-if* results of these decisions taken in conjunction with a specified economic scenario. By contrast, an *optimizer* will help the user find the best solutions, running the model many times and varying the numerical values of decision parameters as required.

- The optimizer would generate a set of decisions guided by goals and constraints, the way they are set by the user case-after-case.
- Whether for descriptive or optimization purposes, however, the model must be very flexible – both in its structure and in terms of the parameters it handles.

One of the more sophisticated models developed in the insurance business simulates a complex combination of risks, reinsurance policies, economic environments and investments. An expert uses this output, interpreting the results the way a professional actuary would do, and calculating corresponding insurance premiums.

The user may choose to simulate an insurance policy at an aggregated level or down to great detail. Flexibility can be achieved by calling into play the required number of basic building blocks which are the logical entities of the model such as:

- Risk classes,
- Treaties,
- Countries,
- Regions,
- Companies,
- Private clients.

Best results are usually obtained through dynamic modeling, simulating the changes in the state of an insurance policy which result from the evolving economic environments or most recent trends, simulating changes which arise from sudden discontinuities, superimposed effects or business cycles, and so on. One of the models currently in operation evaluates the results of changes in the balance sheet and reports accordingly.

In a different example regarding banking loans, financial criteria leading to experimentation can be expressed as a set of rules and numerical parameters which, for instance, determine the minimum solvency margin which a company must have. Correspondingly in insurance hypotheses of imposing more stringent requirements for claims and premiums would be tested.

Claim processing is a highly repetitive job but the estimation of aftermaths needs a fair amount of knowledge and calculation. Hence, it is an ideal application domain for expert systems. However, to effectively contribute to profitable results,

- The knowledge-based artifact must operate online and access a significant number of databases.
- It should also be enriched by knowledge engineering tools that go beyond the capabilities of early constructs, utilizing genetic algorithms, neural networks and fuzzy engineering (see also Chorafas, 1994c).

Competitiveness requires the ability to go beyond present-day solutions. Fuzzy engineering can be instrumental in helping underwriters assess risks and set appropriate premiums. Also in evaluating the risk taken with each type of contract – an application which additionally requires client profiling.

Much of the contribution genetic algorithms make is in optimization and scheduling problems, such as finding the maxima of functions. Also in emulating learning effects, which becomes an important process in modeling.

The ability to provide *full customization* through the use of knowledge engineering is of major competitive advantage. In one of the most advanced banking applications, when an article of interest to an officer arrives, it is selected and instantly sent to his or her workstation. Then, an alert icon warns the enduser that vital information is waiting.

Customization and data filtering are most important to avoid the company's professionals being snowed under with news items and financial data streams. Typically a major financial institution today receives realtime news wires from many different services as well as market information which is channeled into the bank every day.

Intelligence-enriched artifacts are necessary to see that relevant information elements are selected and sent to the relevant workstation in realtime and that the banker is alerted to important news. Every enduser must be offered significant flexibility in requesting information and in the responses he receives. In a recently developed application:

- The knowledge-enriched environment automatically accesses a wide range of outside research databases and returns this information online, neatly catalogued.

- Past decisions on projects, commitments and other issues are also available on the network to all authorized users – through the bank's corporate memory facility.

Using the network and databases, a financial analyst can access quantitative and qualitative information on a company or a group of companies from research sources. Such information is collected and presented in a spreadsheet form or ,in graphics – at the enduser's choice. This is a good example of *quality* customized presentation, as well as of what the effective use of technology can accomplish in terms of greater competitiveness.

MODELS, BALANCE SHEETS AND EXCEPTION REPORTING

A close look at the balance sheet can be instructive in a managerial sense beyond the fundamentals of accounting. This is a domain for the implementation of knowledge engineering, as heuristic approaches capture the skill of the examiner and go well beyond what algorithmic programs can do.

Prior to introducing exception reporting it is necessary to bring into perspective the common ground which exists in regard to two fundamental accounting statements: the *balance sheet* and *profit and loss* (P&L). Both carry valuable information, therefore knowledgeable executives and professionals:

- Examine not only what is formally written on them but also between the lines, and
- Tend to correlate the information elements the two objects contain, to make useful inferences.

Classically the balance sheet is presented in an annual report, but modeling now makes it available much more frequently in an updated form – accessible online as often as necessary. Its contents reflect an instantaneous static picture of the condition of the enterprise as of some particular day. This is true of both its sides:

- Assets, and
- Liabilities.

Corresponding to the dollar value of assets, whether tangible or intangible, there is an equal total amount of claims or ownership (equity). In Figure 9.4, the value of $50,000,000 in assets is exactly matched by claims to ownership through corresponding liabilities. On this fundamental identity every balance sheet rests, and the relation can be written as a simple equation:

$$A = L + NW$$

Assets		Liabilities and Net Worth	
		Liabilities	
Current Assets:		*Current Liabilities*:	
• Cash	3,400	Accounts payable	2,800
• Securities	2,600	Notes payable	3,300
• Inventory	5,000		
	11,000		6,100
Fixed Assets:		*Longer-Term Liabilities*:	
Equipment	21,000	Medium-Term Loans	15,000
Buildings	10,000	Long-Term Loans	10,900
Land	8,000	Bonds Issued	8,000
	39,000		33,900
		Net Worth/Capital:	
		Preferred Stock	2,000
		Common Stock	8,000
			10,000
Total	50,000	Total	50,000

Figure 9.4 The balance sheet of a manufacturing firm
(thousand dollars)

where:

A = Assets
L = Liabilities
NW = Net Worth

We can write the assets relationship in a narrative form which may be a little more explanatory:

Value of Assets = Value of Claims or Ownership
                = Value of Liabilities (owned) +
                  Value of Proprietorship

This is easily computable and can be available tick-by-tick, provided that we carefully define our variables and the operators linking the one to the other. Modeling asks for no different approaches than those followed with accounting – but it automates the linkages.

To better explain the components of each part of balance sheet let us consider the simple example shown in Figure 9.4. The first rule to observe is that a balance sheet must always balance. Net worth, that is the owner-ship of residual claimants, always adjusts itself to make things balance. On the Assets side of the balance sheet we observe that there are two major items:

Debtors		Creditors	
Cash on hand	2.000	Share capital	2.800
Other banks	1.500	Reserves	1.5000
Loans	25.000	Total own capital	3.500
Bonds & shares	8.0000	Deposits	30.000
Foreign		Other banks	1.000
correspondents	6.0000	Central bank	3.000
Guarantees	7.000	Foreign correspondents	4.000
Fixed assets	1.000	Guarantees	5.000
Sundry	2.000	Sundry	2.500
Balance	52.500	Balance	52.500

Total loans	25.000
Total deposits	30.000
Deposit surplus	5.000
Average working capital	
(Balance less guarantees)	45.500

Figure 9.5 A bank's balance sheet (thousand dollars)

* Current Assets (CA), and
* Fixed Assets (FA).

Current assets are defined as being those which can be quickly liquidated if need be. For instance cash, securities and inventories. *Fixed assets* are mainly land, buildings and equipment; and they account for a large part of the fixed costs. On the Liabilities side, too, we have a distinction among types of debt:

* Current Liabilities (CL)
* Longer Term Liabilities (LTL), and
* Net Worth (NW), or Capital

Current liabilities are composed of accounts payable (suppliers, invoices, salaries, premiums) and short-term loans as well as other notes. A good deal of *what-if* experimentation concerns current liabilities and the examination of hypotheses about what happens when they become due.

Longer-term liabilities include medium- and long-term loans as well as bonds which have been issued. The component parts of *capital* are common and preferred stock which represent a sort of debt towards the ownership of the firm.

Because the items to be included are largely financial assets, a company's balance sheet can be differently structured, an example being given in Figure 9.5. Even within the same industry, balance sheets are not necessarily

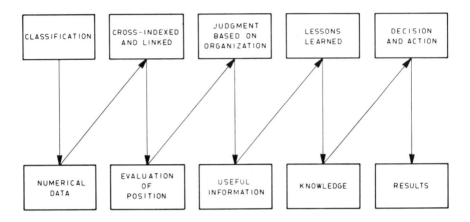

Figure 9.6   A step-by-step approach to evaluation of financial data, judgment and action

homogeneous but in the background they do share a step-by-step conceptual approach to evaluation and judgment which permits both decisions and corrective action, as shown in Figure 9.6.

MULTIDIMENSIONAL ANALYSIS AND THE ACID TEST

A number of interesting facts can be revealed even by a simple balance sheet. Let's take as a reference the balance sheet of a manufacturing company presented in Figure 9.4. First, it is customary to divide up assets according to whether or not they will be convertible into cash by normal operations within a year, what we called *current assets*.

The *current liabilities* chapter is structured on the criterion whether liabilities fall due in less than a year. The difference between total current assets and total current liabilities, is termed *Net Working Capital* (NWC), and can be expressed as a simple equation:

$$NWC = CA - CL$$

Considerable attention should be paid to the *Working Capital Ratio*, usually known as the *acid test*:

$$WCR = \frac{CA}{CL} = \frac{\$11,000,000}{\$6,100,000} = 1.80$$

If a company's WCR is less than 1, then it is insolvent. The ratio 1.80 is acceptable but not too comfortable. Theoretically this ratio should be greater than 2. Practically, however, every industry and sector within an industry has its own values to the acid test.

Both NWC and WCR are good candidates for reporting by exception. Financial companies, for instance Dun and Bradstreet, publish yearly updated tables with median, upper and lower quartiles values of WCR and they should be used consistently for control purposes.

While NWC and WCR are in themselves simple algorithms, the effective exploitation of ratio analysis for danger signals is the domain of expert systems. For companies more complex than the very simple one with a balance sheet like that we considered in Figure 9.4, it is wise to do *multidimensional analysis* and this calls for knowledge engineering.

The concept of multidimensional analysis has been developed by Yamaichi Securities as a way to better focus on current and expected financial results. The procedure applies to companies with more than one major product line, giving a relative weight to the turnover each line represents. This makes comparisons more meaningful.

For instance, the P + L statements of General Motors (GM) and Ford have no 1:1 correspondence because – while both manufacture cars in the United States and Europe – General Motors also controls Electronic Data Systems (EDS) which does systems development and consulting in computers, and Hughes Aircraft which specializes in radar and space research. EDS and Hughes are other dimensions of GM. Besides this, GM also owns the General Motors Acceptance Corporation which specializes in financing.

When it comes to the analysis of financial statements, it is as well correct to keep under perspective some other facts:

- An important issue about the balance sheet is that its two sides must balance *in total*,
- But no single item on one side is matched by an item on the other side.

Thus, the capital does not correspond in value to the buildings and land, nor do the bonds correspond to the equipment. Besides this the fair value of buildings, land and other assets (including inventories) can be a highly disputed item. One thing sure is that *fair value* has little to do with *book value.*

Yet even if some of the items and their values are fuzzy (and the way to calculate them can vary from one country to the other), the usual statement about a balance sheet is that creditors have a general claim of a definite value against the firm. The owners have a residual claim against what remains.

- Exception reporting is usually addressed to the interests of the owners and of management,
- Therefore, it clearly concerns the creditors' side – but experimentation can be done both for the owners and for the creditors.

A normal comparative report might show the difference between actual and planned expenses, identifying reasons why, for example, larger than planned loans were needed. An expert system will evaluate for each and every line if the variance was acceptable, each time there is new information about planned and actual values.

The allowable variance can be computed by the system or entered for each detailed line as, say, a dollar amount, a percentage figure, or some combination of $ and % – in short, as an exception parameter code. The system will do the checking and the graphical visualization.

This discussion identifies how flexible the evaluation of company balance sheets through modeling can be. The financial analyst simply decides which types of accounts he wishes to examine and the expert system:

- Checks the $ levels as well as the ratios,
- Elaborates the details of assets and liabilities, and
- Ensures compliance or identifies deviations.

Subsequently, a visualization routine will do the presentation. The notion to retain is that the more sophisticated work cannot be accomplished algorithmically. More sophisticated approaches are necessary.

Legacy-type applications are usually done step-by-step. Procedural approaches, however, are more costly to program – while non-procedural approaches cannot be handled through classical means which are inflexible, and require a quite significant maintenance cost. This underlines the interest in intelligence-enriched systems which give results beyond the simple transactional chores and provide qualitative evaluation as well as flexible reporting.

MANAGERIAL RESPONSIBILITIES AND THE BALANCE SHEET

As we will see in Chapter 10, one of the new themes in trading and investing is off-balance sheet operations (see Chorafas and Steinmann, 1994a). It is an activity which over the last six years has provided financial institutions with a new avenue for profits, but also involves significant credit risks and market risks. But before talking of derivatives let's return to balance-sheet basics.

Prior to the October 1987 market crash, billions in the corporate treasury were often looked at as an embarrassment or a sign that management lacked imagination and was not providing full value to shareholders. But since October 1987 *cash* is king, and will remain so for some time.

- The financial strength of companies becomes most critical in a relatively uncertain and unsettled business environment.
- As a result, both a company's own management and the securities analysts are going back to looking at cash flows rather than earnings momentum.

When analysts carefully evaluate cash flows and balance sheets, they find quite a number of companies whose financial situations are simply dazzling. Poor management is magnifying the distance between cash rich and cash poor companies.

As we will see in Chapter 11, cash serves as an insurance against a skidding economy. Fear of what the future holds drives up the savings rate for corporations – as it does for security-conscious individuals. Correctly:

- Companies with sound management are unwilling to depend only on bankers in a period of uncertainty, and
- The market appreciates that cash also means the ability to take hold of opportunities as they develop.

A big war chest available at the right time has allowed companies to purchase assets that become a lot cheaper after a financial crisis, eventually passing that value along to the investors. A part of the job is figuring out how to tap resources and handle them ingeniously, which is after all the foundation of financial engineering.

Good management requires sound policies and the resolve to apply them, but also the tools. One of the problems, however, is that many small and medium-size companies have neither the knowledge nor the personnel to find solutions by themselves. Yet to manage their financial resources properly they need:

- Simulators which work out cash flow, matching current assets and current liabilities under alternative scenarios,
- Optimizers addressing a variety of earnings profiles in regard to alternative investment decisions, and
- Analytical models which produce breakeven evaluations and calculate targets in business.

This is done with the help of business data from previous years and turnover forecasts. In Part Two we spoke of flexible budgets. A similar approach to financial engineering can be taken with the advanced evaluation of projected annual statements for the coming years.

The better managed companies are particularly well placed in this field. Their portfolio analysis service looks at more than just financial status. It compares the individual figures with industry data and is, therefore, able to tell about the company's competitive position.

As an example of this type of balance sheet analysis and experimentation we will take the XYZ financial institution, and examine the practice which it follows as a case study on sound management.

- Figure 9.7 shows the balance sheet for the last five years (1989–1993), concentrating on assets, advances, deposits, investments, and equity.

Averages	1989	1990	1991	1992	1993
Assets	802.0	840.7	908.5	1,419.3	1,550.8
Advances	526.0	559.0	606.4	955.6	1,050.9
Deposits	715.4	752.6	817.2	1,243.9	1,350.0
Investments	108.1	131.5	165.0	226.5	226.5
Loan Capital	n/a	n/a	n/a	n/a	n/a
Equity	39.0	46.8	54.9	59.8	67.8

Figure 9.7   XYZ: balance sheet
(thousand dollars)

	Deviation from 1989 target	Deviation from 1989 target	Deviation from 1991 target	Deviation from 1992 target	Deviation from 1993 target
Net interest Income					
Noninterest Income					
Debt Provisions					
Risks Provisions					
Total Costs					
Pretax Profits					
Tax Levy					

Figure 9.8   XYZ: profit and loss statement
(million dollars)

	This year	Last year	Average in the industry	Best in the industry
Gross Yield (%)				
Price/Earnings (P/E)*				
Gross Dividend				
Earnings per Share (EPS)				
Net Yield (%)				

Table 9.1   XYZ: critical ratings in evaluating performance

* The Price/Earnings ratio is expressed as stock price divided by last 4 quarters of per share earnings.

- The outline of a profit and loss statement is shown in Figure 9.8, including net interest income, noninterest income, debt and risk provisions.
- Table 9.1 presents the ratings management particularly watches. We will be talking about critical ratios in Chapter 13.

The balance sheet, P&L and ratings figures can nicely be integrated into a functional planning and evaluation model, as suggested in the two parts of Figure 9.9 (shown in pp. 197–8). The suggested procedure ensures a basis for judgment on current operations, permitting us to evaluate trends and identify anomalies. It also provides background information to facilitate a factual and documented next year's budget.

At XYZ, a properly constructed profitability statement lists the major sources of income derived by the bank from the relationship with its customers; and it is enriched through interactive graphics. The most important entries are:

- Interest accruing on loans during the period under analysis and experimentation.
- Profits made in the treasury, forex and securities domains after reserves for extraordinary risks – which is a new concept.
- Amounts paid to the bank, such as service charges and fees for portfolio management, trust and other services.
- Interest imputed on loanable funds supplied by customers and interbanking loans.

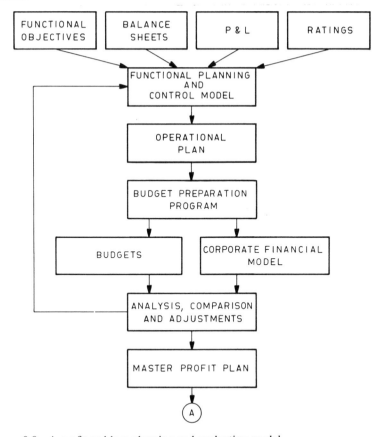

Figure 9.9   A profit and loss planning and evaluation model

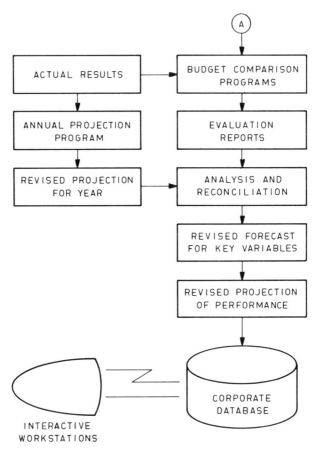

- Noninterest expenses incurred during the period under examination, with particular attention to overhead.

Interest accruing on loans is the classical income of the bank in its role as financial intermediary. Service charges represent any sum paid to the bank to cover deposit activity costs as well as charges associated with investment transactions and fund management. The more dynamic the financial industry becomes, the more income sources other than loans are underlined.

Since, as we will see in Chapter 10 on off-balance sheet financing, new instruments introduce risks with which classical bankers are unfamiliar, tier 1 banks have developed a system which permits them to make additional reserves commensurate with the risks being taken. This is a new concept which also brings management's attention to the fact that statements about some types of profits are exaggerated because they don't account for perversive risk factors.

AN EXERCISE IN FINANCIAL ENGINEERING

No two banks have the same concept about what financial engineering is, or what it tries to do. The wider view is that of an ingenious application of analytics in banking operations – with the aim of uncovering new business opportunities and estimate their risks. A much more limited (and short-sighted) notion is that of manipulating financial statements. Questions like:

• Which products do our current and potential customers wish to buy?
• Where can our products be sold with most profitability? and
• Which areas offer the greatest potential for profits?

are typical management queries which should receive a factual and documented answer. Some of the evaluations required for a valid response are creative and have to be done by experts. But many are repetitive, hence the wisdom of using knowledge engineering to automate that part of the job.

While strategic measures have to be taken to remedy any deficiencies, at the tactical level attention must be paid to the proper infrastructure. The latter should carefully reflect the changes taking place in the nature of business conducted by banks:

• Priority must be given to fee income and services, by means of innovative new products.
• Securitization of existing assets must be examined as a method of generating cash and creating new business.
• Disintermediation via the capital markets makes it advisable that banks provide consultancy and ancillary services.
• Business done off-balance sheet raises return on assets and equity and permits us to hedge – but also involves significant risks which must be controlled.

Activities in these domains are not classical banking exercises and therefore require financial engineering support. This uses a significant amount of computer power, communications and knowledge-enriched software, to accelerate product delivery and reduce production and distribution costs.

But computers alone will not change the way in which a financial institution is managed. An integral part of the new infrastructure needed is a fully automated, properly planned and capillary accounting system electronically capturing all vouchers at their point of origin, and also, providing for exception reporting. This, too, is a financial engineering area of activity.

Figure 9.10 gives as an example a matrix developed for the assignment of general ledger accounts with a view to profit center evaluation. An increasing number of financial institutions are using artificial intelligence to improve exception reporting by type of activity and risk, thus enhancing the

Figure 9.10 Assignments of general ledger accounts

Account and Title	Unit of responsibility Single Multiple	How Assigned Daily entry Monthly distribution	Requirements to accomplish proper distribution	Profit center reporting (P&L)

General instructions
List every account; group by major category–for instance, Loan accrued
interest receivable, investment instruments, fees sources, and so on.

quality of the decision processes. A case study from Bankers Trust documents what can be achieved in terms of results.

The Magellan system is currently deployed over 750 networked workstations in North America and Europe. It is a fully automated decision support environment implemented in the Corporate Finance and Capital Markets areas. Its strong point is that of using technology to leverage financial expertise.

1. Magellan provides the Bankers Trust professionals with the ability to access necessary information right on desktop.

Such information is interactively available online and concerns databases external to the bank as well as information elements generated within the bank. At the user's request, Magellan is able to integrate data streams and database contents in an ad hoc manner.

2. The network allows professionals across distant physical locations to work on vital information cooperatively.

Using electronic mail, anyone on the network can instantly send to anyone else multimedia information – text, graphs, tables, images, or spreadsheets. New product term sheets, proposals, immediate response to customer requests, customer contracts and master agreements can be made available in realtime throughout the bank.

3. This facility is instrumental in creating new products and services, as well as in marketing them effectively to clients.

Magellan makes communications much more effective, especially across geographic boundaries, and assures that *each new financial product and/or client proposal does not require total reinvention*. Voice annotation allows product specialists to:

- Pitch their latest ideas to the multimedia document, and
- Explain intricate issues concerning the proposal's or decision's rationale.

Through knowledge engineering artifacts, each one of the interconnected workstations can flash *alert* icons. Also, as huge amounts of news and financial data are brought into Bankers Trust each day, special, individually tailored filters scan the news items and financial data for issues important to each officer.

10 New Financial Instruments and Off-Balance Sheet Transactions

INTRODUCTION

Major changes have been taking place in banking, altering the structure of the industry. The financial institutions and their customers are no longer what they used to be. In the late 1950s, 90 percent of all loans made by American money center banks went to the large American companies. Today, that figure is about 4 percent.

It is evident that banks try to compensate for this loss of income by introducing new financial products and opening new markets. The lion's share of this effort centers on *off-balance sheet* (OBS) activities which typically include the business that does not involve the classical way of booking assets and liabilities. Examples are trading in:

- Options,
- Swaps,
- Futures,
- Interest rate agreements,
- Foreign exchange forwards, and
- Other derivative products.

Other examples include the granting of standby commitments and letters of credit, though the latter are taken on-balance sheet in some countries. While some people tend to think that the whole issue of the OBS book has been and is still one gigantic loophole, in reality this business started because there are a number of items that do not necessarily fit into the balance sheet definition. Then it expanded in all directions.

Over the years, the whole concept underpinning *financial instruments* has changed. Classically, a financial instrument is defined as cash, evidence of an ownership in an equity (or debt), or contract that meets certain criteria which have been primarily characterized by balance sheet operations – but this is no longer the exclusive description.

- Whether on-balance sheet or off-balance sheet, criteria characterizing a financial transaction have to do with contractual obligations and rights.
- The sense of *financial responsibility* connected with a given product is integrative, and it comes from the fact that financing imposes contractual obligations.

For instance, a company agrees to deliver cash or other means of wealth transfer to another company or to exchange financial instruments with this second entity on potentially unfavorable terms. The transaction which is made conveys to that second entity a contractual right.

Examples of such a right are receiving cash from the first company or, alternatively, exchanging other financial instruments on potentially favorable terms with the first firm. Such obligations, however, involve *credit risk* and *market risk*. We will now see what these terms mean in connection to OBS operations.

USING DERIVATIVE FINANCIAL INSTRUMENTS

Derivatives are financial instruments whose value, at any point in time, is based on more fundamental real or financial assets. This market started to develop after three events, which at the time seemed to be independent of one another. But, among themselves, these provided the necessary infrastructure and the motivation for a new market thrust.

All three events happened in the early 1970s. First, the Nixon Administration in 1971 practically ended the Bretton Woods accords of fixed exchange rates, by cancelling foreign governments' ability to convert dollars into gold. Over the years, flexible exchange rates created a new mechanism of market action and, with it, a tremendous trading opportunity.

The second major contribution to the creation of a new market has been the advent of exchanges able to support futures trades. While in their fundamentals deals in futures are not a new business, this market was more or less limited to agricultural products until, in 1972, the Chicago Mercantile Exchange (CME) instituted futures trading in precious metals and other commodities – to which have been added currencies.

However, apart from exchanges, to be successfully dealt with, options and futures need a pricing mechanism. The third basic reference is that of an analytical framework for calculating the *fair value* of options contracts. This was established by Dr Fischer Black* and Dr Myron Scholes in their seminal paper, which was submitted for publication in 1970 and was published in 1972.

- The existence of *modeling* permits both active trading and the efficient redistribution of profits and risks in the financial community.
- Derivative trades, as we know them today could not be possible without technology, because many OBS deals are bilateral and have, so to speak, no fair market value.

---

* In May 1994 Dr Fischer Black has been awarded the Dimitris N. Chorafas prize of the Swiss Academies of Science for his development of the Black–Scholes option pricing algorithm. The award carries an SF 100,000 reward.

Relying on the mathematics of continuous-time stochastic processes, the analytical framework advanced by Black and Scholes has been followed by more sophisticated versions. It is however the original model which has become part of the infrastructure of financial analysis.

Besides these three fundamental reasons underpinning the development of derivatives trades, two other factors have also significantly contributed to the exponential growth of the OBS market, after the dozen years or so of its incubation.

1. In the early 1980s, the Federal Reserve Board permitted banks to write some items, which did not quite fit the established balance sheet structure, off-balance sheet, and
2. Experts in the financial industry were fairly quick to grasp the fact that derivative instruments, especially option contracts, often provide *nonlinear payoffs* which are not available from the fundamental underlying assets.

The derivatives market took off in America and it quickly went beyond CME, through the use of customized over-the-counter (OTC) procedures. Then it spread to Europe and (to a lesser extent) the Pacific Rim – while remaining primarily an American game.

There is no surprise with regard to involvement of the world's major financial institutions inasmuch as a key factor permitting derivative trades is the increasing availability, at an ever decreasing cost, of the computational power necessary to analyze and manage complex financial instruments. The high technology reference includes sophisticated software with knowledge engineering as well as object oriented paradigms for programming and database management at centerpoint.

- But the able handling of off-balance sheet transactions requires much more than high technology.
- It calls for a significant amount of skill as well as a new culture in financial transactions.

Every new instrument and every new procedure has its challenges. Foremost among them is the fact that today, for all practical purposes, there are no norms on how to really evaluate exposure. While the reserve authorities are working hard to establish new norms, each institution tends to follow its own directives.

The most successful of these efforts have been characterized by a long-term perspective, which is particularly important for risk management. As Figure 10.1 demonstrates, risk calculation is a steady business to be done 24 hours per day – but this, while necessary, is not enough:

- Banks which really wish to bring derivative financial instruments and other risks under *control*, target the longer term.

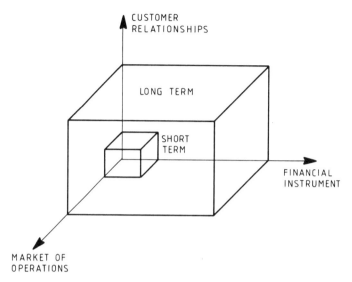

Figure 10.1   Risk calculation is a steady business to be done 24 hours per day, targetting the longer term

- Banks which are trigger-happy or lack the management culture necessary to master derivatives, limit themselves to a short-term perspective.

Long-term risk management should take place in a frame of reference which includes all customer relationships (corresponding banks and other firms), each and every financial instrument, and each market in which dealing in derivatives takes place. All this should be done in *realtime*.

Unlike what is usually taught about the classical banking book, the composition of a trading portfolio today often changes significantly hour-to-hour, not just day-to-day. As a result, a hedge judged to be valid one day may shrink, altogether disappear or even become a liability a few days later. OBS trades defy the traditional concept of double-entry, where assets and liabilities should balance out.

- Intensive, deregulated global trading and the rapid evolution of new financial products sees to it that complete offsetting is not a realistic proposition.
- Yet the bank's trading books have to be evaluated in the context of credit risk and market risk, as we will see in the following pages.

The existence of different accounting rules for different categories of assets and liabilities suggests the need to consider measures able to respond to polyvalent aspects of risk. It is also advisable to take into full account *legal risk*. Laws, rules and regulations vary often significantly from one country to another, and sometimes within the same country.

CREDIT RISK AND MARKET RISK

The meaning of these two terms is practically the same whether we talk of balance sheet or of off-balance sheet financing. *Credit risk* is the more classical and it relates to the counterparty. It represents the possibility that a loss may occur from failure of another entity to perform according to the terms of a contract.

- A failure to live up to contractual requirements engages the financial responsibility of that counterparty.
- But the impact of the failure is felt by the company that stood to benefit from the clauses the exchange of the financial instrument stipulated.

To face part of the credit risk, some banks have introduced the notion of *settlement exposure*. This represents the risk that they will deliver under a contract but that the customer will fail to deliver the countervailing amount. Day-in and day-out, year-in and year-out the credit risks a bank is taking can be divided into the following two larger classes:

1. The positions opened with other parties at the *dealing room*, which today represent roughly two thirds of the total exposure, but
2. *Credits and loans* are under the commercial division and concern the other third of the bank's global credit risk.

Treasury operations at the dealing room involve not only credit risk but also *market risk*. Market risk represents the possibility that future changes in market behavior, and in market prices, may make a financial instrument less valuable or more onerous. Two examples are interest rate risk and currency exchange rate risk.

- The distinction between credit risk and market risk is important because the two are differently motivated.
- Besides this, disclosure requirements differ for each from country to country and within the same country.

The measurement of market risk associated with financial instruments is meaningful only when all related and offsetting on-balance sheet and off-balance-sheet transactions are handled in a comprehensive manner and the resulting net positions are properly identified. Hence the need to maintain risk management policies that monitor and limit exposure to market risks and to take the necessary steps to handle a number of other requirements.

Market risk can be divided into two major components. *General market risk* is that of a general market movement arising from, say, a change in official policy, interest rates, a major bank failure, or the perception of a coming illiquidity in the market. The other is *specific market risk.*

Specific market risk addresses the credit-related and liquidity risks associated with an underlying financial instrument. With off-balance sheet products this is usually a hybrid of credit risk and general market risk.

General market risk applies to positions taken with each and every derivative product, subject only to an exemption for fully or very closely matched
positions in identical instruments, which is an imprecise art. Its handling
requires the use of analytical approaches. For instance,

- For risk calculation purposes the various categories of instruments are
  typically slotted into the maturity ladder.
- To these maturity ladders the Bank for International Settlements (BIS)
  suggests applying offsetting procedures.

Known as horizontal and vertical *offsetting* these procedures are controversial. The more advanced financial institutions do not believe they are
netting or offsetting anything. One of of these banks said in the course of
my research: 'This is junior highschool stuff.'

Opinions on how risky derivatives are do, however, vary. Many banks,
particularly among the least technologically advanced and more trigger-happy
(two conditions which have been found to correlate in a significant manner)
consider that interest rate and currency swaps, forward foreign exchange
contracts, and interest rate futures and options are not necessarily subject to
a specific risk charge. This exemption is also thought to apply to futures
and options on a short-term interest rate index.

Serious banks which care about their exposure, and give a much greater
value to their long-term survival than to the cosmetics on profit figures, do
appreciate that credit risks and market risks should not be taken lightly.
Too much exposure can be counterproductive, as there is a correlation of
risks:

- In the case of futures and options contracts where the underlying security
  is a debt, or an index representing a basket of debt securities, specific
  market risk applies according to the credit risk of the issuer.
- Only for First World governments is specific market risk taken to be
  zero. And other cases require sophisticated simulators to evaluate specific
  market risk and fair value in conjunction to credit risk.

Tier 1 banks are always ready to evaluate the credit and market positions
they are holding. They are eager to highlight weak or negative performers,
taking care of them before it is too late. This is quite understandable if we
account for the fact that major banks tend to allocate about two thirds of
their credit line toward counterparties to off-balance sheet operations.

Just as significant is the fact that 50 percent or more of OBS trades are

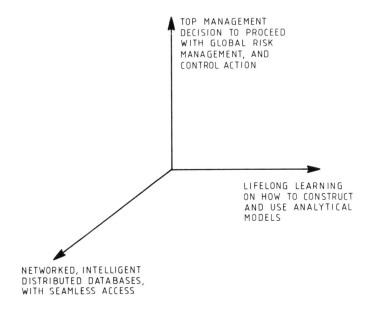

Figure 10.2   A solution space for successful operations with off-balance sheet instruments

made between corresponding banks, not with other types of companies or government authorities. Huge amounts of money are involved in such transactions. Daily trading in New York reaches the level of $2.5 trillion – though this is not the average figure.

The market with the largest risks taken with derivative instruments is New York. There is also a concentration of OBS trades, with the top 9 US banks representing 90 percent of American exposure. Knowledgeable financial experts predict that there will be a shakedown among the financial players.

- The current top team involves thirty or so major money center banks.
- Some central banks think that by the end of the 1990s the top team will be reduced to five or six really active in OBS deals.

The question is often asked: 'Which banks may be best fit to survive?' This is not an easy one but, other things being equal, the survivers will be the banks who make their trades and track their exposure within the solution space defined in Figure 10.2.

Knowledgeable readers will appreciate that in the frame of reference defined in Figure 10.2, the first and foremost issue is management culture in respect to risk control. In a derivatives trade characterized by rapid change, the second axis of reference is lifelong learning, the third the ability to develop and use high technology solutions which permit us to see clearer in situations which are, by their nature, rather fuzzy.

NOTIONAL PRINCIPAL AMOUNT

Typically, a money center bank today has an off-balance sheet exposure in the range of $1 trillion–$2.5 trillion in *notional principal amounts*, with the average OBS exposure being in the range of $1.2–$1.5 trillion. These numbers do not exactly reflect the money traded in the exchange and clearing houses. To understand what they mean, we must appreciate the sense of 'notional principal'.

Widely used with derivatives, the term notional principal has been borrowed from the swaps market where it signifies the quantity of money never actually to be paid or received. Rather, notional amounts are used as the basis for calculating the periodic payments of *rate interest*:

- Fixed, or
- Floating.

The same notional principal concept applies to caps and floors, forward rate agreements, futures or forwards contracts for treasury bonds, guilds and bunds. However, the concept of notional principal is not so useful with some derivatives such as:

- Stock index futures, and
- Commodity options

where the basis for calculations is number of shares, or bushels of wheat and soybeans. These quantities cannot be meaningfully aggregated. Can we use a demodulator to convert *from notional amounts to real exposure figures* with which bankers are better acquainted?

The risk concept most widely appreciated in the financial industry is that which is associated with *loans*. Therefore, to bring the notional principal amount to the equivalent level of loans exposure, banks apply a reduction factor or *demodulator*. This is different by OBS instrument, but some banks also use an aggregate demultiplier – after having summed up all their notional principal exposure. The demodulator ranges:

- From 1/10 used by the most conservative banks
- To 1/60 used by institutions which are the least adverse to risk exposure.

Not every financial institution agrees with this policy. Some consider it to be irrelevant, just as they think that the notional principal amount is meaningless as a measure of exposure. But which are the alternatives?

There are not many alternatives and for this reason the reserve banks back the *notional principal amount* as a metric of risk. Among other reasons, it constitutes a common level of reference. Some reserve banks, however, prefer to control the risk taken by commercial and investment banks through their *cash flow*. Another alternative, or supplementary metric depending on the case, is *fair value*.

For their part, some of the high technology banks not only adopted the notional principal metric but also developed a statistical system which permits them to adapt the demodulator to the prevailing uncertainty in the market, depending on volatility, liquidity and other factors. For instance:

- A 1/30 ratio characterizes a less stringent control, if the markets are calm.
- A 1/20 ratio is applied if more conservative policies should be followed because there is turmoil in the market.

As a numerical example, the use of a 1/30 demodulator would mean that if a bank has $1.2 trillion in off-balance sheet exposure its loans equivalent exposure will be $40 billion. That's a colossal sum which may represent many times the bank's capital and its reserves.

- As it will be appreciated, $40 billion in real money represents a tremendous risk not only to the bank which carries it but the financial system as a whole.
- No financial institution's capital and reserves have been adapted to face that high level of risk – not even the reserve banks have in liquid form the money to confront it.

For a $150 billion bank, for instance, the reserve requirement stipulated by the Basel Committee on capital requirements will amount to $12 billion – or only 30 percent the OBS exposure which it probably has. At the same time, there are also major risks to be covered in the area of classical loans – for which the 8 percent reserve requirement was stipulated in the first place.

It is in everybody's interest to have a sound system for risk management. Based on an extensive research project which I did in 1993 and 1994 in the United States, England, Scandinavia, Germany, Austria and Japan, Figure 10.3 suggests a reporting framework on financial exposure along three axes of reference: notional principal, fair value and cash flow. We will be talking about cash flow in Chapter 11, hence in the present section let's focus on fair value.

THE CONCEPT OF FAIR VALUE

The concept of fair value and its estimate did not start with off-balance sheet financing, but derivative instruments shed a new light on it. When a

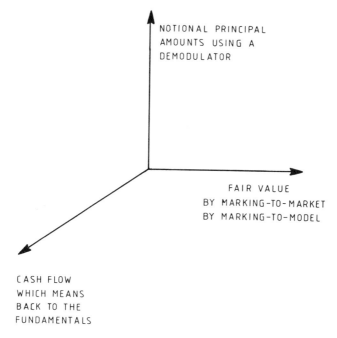

NOTIONAL PRINCIPAL
AMOUNTS USING A
DEMODULATOR

FAIR VALUE
BY MARKING-TO-MARKET
BY MARKING-TO-MODEL

CASH FLOW
WHICH MEANS
BACK TO THE
FUNDAMENTALS

Figure 10.3 The reporting of financial exposure by commercial and investment banks can be made along a 3-dimensional frame of reference

company estimates the value of its inventory, it usually tries to be 'fair;' this, however, is not so easy. For this reason there exist rules which are legally admissible for tax reasons:

- First-in, first-out (FIFO),
- Last-in, first-out (LIFO), or
- Weighted average.

These rules do not apply with derivative financial instruments, therefore regulators have looked for alternatives which can pass the market test. In America, as defined by the Financial Accounting Standards Board (FASB) Statement 107 as a reporting criterion,

- *Fair value* stands for market value by marking-to-market.
- It is *not* a value responding to *worst-case scenario*, or market collapse.

The desired fair value price is the amount at which a financial instrument could be exchanged in a current transaction, between a willing buyer, and a willing seller. This is considered in the perspective of other cases than forced liquidation.

If the market has collapsed, Statement 107 requires the reporting bank to make its best estimate of fair value. This is not easy either and it can lead to a great heterogeneity in reporting:

- For some derivatives the market value may be zero or simply trivial – just as with loans and other investments.
- But no bank will zero out many of the assets it has written in its books – unless forced into liquidation.

On the other hand, as long as there is a market for a given financial instrument, commercial and investment banks are required to *mark-to-market*. If there is no market, either because it has not yet been really created or it is past, then banks *mark-to-model*. These two issues:

- Marking-to-market, and
- Marking-to-model

should not be confused even if they serve the same purpose and, in many cases, complement one another. If there is no market for the instrument, then fair value must be computed. This is done through *option pricing models* such as Black-Scholes, binomial approximation, Poisson distribution, or Monte Carlo.

A common weakness of current models targeting a derivative's fair value is that they don't examine *worst-case scenarios*. Yet, it is very important to account for what is left of the fair value in case of market collapse. Banks will be well advised to do so for their own portfolio, that of their clients, and for what is known about counterparties.

- This can be done through *fuzzy engineering*.
- But few banks have the necessary knowhow to proceed along that road.

There are also legal problems raised in connection to the fair value concept, as well as in regard to hedging. Bankers may be getting smarter in regard to derivative financial instruments, but judges in the courts are not yet acquainted with their risks.

In June 1992, a Court decision in America brought nearer the day when board members have a legal duty in OBS. The case of *Brane v. Roth* started back in 1980 and it involved a small grain coop in Indiana.

- The accountants had advised the coop manager to hedge at the Chicago Board of Trade
- But the coop manager only hedged $30.000 out of $7.3 million
- The resulting loss was $424.000 because of the grain market collapse

The Court ruled that managers and board members had the duty to understand hedging techniques and they were liable for damages. This placed squarely at director level the responsibility to understand *market risk* and be able to hedge the odds so as to protect the company from adversity.

The problem with this strategy is that hedging can sometimes turn against the hedger, particularly if he is overexposed. Since the estimation of fair value is not an exact science, there exists *no perfect hedging* – as we will be discussing on p. 220.

Most hedges are imperfect; and some may actually increase the market risk rather than cover it. It is not surprising that it is difficult to get an admission of this fact from the people who sell the derivative financial products. The surprise is that some judges also take the same liberal attitude in terms of fair value and exposure.

WHAT IS MEANT BY OPTIONS?

A better understanding of derivatives will help to appreciate the meaning of this last statement. One of the most popular derivatives is options. An *option* is a security giving right to buy (call) or sell (put) an asset, within a specified period of time, subject to certain conditions.

A *call* option gives the holder the right – but not the obligation – to enter a long futures position at a specific price. The buyer gets into an options contract by paying a certain price. This contract obliges the writer (seller) to:

* Enter a short futures position at that specific price
* If he is assigned by the holder, who exercises his option.

A *put* option gives the holder *the right* to enter a short futures position. The writer will be obliged to enter a long futures position, should the option be exercised.

The simplest kind of option is one that offers the right to buy or sell a share of common stock. Other things being equal, the higher the price of the stock the greater will be the value of the option.

* When the stock price is higher than the *strike price* of the option, the latter is sure to be exercised.
* When the stock price is lower than the strike price of the option, its holder will forgo his right to exercise it.

Options have *volatility*, which is a function of both stock price and maturity. The potential gain of an option holder, and the potential loss of an option buyer increases with the volatility of the market.

An option is *at-the-money* when the exercise price is equal to or near the current underlying futures price. An option is *in-the-money* if it has *intrinsic value*. For call options this is the difference between:

- The futures price, and
- The strike price.

Out-of-the-money is an option with no intrinsic value. For instance, in the case of a call option, if the underlying futures price is lower than the strike price.

The *intrinsic* value of an option is the value it would have exercised immediately. The *extrinsic* value of an option is its current price less its intrinsic value. Extrinsic value is sometimes called *time value* because the time remaining for the option to make a move is the key to its worth. Such extrinsic value of an option is the amount of its value that is not in-the-money.

By contrast, the intrinsic value is the amount an option is in-the-money. Intrinsic values are determined by the underlying market. Extrinsic values are determined by the option market. The two are loosely coupled: when one changes, the other may or may not change.

Options appear in many financial deals with exchange-listed and over-the-counter (OTC) markets. Callable bonds and mortgage-backed securities (MBS) are examples. We typically distinguish:

- American-type options which can be exercised at any time up to maturity, and
- European-type options which are exercised near their maturity.

Options are often compared to insurance which is subject to the laws of supply and demand. When demand is low, the price goes down. When demand is high, prices go up. When a market starts to move or heat up, traders are more uncertain about what might happen. Because of this, options become more valuable and their prices go up.

- As options prices change, their extrinsic value is increasing.
- While for any price in the underlying market, the option's intrinsic value will be the same, whether the underlying market is active or not.

In addition to the close relationship between option prices and implied volatility for a given underlying price, a 1:1 relationship exists between option prices and extrinsic values for a given underlying price. Hence the implied volatility is a measure of the extrinsic value of an option price.

Futures		Forward	
1	Standardized	1	Non-standardized
2	Traded in exchanges	2	Bilateral agreements
3	Settled daily	3	Exercised usually at maturity
4	Buyer deposits a margin	4	Depends on agreement
5	Buyer called to upgrade margin	5	Depends on agreement
6	Commission to broker	6	No broker involved
7	Price set by the market	7	Price fixed by writer or common accord
8	Traded on items for which is market demand	8	Developed and traded to fit the two parties
9	Easy offset by opposite position	9	Thorough analysis needed for offsetting
10	Mainly market risk	10	Both market risk and credit risk

Table 10.1 Ten crucial differences characterizing futures and forward contracts

FUTURES CONTRACTS AND FORWARDS

A *futures* contract is an exchange-traded commitment which generally calls for the delivery of a specified amount of a particular grade of commodity or financial instrument. The price of futures fluctuates since they are exchange-traded.

Forward is a bilateral commitment to buy or sell an asset at a future date for a price determined when the deal is made. Futures are standardized; forwards are not. Table 10.1 expresses the ten most important differences between futures and forwards.

Many types of forwards are foreign exchange contracts, promoted by the fact there is fluctuation in exchange rates even within regional market agreements. Dealing made in foreign currency between two parties can be of two types:

1. Foreign currency *denominated* contracts

where settlements are performed in a single currency. These include the popular forward rate agreements (FRAs) that bet on the future interest rate in a foreign currency; *bonds* payable in a foreign currency; and commitments to sell *goods or services* for foreign currency.

2. Foreign currency *exchange* contracts

Obligations include the exchange of currencies, such as traditional *currency swaps* and *forex options* – but not forward rate agreements which are of the forex denominated rather than exchange category.

Forwards have become important as increasing emphasis is placed on bilateral contracts traded off-exchange. By all accounts, the beginning of the

21st century will see banking and financial services as a key competitive ground with battles fought off-exchange. At a premium will be:

• Bilateral agreements, and
• Transnational realtime networks.

Institutional investors will operate cross-border on-balance sheet and off-balance sheet. Financial analysis, simulation and knowledge engineering will be used for the rapid development of new instruments, their optimization and the online execution of complex transactions.

Up to a point, options, futures and forwards permit us to determine and control the risk the investor or trader is willing to take, even if he will sell the contracts rather than buy them. But as with all financial products, there are constraints.

• *Time value* is a wasting asset, which is why many option traders prefer to sell calls and puts rather than to buy them.
• But astute investors can make time work in a way that will be favorable to them, in a *profitability* sense.

A key factor to profits is to know when to cut one's own losses and when to let his profits run. Understanding the dynamics of an option spread means appreciating how the value of the spread changes over time. This helps decide when to hold positions and when to liquidate them.

SWAPS AGREEMENTS AND SPREADS

The three most important classes of swaps are physical commodity, currency, and interest rate. Interest rate swaps (IRS) are one of the two most popular derivative financial instruments today because of the fact that many banks believe that:

• Interest rate swaps, and
• Forward rate agreements

can enhance their ability to manage interest rate risk. This is not necessarily true given that each party entering an IRS or FRA is exposed to the other in terms of credit risk, market risk and legal risk – among other risks characterizing bilateral deals.

As with all aspects of banking and of financial transactions at large, parties engaging in swaps trades must pay attention to the nature of the instrument they are dealing with. A *swap* is a financial transaction in which two counterparties agree to:

- Exchange streams of payments over time,
- According to a predetermined rule applying to both of them.

A swap is a *legal agreement* which specifies a notional principal amount, payments to be made, termination (and hence maturity) and terms of default. A *standard swap* involves receipt of a predetermined amount of the spot value of the unit of the agreed commodity – over a given period.

Differential swaps provide a good example of the technology needed to handle new financial instruments. Though they are known as derivatives players, some banks avoid making differential swaps if they can, not because these instruments imply taking risk, but because the bankers feel they do not have a complete *model* to cope with the challenges.

Indeed, there are many unknowns with cross-market operations, the instruments used in such transactions and the resulting exposure. *Volatility* per se and pricing accounting for volatility are examples. On many transactions in options, futures, and derivatives – and most particularly on differential swaps – banks do not properly *price the risk*. Somehow, they tend to ignore:

- The future hedging costs, and
- The exposure they take.

Hence the tendency to keep closer to lower risk option spreads which, at times, can mean attractive returns. For instance, option spread strategies can be constructed to capitalize on an essentially neutral market where futures traders don't see great profits opportunities.

- In an option spread, a call or put can be bought at the same time another call or put is sold.
- However, the purchase and sale cannot be of the same call or put or the net position would be nil.

This is not difficult to avoid as option contracts vary with strike price, expiration or both. The most fundamental kinds of option spreads are vertical, horizontal and diagonal. We will briefly look at the vertical alternative.

A vertical spread is the purchase and sale of calls or puts in which the two legs of the spread have different strike prices but the same expiry date. The term originated in the stock option market, where options were quoted in the financial press with expiry months running across a row and strike prices running downward in a column.

Vertical spreads may be constructed to take advantage of a sideways trading market, but they are generally classified as either bullish or bearish. Such trades may profit in advancing or declining markets. Since the strike prices of the two legs are different, these strategies also have been called 'money' spreads.

- With a bull spread, the trader or investor buys a low-struck option and sells a relatively high-struck option.
- With a bear spread, he buys a high-struck option and sells a relatively low-struck option.

Whether we talk of swaps, forwards or spreads, a definite asset is the amount of homework which was done *prior* to engaging in a trade. Also the ability to follow in *realtime* minute market changes, experimenting on 'What-if' and dynamically adjusting portfolio position. Hence the emphasis on financial engineering in connection with off-balance sheet operations.

THE ROLE OF PREDICTION IN FINANCIAL ANALYSIS

As we saw on many occasions in Part One, *analysis* is a compelling metaphor for the way the financial industry works. Through *financial engineering* we examine the key variables, sensitivities, profit potential and embedded risks – to be further studied by means of analytical techniques.

Analytical models help to evaluate the financial market, experimenting on products and their behavior. For instance, we may wish to know about *trends*, *volatility* and *liquidity*. Or we may wish to study pockets of inefficiency, short-lived *anomalies*, and the like.

- Key to financial analysis is *nontraditional* research.
- Hence the need for the new methods and tools we put in place for reasons of *prediction*.

The object of prediction is the future impact of current decisions. Contrary to what many people think, forecasting and planning are not really concerned with future decisions – but with the future impact of *current* decisions. Prediction is a task made much more complex in times of turbulence, which is by definition:

- Nonlinear,
- Irregular, and
- Erratic.

Algorithms and heuristics are used, for example, to stochastically examine volatility, detect pricing errors created by simpler models and personalize a prediction process to a given trader, investor, or speculator.

The analysis of stochastic patterns can not only reveal investor and speculator characteristics, and try to match them to market behavior, but also lead to better risk management procedures. This is important because of the leverage factor:

- Considerably less capital is required to participate in the options market than in the stock market.
- Investors are often present in the options market to hedge risk as well as to optimize their portfolios.
- Speculators are attracted to the options market because of the potential for higher profits.

The future impact of current decisions is important to all of them, but each has his own way of looking at aftermaths or reacting to a panic. While the customization of models to the instrument and to the player is an asset, it should also not be forgotten that at least some of the elements in financial modeling are common. Basic parameters include:

- Volatility of underlying assets,
- Variance of volatility,
- Correlation between option price and volatility, and
- Experimentation on possible distribution of values.

One of the areas where experimentation is necessary is the comparison of a set of option pricing models against knowledge to be derived from historical market data. Such comparison requires high performance computing, in order to give results which are meaningful in a realtime market sense.

Experimenters with experience in the modeling of derivatives use optimization techniques to estimate model parameters, and devise figures of merit based on the bid/ask spread. They act this way to gauge model performance.

- This approach permits them to improve the results of existing pricing models, and
- Leads toward a trading strategy enriched with prediction capabilities.

Financial analysis at the edges of the banker's knowhow in terms of instruments and market behavior plays a dual role which is not as generally appreciated as it should be. The objectives of simulation and optimization are generally well-known. Less understood is the fact that *prediction* on the *future* course of *current* decisions helps in developing dissension.

In his book *My Years with General Motors* (1900), Alfred Sloan recounts how, as chairman of the board of GM he: 'Never accepted an important proposal without having dissension, hence critical discussion about its merits and demerits.' And Dr Robert McNamara advises: 'Never go ahead with a major project unless you have examined all the *alternatives*. In a multimillion dollar project you should never be satisfied with vanilla icecream only. You should have many flavors.'

MODELS, VOLATILITY AND HEDGING

It is important to appreciate that the dual role of financial analysis has a significant effect on pricing models. We can use a valid option-pricing formula to calculate the fair value of a derivative. But we can also use it in reverse to find a volatility level that makes a certain option worth a certain price, for instance, the current market price.

- Originally, option-pricing models were designed to produce a computed, and therefore theoretical, value or price for an option.
- But their greatest worth proves to be in calculating implied volatility, as well as in providing a common frame of reference.

Because fairly precise models for calculating implied volatility are computing-intense, the way most financial analysts go about option pricing is by trial and error – or more precisely through heuristics. An initial guess is made and the resulting value is compared to the actual option price.

- If the theoretical value is too low, then the volatility guestimate is too low.
- If the theoretical value is too high, then the volatility guesstimate is too high.

By means of high performance computers, this process is repeated time and again, until the calculated value equals the current market price for the option (if there is one) – keeping in mind that for every different price that an option trades at in the market, there is a unique implied volatility value. When this changes,

- Option positions can change in value.
- This is true even though the underlying instrument may not change.

There are different definitions of volatility and it is at least wise to distinguish between *historical* or actual volatility and *implied* or future volatility. Both are important with financial instruments, and particularly so with derivative products.

Historical volatility refers to price fluctuations over some specific period of the past. For instance, the volatility of the crude oil market over the last 30, 60 or 90 days; or stock market volatility. The best use of historical volatility is that it permits an educated guess about what the future volatility might be.

The real goal, of course, is future volatility – which is what every investor and trader will like to know. Forecasted volatility is calculated by means of models:

- Many financial analysts try to do this for a period covering the life of an option.
- This is, however, tough, with the results that future volatility is essentially a guesstimate.

An implied volatility typically measures the price of options on a scale which does not depend upon strike price, underlying price or time. Given basic inputs required for option evaluation, exercise price, underlying price and interest rates – we run these inputs through a mathematical pricing model to obtain an estimated value for an option, as stated already concerning fair value.

The volatility factor, or *beta* (β), is very important in all financial trades. But there are also other, more recently developed, critical measures of a growing impact in connection with the trading of financial instruments. They are known as delta, gamma, theta, kappa, rho (δ, γ, θ, κ, ρ).

- *Delta* is the expected change in an option's price, as a proportion of a small change in the underlier.
- *Gamma* is the partial derivative of *delta*, and the second derivative of the price function.
- *Theta* expresses the rate at which an option loses computed value, for each day that passes with no movement in the price of the underlier (time decay).
- *Kappa*, (or vega, lamda, beta prime) addresses the impact of fairly small changes in a given position, for example, a 1 percent change in beta.
- *Rho* is the change in the option's price per 1 percent change in the interest rate that reflects the option's carrying cost.

For instance, an option with a delta of 40 can be expected to change its value at 40 percent of the rate of change in the price of the underlying security. If the underlying security goes up 5, the option's theoretical value can be expected to go up 2.

Delta is also known as *hedge ratio* because it expresses the ratio of underlier to option contracts, for reasons of neutral hedge. Delta-neutral, gamma-neutral and other positions in relation to the forementioned metrics are established through hedging, but not all metrics can be hedged at the same time.

MARKING-TO-MARKET OR MARKING-TO-MODEL FOR OPTION PRICING?

A basic question in the science of evolution as well as in prediction theory is how to determine the macroscopic variables which characterize the behavior of a complex system. This has many similitudes with the quest to quantify unpredictability in the study of chaos, whether the underlying system is:

- The behavior of financial markets,
- Astronomical observations in the cosmos, or
- Patterns connected to weather prediction.

In visual pattern recognition connected to any of these cases, the typical formulation of the problem tries to classify spatial information in a manner amenable to interpretation. This requires identifying then handling in an effective manner *independent* variables and *dependent* variables.

Usually the independent variables provide the *inputs* from which, through the *model* we have made of the real world, we aim to obtain *outputs* telling us about the behavior of the dependent variables. The outputs may, for instance, be those defined by Black and Karasinki (1991):

- Yield curve,
- Volatility curve, and
- Cap curve.

In the path to maturity, the cap curve gives the price of an at-the-money differential cap – which maps a rate equal to the positive difference between the short rate and the strike price. For any maturity, an at-the-money cap has a strike equal to the forward rate for that maturity.

This sort of study helps the financial analyst in getting a better perspective, but how good this is going to be largely depends on his ingenuity, the data he has available and the model he chooses. Also, how well he exploits the potential this model is offering.

As we have seen since the beginning of this chapter, different modeling techniques have been used over the years in connection to option pricing. The more popular are: the Black–Scholes method, binomial approximation and Monte Carlo, each having its strong points as well as its limitations.

The *Black–Scholes option pricing model* assumes constant volatility and European pricing. It is a fairly approximate method as it makes many assumptions and employs a nonstochastic equation for call price. By contrast, other models treat volatility as a stochastic process.

The *binomial approximation* allows us to incorporate stochastic volatility and American-type option trading. Binomial models are also an approximation, using a set of fixed input parameters such as:

- Stock price,
- Stock price/exercise price ratio,
- Volatility,
- Variance of volatility,
- Correlation between parameters.

1 *Fair Value* is function of intrinsic value and time value.
It provides the basis for estimating a *risk premium* in connection to intrinsic value and time value.
2 *Intrinsic Value* is the value of an option at any time it is exercised.
It can be expressed depending on the condition:
in-the-money, out-of-the-money, at-the-money.
3 *Time Value* is a function of time to maturity, beta, interest rate, critical ratio.

4 Critical Ratio $= \dfrac{\text{Strike Price}}{\text{Spot Price}}$.

5 *Hedge Coefficients* are delta, gamma, theta, kappa, rho.
Plus an uncertainty factor to account for the evaluation done by the market.

Table 10.2 Key factors entering an options pricing model

Monte Carlo models are more accurate for option pricing purposes. They make it feasible to directly incorporate volatility and stock price change, as stochastic processes, and are easy to parallelize. However, Monte Carlo models are too computationally intensive.

Table 10.2 presents in a nutshell the key factors which enter an option pricing model. These include: fair value, intrinsic value, time value, critical ratio and the hedge coefficients discussed on p. 221. The last two sections of Chapter 14 continue the discussion of OBS transaction, following the explanation on the use of balance sheet ratios.

11 Cash Flow and its Management

INTRODUCTION

Cash flow means financial staying power. In the long term, it is a function of *our* products, their market appeal and the ingenuity of the salesmen. Cash flow is an important criterion in financial analysis because in the very short term (90–180 days), it makes the difference between the company's solvency or insolvency – while in the longer term it contributes to its financial freedom, from loans and indebtedness.

The management of cash flow has been a concern of financiers, merchants and industrialists for all of recorded history. This is as true of relatively small enterprises as it is of large ones. In both cases, it reflects the company's capability for managing projects which involve time, skill and financial resources to develop and support.

The absence of policies and procedures to assure a sound cash flow has been a recurrent theme in business. Few people realize that, in its fundamentals, the challenge of:

- Projecting,
- Measuring, and
- Controlling

the cash flow is one of aggregating financial resources, adding up all the support functions required during each time period, and for each endeavor, with particular emphasis on financial means and their evolution as time goes on.

The crucial test is one of taking all business parameters into account developing factual and documented cash flow scenarios. This is an approach which can be effectively used as well in risk control and in budgeting.

- There is a close connection between cash flow, budgeting and risk control.
- Forecasts made for new commitments and with realtime evaluation of current positions are a highly recommended business practice.

An able management will use the results of sound cash flow calculations very quickly. They help in judging whether the company requires more financial resources than are available at any given time, and assist in demonstrating what sort of action needs to be taken in order to improve upon current conditions.

DEFINING THE MEANING OF CASH FLOW

To treat a given subject in an effective manner, we must first define its meaning. The term *cash flow*, however, does not have just one definition and method of computation, as some textbooks suggest. Much depends on the type of company and the practices which it has adopted. Therefore, it is wise to start with the fundamentals: more precisely, with the meaning of *cash*.

Cash assumes many forms. There is: cash in the bank, cash on hand, undeposited cheques and money orders, undeposited drafts, change funds, payroll funds and so on. Typically, cash is classified in the balance sheet as either:

* Cash on hand, or
* Cash in bank.

Cash on hand includes coins, paper money, cheques, bank drafts, cashier's checks, express money orders, and postal money orders. Cash in bank consists of demand deposits in cheque accounts. Demand certificates of deposit may be classified as cash, but this is not true of time certificates.

Safeguarding the cash is only one element of a good system of internal checks and balances, but it is a very important one. An adequate internal check upon cash requires a control over both *receipts* and *disbursements*. The methods of effecting this control vary greatly in different organizations, and the same is true with regard to the concept of cash flow and its handling.

Cash flow is typically generated through business transactions, and we all know that such transactions are of a *circular* character. This cyclical process begins with a *cash debit* and ends with a *cash credit* – which creates the basis of the cash flow and its computation.

* Productive resources are acquired by bargaining transactions, and
* They are used to create products which are sold to the market also through transactions.

Cash flow, in its simplest form, is net income plus items such as depreciation. *Net income* is both the bottom line and the starting point when figuring out a company's cash flow.

$$\text{Cash flow} = \text{Net income} + \text{Depreciation} + \text{Depletion} + \text{Amortization}$$

Through *depreciation* we write down the cost of an asset, such as a factory or a machine tool, over its useful life. This charge is made for shareholders and tax reporting, it is a bookkeeping charge which does not require cash outlays.

The fact that in current industrial accounting practice, depreciation costs are subtracted from net income, is a big reason for the depressed profits of many companies. But it also means that much of the cash that would otherwise be visible is hidden from view.

* A company which depreciates $100 million shows net earnings of another $100 million and pays no dividend,
* Has actually generated a cash flow of $200 million, twice its earnings.

The concept of *depletion* is the write-off when the asset being used is a natural resource, such as oil, gas, coal, or minerals. *Amortization* is also a write-down but of specific terms or of intangible assets.

Acquisitive companies often have an entry on the books called *goodwill*, the difference between what they paid for a firm and the lower book value. Goodwill is amortized over a long period, usually 40 years, and requires no cash outlay.

Simple cash flow is not a particularly useful figure by itself, what is important is *operating cash flow* (OCF). Operating cash flow is the money generated by a company before the cost of financing and taxes come into play.

In recent years, investing in companies based on their price-to-OCF multiples has been one of the best strategies, and one which can be significantly assisted through financial analysis.

$$\text{OCF} = \begin{array}{c}\text{Operating}\\ \text{cash flow}\end{array} = \begin{array}{c}\text{Cash}\\ \text{flow}\end{array} + \begin{array}{c}\text{Interest}\\ \text{expense}\end{array} + \begin{array}{c}\text{Income tax}\\ \text{expense}\end{array}$$

Interest expense is added back to the simple cash flow, to get the broadest possible measure. In case of takeovers, *income tax expense* is added because it will not have to be paid after the new owner adds so much debt that there is no book profit and hence no tax due.

Another money indicator to watch is *free cash flow* (FCF); it tells how much cash is uncommitted and available for other uses. Its computation takes cash flow and adjusts certain balance sheet items, subtracting current debt and capital expenditures.

$$\text{FCF} = \begin{array}{c}\text{Free}\\ \text{cash flow}\end{array} = \begin{array}{c}\text{Cash}\\ \text{flow}\end{array} - \begin{array}{c}\text{Capital}\\ \text{expenditures}\end{array} - \text{Dividends}$$

To calculate the free cash flow, those *capital expenditures* are subtracted which are necessary to maintain plant and equipment and keep the company competitive, but no optional ones. A similar logic is applied to dividends.

LOOKING AT CASH FLOW AS A CRITICAL RESOURCE

The algorithmic expressions which we have seen in the previous section can be nicely programmed for computer processing the classical way, but they can also be mapped in a more sophisticated way by means of expert systems rules. The expert systems exercise is rewarding, provided that management has decided which cash flow notion it wishes to target.

While operating cash flow is the broadest measure of a company's funds, some prefer to zero in on the narrower free cash flow, because it measures truly *discretionary funds*. That is, company money that an owner could manage at his discretion.

- In terms of acquisitions, companies with free cash flow are those particularly sought after.
- Free cash flow can be used to boost dividends, buy back shares, or pay back shares, or pay down debt.
- Some businesses that look pricey based on earnings may be bargains when measured by the yardstick of free cash flow.

Many companies estimate their operating cash flow in a way matching their commitment. Some compare this exercise to *resource leveling*, a process of modifying the schedule of their activities in order to reduce any peaks in financial requirements which cannot be matched through cash flow. Such peaks are typically calculated during resource aggregation.

Nobody can lose sight of cash flow estimates or of *resource allocation* and prosper. Resource-leveling schedules are known from project management. There are two leveling algorithms for doing this:

- Resource limited leveling, and
- Time-limited leveling.

In resource limited leveling the known capacity, or availability level, of each resource is never to be exceeded by the schedule. Activities are delayed in the resource limited schedule until the means needed are available, with particular attention paid to not-exceeding the availability level.

In time limited leveling, activities are delayed only if they have float, and only if the completion date of the project is not affected. Time limited leveling will reduce the peaks in the financial resource profiles, but it is not guaranteed to reduce the peaks to a level below the known capacities of the resources.

We said on p. 225 that one of the problems with the definition of the cash flow (and its handling) is that it tends to mean different things to different companies. In banking, for instance, the cash flow characteristics of a holding company can be entirely different from those of the bank(s) which it controls.

This variation which may exist in cash flow definition is not always appreciated. In the first few years following the massive creation of bank holding companies, back in 1970–1, problems in bank analysis associated with cash flows were masked by:

- The issues connected with the fully consolidated statements at holding company level, and
- The widespread belief that growth would take care of those who worried about cash flow by individual unit or at the holding.

Facts show that this is not necessarily true – the case of Drexel, Burnham, Lambert being an example. The cash available at banking holding companies as well as their profitable subsidiaries must do more work than pay for dividends to shareholders and service double-leveraged debt.

Whether the analysis of cash flow and associated scheduling algorithms concerns banks, bank-related firms or other companies, the dividends received by the holding from its subsidiaries must:

- Cover any operating loss of the parent, and
- Help in the funding of newer affiliates.

Dividends from subsidiaries should perform several jobs, but typically those dividends are effectively limited – often to half of the bank's earnings. As a result, the analysis of fully consolidated earning power is key to effective parent company evaluation. This is a process essential to:

- Investors in bank holding company securities,
- Lenders to bank holding companies, and
- Large depositors in subsidiary banks.

In conclusion, cash flow forecasts should be elaborated with great care. They should definitely cover at least a one-year period – including accounts receivable and to be paid during *this* time period, plus other income, for instance, patents and other accords on knowhow, portfolio and interest from deposits, sales of property and so on. In the last analysis cash flow and assets are two critical subjects which are closely related.

FOCUSING ON CASH FLOWS AND OTHER ASSETS

One of the most important issues to any company is the timing of *cash flows*. Heuristics are more helpful than algorithms in terms of this mission. Underlying the calculation of discounted cash flows are assumptions about the timing of these flows within a year. The user tells the expert system when cash flows are expected to occur, but he may not be sure when they will really occur within the year.

Through rules or by means of fuzzy logic (see also Chorafas, 1994c), the knowledge engineering construct makes a number of assumptions about cash flow timing, both in terms of receipts and expenditures. It accounts for the fact that:

- Commitments regarding capital investments are made at the beginning of the year.
- But operating flows (revenues and expenses) occur throughout the year.

The mission is to study the characteristic pattern. The operating cash flow which we defined as the most important measure of a company's ability to service its debt. To raise cash:

- Capital assets specified by management are sold according to market opportunity within a given timetable.
- Depreciated items with, say, a six- or seven-year lifecycle, will be sold at the beginning of the year following the year they were purchased.
- Disposable inventory is liquidated on the last day of the year, but taxes on its sale are treated as operating cash flows.

Cash on hand and cash in bank are the only assets whose value is exact rather than an estimate. All other valuations involve some guesswork, albeit a careful guess, as all accounting valuations must be made relative to the actual intended purpose or use of the asset in question.

If a business is a going concern and not in the process of liquidation, the financial analyst will be careful not to value the assets at the low figure that they would bring at a forced sale. He should rather value them at their worth to the company in its normal day-to-day operation. The opposite is true in the case of liquidation.

One of the uses of cash flow is to purchase materials. There are different methods of valuing inventory, three of them being weighted average, Last-in first-out (LIFO) and First-in first-out (FIFO). Conservative companies use original cost of the inventories or present market value, whichever is lower.

Difficult problems arise when the prices of materials vary from month to month. Hence the wisdom of following the accounting convention which states that 'At time of purchase, a thing is presumed worth what the company pays for it.' The problem is what happens afterwards, as prices always fluctuate:

- Many companies use hedging for raw materials with high volatility, by means of derivative instruments.
- But many hedging plans are incomplete, leaving the company exposed to market swings, as the crash of Metallgesellschaft in 1993 helps to document.

Another use of cash flow is to face the demands posed by accounts payable which, as their name implies, are the sums owed for goods and services bought and charged. Notes payable represent promissory notes owed to the banks or to a financing company.

Cash flow also serves to pay bank loans, and *bonds* which represent a long-term loan. Typically bonds are floated at a given coupon rate. Bullet bonds (straight bonds) are not due prior to maturity, but this is not true of callable bonds. Dividends and capital due for high interest bonds (junk bonds) consume a significant amount of cash flow.

- The diversity of financial obligation to be faced through the company's cash flow requires very careful study and experimentation.
- Both simulation and knowledge engineering can be of significant assistance to the financial analyst and to the company's management as well.

Working parametrically an expert system might deduce from past practice that management typically discounts cash flows back to the middle of the year, using this measure, by default, to specify the *present value date*. The expert system will then experiment on the results of discounting at different timeframes – experimenting in terms of obtained results.

Another module of the expert system may optimize commitments in function of interest rates and interest rate forecasts. The artifact knows from its knowledgebank that starting in the 1980s, inflationary booms have been quickly dampened by rising interest rates, with market forces keeping the economy from overheating.

- In the global credit markets, bondholders pushed yields up rapidly when they perceived an inflation threat.
- Such preemptive strikes reduced the chances that inflation would become a serious problem in the immediate future.

Today booms and busts are not necessarily engineered by the monetary authorities but by market response. This is one of the reasons why some reserve banks, like the German Bundesbank, look at cash flow as a means for controlling undue exposure with derivatives. Leading-edge banks with a premier system for risk management are taking a similar approach.

DEVELOPING EFFECTIVE MEANS FOR CASH MANAGEMENT

Cash management directly affects the bottom line of every company. Inherently slow or sloppy cash management operations not only cannot help maximize profits but also involve lots of dangers – particularly the risk of being out of step with the market, or with the cash flow requirements of the company.

Like timely financial control which serves the purpose of optimizing the use of resources, cash management must be able to safeguard a company's liquidity. But to deliver a reliable approach to cash management requirements, the information system must be able to respond to ad hoc queries by supplying in realtime:

- Up-to-date bank balances by value date in any place and in any currency,
- The output of models optimizing borrowing and investment decisions,
- Target planning and analysis of sources and uses of funds, and
- Accurate daily forecast of cash requirements, including availabilities in local and foreign currencies.

One of the elements the models should interactively provide is a cash management position that includes a rolling value-date forecast for the following days. This must include open items, purchase orders, customer orders, outstanding bills and so on – as well as a link to electronic banking services. Computer-based experimentation is necessary since:

- Some accounts showing a positive balance must be cleared; while others having a negative balance must be balanced.
- Minimum balances and clearing procedures must be taken into consideration for their immediate and longer-term effects.

Not only should these procedures be carried out online but also the experimentation necessary to optimize every one of them should be executed in realtime. Knowledge artifacts must see to it that the bank accounts are reconciled, including all cash flow operations, financial deposits, payments, borrowings and clearance for the next day.

In terms of bank correspondence, there is a clearing result in the form of bank transfers or bank confirmations and other memos, which must be generated to determine the new bank account balance in any currency, anywhere in the world, by value date. Secure database-to-database transfers is the better policy.

Cash forecast procedures must be an integral part of the system, with comprehensive interactive screens assisting decisions regarding short- and longer-term deposits and borrowing of funds. This information needs not only to be databased and steadily updated but also analyzed. Interactive cash flow statements must be both consolidated and itemized in terms of the company's sources and uses of cash.

- Cash provided by (or used in) operating activities consists of net earnings (loss), adjusted for items that do not necessarily involve the outlay or receipt of cash.
- Cash provided by (or used in) financing activities includes net proceeds from each and every financing-related proceed and payment.
- Cash provided by (or used in) investing activities must be accounted for, identifying and outlining investments in assets to provide future benefits to shareholders.

Net increase or decrease in cash and cash equivalents should be highlighted in every currency in which they occur, anywhere in the world, with approximate justifications accessible as necessary. Balances should indicate the amount remaining as the result of these activities, in any currency, at any time, anywhere in the world.

It used to be an accounting principle that in preparing for the next day of operations, transactions must be cleared and decisions documented. This principle is still valid, but for the next hour – and eventually the next minute – of operations, rather than the next day. The cash management position must be available on request with fully updated information.

It should also be feasible to enter memo records, such as additional forecasts, like payroll or tax payments, to cover a complete planning period. A cash forecast analysis should be carried out with exchange rate risks pinpointed by simulating exchange rate developments on the basis of hypotheses and trends projected by the treasurer.

NET PRESENT VALUE, NET WORTH AND HEURISTICS

State-of-the-art organizations have been successful in managing their cash flow – from the leveling of peaks to the optimization of investments. They do so through the use of financial models, but the majority of companies are not so advanced in the use of technology. Therefore, a crucial question management should ask itself is:

- Do we have the skill and the tools to take advantage of the opportunities propelled through the market forces?
- If not, what should we be doing to significantly improve our technology? Who should have the responsibility for this effort?

Both the methodology and the metrics connected to financial instruments and their evaluation, should be fully reviewed and upgraded. One of the metrics to which management must pay attention – and can do so through expert systems – is *net present value*.

Net present value is a single value measure of cash flows, adjusted for *risk* and the cost of money. Few companies are properly tooled to take advantage of the three key factors affecting this discounting process:

1. Well-documented timing assumptions.
2. The rate the system uses to discount cash flows (hurdle rate) (more precisely, the internal rate of return (IRR), or the rate at which the net present value equals zero.
3. Present value date.

A standard present value calculation assuming noncontinuous discounting can be done through algorithms. The same is valid for *asset recovery* with discrimination between assets that were sold on the first day of the year (because their useful life had ended) and assets sold on the last day of the year and/or some other timeframe (maybe for working capital liquidation).

While the measurement of cash in coins and banknotes is a relatively simple issue whose valuation depends on arithmetic calculation, net present value of current assets represents a challenging subject which can best be approached through knowledge-enriched solutions.

- This process is quite like the actuary's job in an insurance company.
- Judgmental evaluations require heuristics and must be assisted through expert systems.

As a matter of fact, every one of the long list of items which we consider in this chapter can be amenable to a more sophisticated analysis when combined with the positive or negative cash flow perspectives which it generates. The same is true of net sales, cost of sales, direct labor and direct materials.

An all-embracing model should also incorporate research and development expenditures, as well as general and administrative expenses. Other items include pretax income, taxes and tax rates, net income, earnings per share, return on assets, and return on equity.

Both heuristic and algorithmic approaches can be taken in evaluating operating costs to be met by the cash flow. Estimating the operating expenses and timing them properly can be a complex job as the block diagram in the two parts of Figure 11.1 demonstrates. Three intermediate balances are computed in this example, with the whole process divided into four parts for simplification reasons.

In Figure 11.1, Balance 1 includes those calculations representing the direct effect of the envisaged sales and production volumes. Balance 2 focuses on the requirements of direct labor in the factories, maintenance shops, transport

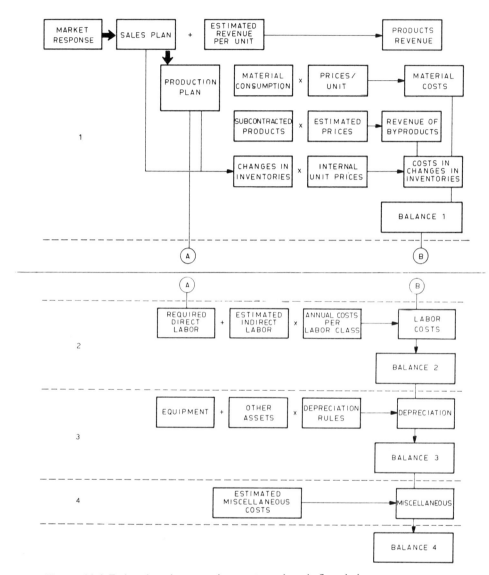

Figure 11.1 Estimating the operating costs and cash flow balances

services, and so on. They can be derived from the production plans according to rules laid down to that end.

These are activities which will consume cash, while depreciation will contribute to it. But depreciation is an aftermath of capital expenditures which also consumer cash, and are the subject of Balance 3. Finally, Balance 4 is added to account for the miscellaneous costs, including several heterogeneous items which have in common demand for cash.

Operating income	*Operating expenses*
	Noninterest
1 Interest earned on loans	1 Salaries and benefits
• Wholesale business	2 Occupancy
• Retail	3 Supplies and equipment
• Direct consumer	4 Utilities
• Residential mortgage	5 Communications and computers
2 Credit card	6 Travel
3 Medical plan	7 Service fees
4 Fees	8 Other operating expense
5 Deliquency charges	
6 Interest on participation	*Interest*
7 Investments in portfolio	1 Interest on deposits
8 Foreign operations	2 Interest on borrowed money
9 Documentary export credit	
10 Real estate	*Extraordinary provisions*
11 Information system services	1 Provision for loan losses
12 Other income	2 Other provisions

Figure 11.2   A bank's income and expense statement

Alert banks would say that something similar is true in their case regarding the way they approach operating income and operating expenses. In Figure 11.2 (which represents the income and expense items of a medium-sized American financial institution) practically each item can have discounted values, much depending on the level of sophistication at which we wish to treat income, expense and cash.

PREREQUISITES TO A DYNAMIC FINANCIAL ANALYSIS

Like dynamic budgeting a dynamic cash flow analysis involves strategies for replacement of maturing financial instruments as well as their effects on the balance sheet. Good management requires forecasting the maturity structure as well as mapping new commitments as they happen.

If different algorithms exist for calculating cash flow, up to a point this is a choice management makes. The same statement can be made for calculating net present value. As we saw on p. 233, *net present value* should not be confused with *net worth*, of which we spoke in connection with the balance sheet:

• Net worth is a bookkeeping calculation, largely reflecting capital and past investments which have been influenced by income and expenses.
• Net present value is a market valuation, though it is often done in an algorithmic way – marking-to-model rather than marking-to-market (see also the discussion in Chapter 10).

1 *Current Ratings*
  • Price/Earnings (P/E)
  • Dividend Yield
  • Premium on Book Equity
2 *Historical Record in %*
  • After Tax Return on Assets
  • After Tax Return on Equity
3 *Current Returns in %*
  • After Tax Return on Assets
  • After Tax Return on Equity
4 *Capital Adequacy*
  • Core Capital (%)
  • Total Capital (%)
5 *Third World Debt*
  • Third World Debt as % of Equity
  • Cost of Increasing Provisions to 50%
6 *Domestic Diversification*
  • Wholesale Banking
  • Business Banking
  • Retail Banking
  • Securities
  • Foreign Exchange
  • Leasing
7 *Geographic Mix (%)*
  • Area 1
  • Area 2
  • Area 3

Figure 11.3 A critical analysis of income statements

As an asset, net present value is essentially a discounted future value of the company as perceived by investors. Hence the increasingly important role which it plays in connection with derivative financial instruments.

But while net worth and net present value are two different concepts, there also exist some similarities. If we turn back our attention to Chapter 9, we will see that in Figure 9.4 we have defined net worth as belonging to the liabilities side of the balance sheet. In that particular example, it was composed of two items:

• Preferred stock, and
• Common stock.

There are no standard ways of analysis of net worth in a market-wide sense. However, well-managed organizations have chosen a more structured approach which is reflected in Figure 11.3.

First and foremost, the main element net worth and net present value have in common is that they both contribute to the financial staying power of the

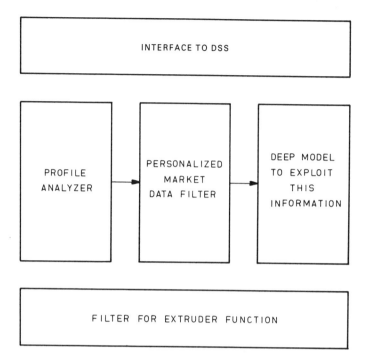

Figure 11.4 Expert systems interfacing to a decision support infrastructure

company. But there is also a sense of a common algorithmic background. This rests on a critical analysis of income statements and is particularly applicable in the banking sector.

One of the known financial institutions evaluates bank holding companies through a matrix approach which we will examine in Chapter 12. This is a multidimensional classification which requires sorting out the lines of strength (retail banking, business loans, leasing and so on):

- Assigning percentages by product line, the way each channel weights on the yearly business.
- Then evaluating these weights in terms of marketing perspectives and yield by country of operations.

It is beyond doubt that no matter which evaluation scheme is adopted, its output should be kept dynamic. At least one financial institution is doing that through expert systems which interface to an established decision support infrastructure.

Figure 11.4 shows that this expert system is composed of five modules: the interface to the already existing decision support system (DSS), a profile

---

Add: Net Sales (after all discounts and rebates)
Deduct: Manufacturing cost of goods sold:*
    Direct Materials
    Direct Labor
    Depreciation
    Manufacturing Overhead
Add: Beginning inventory:
Deduct: Closing inventory:
Gross profit (or gross margin):
    Deduct: Selling and administrative costs
Net operating profit:
    Deduct: Interest charges and local taxes
Net earnings before income taxes:
    Deduct: Income taxes
Net earnings after taxes
    Deduct: Dividends on preferred stock
Net profits on common stockholders:
    Deduct: Dividends paid on common stock
Addition to surplus

---

*Manufacturing cost of goods sold is the sum of all deducted items.

Figure 11.5 Statement of profit and loss: first quarter of an operation
year based on analytics

analyzer, a market data filter, a deep model to explore the retained information and an extruder function to prune the database.

A similar modular approach to the evaluation of financial data can be used with net present value. It can be applied in banking as well as for manufacturing operations. Simple analytical procedures can be done algorithmically. For instance, the case presented in Figure 11.5 reports:

* Income from sales in the quarter
* Expenses to be charged against such sales, and
* Profit remaining after expenses have been deducted.

This is something a procedural approach can provide. But this statement ceases to be valid if instead of addition (*Add*) subtraction (*Deduct*), and multiplication we talk of profitability evaluation, of asset management or, by extension, of net present value.

Prior to closing this example, let's notice that in the last line of Figure 11.5 is written the word *surplus*. This is often done but it is misleading, as it sounds like an extra sort of cash which the company's stockholders might hope to receive. Actually, surplus is not an asset account, much less a pool of liquid cash. It simply indicates a part of the *ownership*, over and above liabilities to creditors and original subscribed capital ownership.

As this discussion on cash flow, net worth and net present value, it brings together some of the elements in financial analysis which permit us to talk of *profitability* as a measure of how much we get for our investment. Profitability is the theme of Chapter 12, but as an introduction to the subject it can be said that to calculate profitability, the *net cash inflow* from operations has to be divided by the *net cash outflow* for investments.

- Both sets of cash flows must be discounted.
- The higher is the ratio, the higher the inflow relative to the outflow.

In this ratio, the numerator: operating cash flows, includes both the outflows (cash paid) and inflows (liquidation) related to working capital. This is valid since working capital is a current asset used to finance operations and not a long-term asset. Notice, however, that working capital liquidation is included in the denominator: investment cash flows, as part of total asset recovery.

In conclusion, we have seen that more than a procedural, algorithmic-type solution is needed for profitability analysis. For this reason, one of the leading financial organizations built a family of expert systems able to capitalize on economic perspectives and their aftermaths. This was done after a thorough study documented that valid profitability evaluations can only be done through heuristics.

After examining both financial and economic factors entering into the profitability equation, the study in reference provided solid evidence that since about 1983 and for a period of nearly ten years the factors underpinning profitability have changed because:

- Economic growth has been much more stable than in previous time periods,
- While interest rates and exchange rates have been much more volatile than in the past.

These are the facts; but finding profitability aftermaths is much more complex. The deregulated credit markets are doing a good job in keeping the economy's engine running at a sustainable speed, even if there is no steady policy to the end. As the economy continues to grow, we must adapt our systems to the new challenges.

RESEARCH FOCUSED ON CASH-FLOW PROBLEMS

One of the basic financial problems facing, for instance, a bank holding company is that bank regulators exercise an independent power for intervention over its cash-flow lifeline. To a considerable extent, extra dividends from bank subsidiaries are seen as a way of using the banking subsidiary as a cash cow. Therefore, they are carefully watched by the regulatory authorities.

- The steady supervision of such practices aims to protect the subsidiary financial firms.
- At the same time, these controls can bring a parent company which has overexposed itself to bankruptcy.

The case of Drexel Burnham Lambert, the now defunct New York investment bank, documents this statement. The fact that the financial health of the holding company may be totally different than that of its subsidiaries makes it necessary that the careful financial analyst uses knowledge-enriched tools to appraise the:

- Degree of leverage in a parent company and its subsidiaries,
- Extent to which a parent is the financing vehicle for its subsidiaries – and vice versa,
- Work dividends must perform on their way to the shareholders, and
- Cushions needed to cover risk and protect shareholder equity as well as dividends.

During the first half of the 1970s, in the early days of bank holding company expansion, many acquisitions were made on simply a volume approach or 'growth at any cost' basis. Twenty years later, as things have settled down, the better managed holding companies are evaluating in an analytical way the acquisition of an existing bank or the formation of a new one.

Figure 11.6 shows a useful model which has been found to be of significant assistance in financial and market oriented evaluations. There are two focal points: *financial performance* and *market performance*, to which a number of crucial factors contribute.

Both in the banking and in the manufacturing industries the study of these critical variables means experimenting with the price and market perspective of available and projected products. These are the main determinants of a company's cash position, and together with cost factors can reveal if a firm can carry the debt which it has amassed.

- If a holding borrowed the money to buy a company by issuing junk bonds,
- Then, it would be paying back both the interest and principal on that debt primarily from the acquired cash flow and by selling of some assets.

An article in *Business Week* (9 April 1990) had this to say with reference to RJR Nabisco:

Operating cash flow – $647 million in 1989 – is expected to more than double in 1990, making RJR's ratio of *cash flow to cash interest* a bountiful 2.5. And the company has more than a year before it must reset interest rates on two key payments in kind bonds, to make them trade at par.

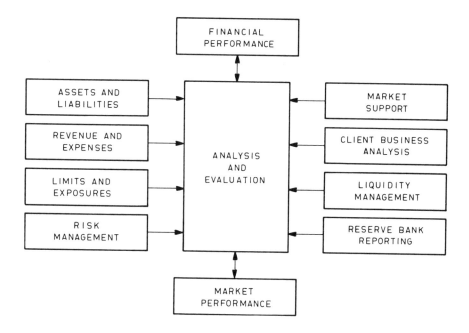

Figure 11.6 Model of financial and market performance based on analytics

One of the most important factors in evaluations of that type is that which epitomizes the economic strengths of a holding company. The potential for future development of almost any banking organization is inextricably tied to its background financial strength – as well as the economic conditions of its market. Metrics which can be helpful in valuation include:

1. Cash flow analysis
2. Assets and liabilities
3. Stock equity and equity to assets
4. Current and projected growth
5. Term debt to total capital
6. Rate of capital formation
7. Emergency cash fund and total short debt
8. Non-performing loans and net charge-offs
9. Earnings coverage of loan losses
10. Double leverage and its payback

Similar standards apply to manufacturing. Doing its homework prior to making firm commitments, the policy followed by Mesa Petroleum was to first evaluate what the output of a company to be acquired through leveraged buy-out (LBO) looked like.

In the case of Unocal, for instance, Mesa ran models with two scenarios: a $20-a-barrel case and a $25. And to make sure it had debt coverage, it ran a worst case scenario of oil falling to $15 a barrel. The deal had to be attractive to the buyers the investment bankers would be selling it to, and its attractiveness depended on profits.

This experimentation revealed some interesting insights. The $20 case was projected to get a 25 percent rate of return. This, Mesa knew, would be very saleable to buyers. Even if the oil price dropped to $15, the debt would have been all paid back, though it would not have resulted in a really good investment for the common shareholders of the new Mesa/Unocal enterprise.

The prospective buyers of these junk-bond securities were sophisticated investors who depended on the raider firm to do a lot of the homework for them. Essentially, they depended on *analysis*, which is precisely the work investment bankers are doing and that is why they need *rocket scientists*. Typically, investment bankers are hired to do evaluations and strategy – not only financing.

THE FOCAL POINT OF ANALYTICAL EXERCISES

A key reason why companies look at investment bankers for mergers-and-acquisitions advice is their analytical capabilities. Investment bankers are paid a fee for that skill. Another basic reason is arranging the commitments and then putting together the subsequent financing, which also requires considerable analytical capabilities.

- Analytical exercises look at cash flow, repayment schedules, and whether some of the securities would have to have interest deferral, which is often the case in highly leveraged deals.
- When the acquiring company cannot afford to pay cash interest on all the securities at the beginning, a significant amount of experimentation is necessary to reveal the better alternative among many.

'When I arrived on Wall Street in 1961 to do financial analysis of the drug industry,' says an old hand in finance, 'I was on the frontier of a revolution in research. Until then, analysts had done statistical work and financial statement analysis, but always combined that with information from members of the Board . . . In these old-line firms, boards of directors were close to the companies and they knew much-sought-after pieces of information – today it is called "insider information"' (Johnson, 1987).

Not only did the laws change but also technology spread. As this happened, rigorous quantitative research increasingly became Wall Street's new tool. Groups of quantitatively oriented young men and women – known as *quants*, or rocket scientists – came into investment banking forming what were initially called *research boutiques*.

Most of these financial R&D laboratories were totally institutional. They offered highly specialized information and therefore the new breed of research analysts became the motor of a fundamental change in the market.

- Ownership of stock was going into the hands of institutions handling billions of dollars, and
- Their large-scale investments required sophisticated research tools and approaches.

Rigorous *quantitative* research also became a tool permitting them to perform in an effective manner the institutional investors' fiduciary duties, an issue which also called for increasingly powerful analytical approaches.

For a number of years, quantitative analyses became the order of the day. Then, it was found that the qualitative characteristics of a financial statement also included standards by which the usefulness of economic and financial information could and should be judged.

Typically, such information is important to management, stockholders and investors – with analytical financial statements being constructed to highlight the most important issues as well as the variation to which they are subjected over time. Cash flows have been instrumental in the able handling of this mission, and this is equally true of:

- The careful outline of original goals, and
- The layout of a procedure to reach them through the intensive use of high technology.

Documented results from financial analysis and high technology are indivisible. Figure 11.7 presents the approach which has been followed by many successful organizations during the last ten years. It starts by setting goals, focuses on the assimilation of technology, then elaborates on the development necessary for acquiring the needed infrastructure. This involves skills and experience, the understanding of algorithms and heuristics, the ability to prove the feasibility of applications, and the provision of links to ensure that solutions are flexible and expanding rather than boxed within a limited framework.

The merging of quantitative and qualitative financial analysis with high technology has provided new vistas in the understanding of financial statement and their contents. Interactive reports should now present to a growing variety of users gap analysis, duration, variability, analysis and What-if evaluations (see also Chorafas, 1994c).

- Algorithms and heuristics assist in making dynamic analyses of assets and liabilities.
- This connects with cash flows since the more short-term liabilities exist, the more cash is needed.

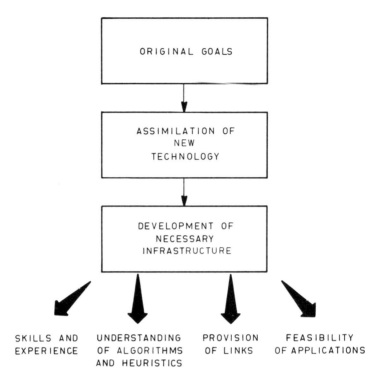

Figure 11.7 From original goals to necessary infrastructure

Through quantitative and qualitative evaluations, financial analysts distinguish net growth from compound growth, evaluate the best repricing strategies, as well as runoffs and exposures.

Any exposure that results from additions to balance sheet and off-balance sheet items must be managed proactively. Careful attention must be paid to dynamic information, with detected shifts in financing focusing on effects and aftermaths. This is the role of nontraditional research.

IMPLEMENTATION OF NON-TRADITIONAL FINANCIAL RESEARCH

Relevance, understandability, verifiability, freedom from bias, timeliness and comparability are qualities which help characterize the usefulness of a financial analysis statement. These characteristics, however, not only complement one another but also conflict; hence tradeoffs might be necessary.

The better documented information coming from a financial R&D laboratory will be both qualitative and quantitative. Qualitative characteristics are typically interpreted in a subjective manner – but this does not necessarily mean that such interpretation is biased.

The sense of a subjective approach is that to a significant degree it is based on criteria dictated by experience and culture. The decision process itself is characterized by evaluator sentences such as:

- A little greater than . . .
- About equal to . . .
- Similar to but not the same . . .
- On the other hand . . .

By contrast, quantitative characteristics rest on metrics, rely on set standards and reflect the accuracy of measurements. The analysis of financial statements, for instance, involves three basic aspects:

- The unit of measurement being used,
- The attributes to be measured, and
- The value which has been measured.

Units of measurement and attributes have to be carefully chosen and this is one of the most challenging jobs the financial analyst must perform. It is a job which requires not only mathematical and analytical skill but also the perception of scales and the ability to reach between the lines of facts and figures.

Some financial analysts suggest that a solution to the problem of attribute measurement is to use different criteria for each type of account depending on its nature and on the goals we are after.

- This, however, would call for a complex and fluctuating standard of measurement.
- While the solutions to be reached should not upset present standards, but provide for evolutionary perspectives.

This apparent conflict in goals has been resolved by what is today known as *nontraditional* financial research. It involves chaos theory, nonlinearities, fractals, genetic algorithms, neural networks and fuzzy engineering in the study of financial information and market phenomena. A great deal of nontraditional studies rest on:

- Analogical reasoning, and
- Patterning.

Thinking by analogy, patterns in cities and buildings affect patterns of movement by people which in turn impact on factors such as merchandising, retailing, banking and communication in the workplace. A method of study of pattern changes is nonlinear dynamics, or *chaos theory*, connected with the theory of motion of bodies under the influence of forces – active, reactive and interactive.

Nonlinear laws in evolutionary processes have been successfully applied to widely different problems in financial modeling and other industrial applications. It has been, for instance, demonstrated that:

- The behavior of time series from capital markets may reflect underlying chaotic behavior.
- This led to the development of tools to characterize and forecast market movements, including cash flows.

Among the mathematical tools used with nonlinear analytical approaches are difference and differential equations, Fourier series, Bessel functions. Genetic algorithms and fuzzy logic provide new opportunities for cash flow estimates, securities trading, portfolio management and risk control. Machine learning techniques have already been successfully applied to a wide range of business and finance processes.

The new tools of nontraditional financial analysis have been used with cash flow patterns, as well as in mapping other market systems. Because they have demonstrated far better performance than conventional approaches, financial modeling is using these tools to address such diverse fields as:

- Foreign exchange trading,
- Stock and bond markets,
- Asset allocation, and
- Off-balance sheet financial instruments.

In conclusion, the final choice of an investment can be made through a thorough analysis of a company's cash flow capabilities and requirements. But the tools used in doing that job are in full evolution.

Algorithmic and heuristic programs can provide good support with the help of high performance computers. As skills develop, current solutions become a springboard to using more sophisticated nontraditional techniques, with rocket scientists and their sophisticated software playing an increasingly critical role.

12 Ways and Means for Judging Profitability

INTRODUCTION

The policy followed by many banks is that an accurate picture of the profitability of a customer relationship can be obtained only if all income and expenses from services are included. Institutions in this group often believe that their executives are not likely to differentiate among individual profit centers and their performance unless they are presented with:

- A P&L of unbundled bank services, and
- Proper customer identification.

Such approach however requires a sophisticated organizational and technological infrastructure, on which can be based a valid analytical methodology. It also calls for *database mining* solutions able to interactively exploit both information and processes (see also Chorafas and Steinmann, 1994b).

Systems designers should never lose sight of the fact that professionals and managers have become *requestors of information* rather than simple accessors of data. Database mining is a process able to provide a common denominator by ensuring:

- A comprehensive general description of available information.
- The derivation source of data streams, as well as update and usage sources.
- Significant references regarding customer, cost, cash flow and other management data.
- Associated statistics such as creation of file, frequency of usage, last update, timestamp and so on.

Astute financial analysts appreciate that these operations are necessary to support *profitability evaluation* for customers, products, markets, operating divisions and the company as a whole. Analytical algorithms and the human skill to exploit them are part of the picture, but the lion's share in presenting factual and documented profitability results is timely and accurate information which can be interactively exploited.

Financial institutions and other organizations which chose to remain with old technology (whether they did so deliberately or did not even know that they had done so), are not able to present their management with sharp

247

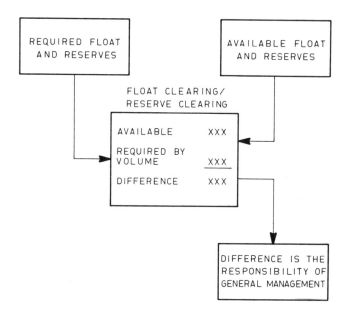

Figure 12.1   Reconciliation of float and reserves required versus available

tools and metrics to judge profitability. Neither can they support their customers, their markets and their products in a way that permits them to remain profitable.

Low technology organizations are steadily losing their market grasp to the profit of high technology companies. They are also taking inordinate risks in an effort to improve their bottom line without appropriate means; risks which will come back to haunt them. By contrast, high technology organizations *steadily* position themselves against the market forces, one of their tools being the nontraditional financial research of which we spoke in Chapter 11, another one the customer mirror.

JUDGING PROFITABILITY THROUGH THE CUSTOMER MIRROR

Among the banks participating in the research project which constitutes the basis of this book, several expressed the opinion that difficulties arise from the numerous possible ways of deriving and allocating the costs of services and funds. These difficulties can at times lead to major disparities in the pricing for standard services and can distort the necessary comparisons of customer profitability.

This statement has its counterparts in the basic analytical functions necessary to guide management's hand. Figure 12.1 brings into perspective a financial institution's plan for reconciliation of float and reserves, emphasizing the difference which may exist between required and available funds. Such differences

- May reside in a center clearing point for funds (the Money Desk), or
- Be isolated in a given profit (or cost) center for inclusion in the bank statement.

Whenever we move out of general accounting, which is mostly regulated by government institutions like the Financial Accounting Standards Board (FASB), we face the problems of diversity in policies, practices and procedures. As a general rule, however, alert managements appreciate that a sound practice calls for:

1. *Required float and reserves* to be determined at profit centers based on deposit volumes
2. *Available* float and reserves to be calculated from average balances of pertinent general ledger accounts – bank-wide
3. The *difference* to be handled as the responsibility of the bank, after being identified by individual profit center.

This organizational approach is necessary to ensure the efficient balancing of funds as well as funds charges and credits, increasing management's visibility down to the level of minute changes taking place due to the stream of daily transactions.

Another basic responsibility of management is to know for each *customer relationship* benefits and costs, and what this relationship brings to the bank. Such a customer oriented analytical approach is fundamental to the bottom line, as the profit and loss statement is in effect the aggregation of profitability results from every business partner relationship.

Some financial institutions call the profit-and-loss oriented report on relationship management a *customer mirror*. Among the issues arising in the preparation of a customer mirror, necessary for analyzing customer profitability, are:

- Which services the customer uses, and hence to included in the analysis,
- How to cost each facet of customer service, and associated transactions,
- How to maintain actual on the standard costs of each service channel,
- How to value by type of transaction bank funds involved in the transaction – from costs to loans and guarantees, and
- How to set the proper level of fees, so that costs are covered and there is a profit.

Effective answers require the ability to support detail, rather than in maintaining some averages. Averages help precious little because differences in the types of activities being costed can give rise to variations in average costs. Therefore, analytical costing by channel and by customer relationship is the better approach (see also Chorafas, 1989a).

Whichever methodology is chosen for the analysis of customer relationships, it must be kept in mind that financial data is dynamic. There is no place for static, fixed and rigid approaches, trying to create a sitting duck repository. By contrast, there is need for a customer information base which:

- Can grow and develop as knowledge and facts change our perceptions of profit and loss,
- Can be steadily exploited with new insights leading to an accurate profitability evaluation.

For a financial database to be effective, or even merely adequate, it must be possible to modify its predictive power as new facts are discovered. It must also be explicit, systematic and comprehensive – exploited online the way we saw in the Introduction when we spoke of database mining.

The aim should be to make the customer database to some degree self-generating, using algorithms and heuristics to systematically enrich the store of captured data. As the database grows, the tools used for its exploitation must become more intelligent and powerful, otherwise the company becomes a sitting duck suffering at the hands of its competitors.

ENHANCING RELATIONSHIP MANAGEMENT BY MEANS OF CUSTOMER PROFILING

In the majority of financial institutions and their current legacy systems, the individual customer is not identified as such. That is bad management because it deprives the bank of the ability to look into the customer relationship at a time when *relationship banking* is supreme.

Because of historical reasons which date back to the 1950s with accounting machines and punched cards, today the computer-based files of most financial instutions are account-based rather than client-based. A client relationship may have only one account, but the way to bet is that important clients – companies and high net worth individuals – have many accounts by banking channel and by branch:

- These are linked among themselves in a weak, error-prone and rigid fashion.
- Such low technology approach makes marketing nearly impossible and handicaps relationship management.

A growing number of financial institutions and other companies start understanding that this state of affairs needs to be changed. The lack of proper focus on the customer makes it nearly impossible to forecast customer behavior in connection with longer-term account handling, most particularly cash management and risk control. Precisely:

- The *balances* the customer leaves with the bank
- The *time* credit balances stay with the bank
- The *currencies* the customer uses most frequently,
- *Patterns* in the covering of debit balances,
- *Exposures* resulting from the customer relationship.

By contrast, Tier 1 banks appreciate that customer behavior can be effectively studied through proper analytical procedures as, for instance supported by fuzzy engineering – provided there is the necessary detail in the database. The fact that in many financial institutions customer details are missing is very bad.

- Paraphrasing an old proverb: 'No money, no commerce,'
- We can say: 'No databases, no business.'

The problem however ends at the IT level, it does not start there. The prerequisite is *organizational work*. Thorough organizational perspectives should definitely precede the implementation of the new generation models such as genetic algorithms and fuzzy engineering, otherwise applications will be built on shaky grounds and this will be visible.

Whether we talk of the analysis of profitability in customer relationships or in any other domain, prior to applying advanced information technology tools the management of the company will be well-advised to study organizational issues connected to the *basics* such as:

- Type of account, and
- Account identification.

For relationship banking reasons, but also for cash management, each individual customer must be properly identified. This is no easy task and therefore in the majority of cases the concept of an account as currently practiced seems to be awfully confused.

Both the previous section and the early part of this section made reference to this fact. Many banks find it quite difficult to properly identify an *account*. There are *client accounts*, which are part of the set of *external accounts*. There are also *internal accounts*, and other accounts such as *profit accounts*. All mixed up.

For someone who does not know the confusion prevailing in legacy systems, it is difficult to see why things should be so messy and disordered. Only leading-edge banks appreciate that in reality the whole issue is rather simple, and they speak from experience as they have already defined in a clear manner the concepts of:

- Clients, and
- Account.

There are prerequisites to the correct implementation of a customer oriented database, and these prerequisites start with a Classification and Identification Code (see also the dual Classification and Identification system in Chorafas 1989b). Let's keep in mind that the clear definition of *client account(s)* can only be made after the issue of *the type of an account* has been sorted out – and *who is a client* has been defined in an unambiguous way.

After the necessary organizational work has been done comes the mission of properly structuring the database. Efficient computational routines can be developed through knowledge engineering but the *database architecture* has its own prerequisites which are structural – not computational.

A distributed deductive (intelligent) database structure will greatly assist in bringing information to the decision centers of the organization, after the datastreams have been appropriately filtered and processed with the objective of:

- Isolating phenomena which the database can still not account for, and
- Higlighting facts which the legacy computer programs cannot recognize.

Interactive access to the financial database must be done in such a way that its contents can be maximally employed by the user community, each professional having a multitude of diverse needs and skills. This requires much more than routines for automatic online access. It calls for sophisticated tools able to provide enhancements, efficiently assisting those who use the data.

THE CLASSIFICATION AND USE OF DATABASE ELEMENTS

The effective use of databased information, starting with the classification and identification of customer relationships, does not only concern day-to-day activities but also the longer-term survival of the organization. We should always be keen to make the best use of the resources we have.

For fine-grain classification reasons there should be families, classes and groups with well-defined subgroupings of information elements. This can be effectively done through object oriented approaches (see also Chorafas and Steinmann, 1993a) which:

- Make feasible the handling of instantaneous but perishable hierarchies.
- Substitute for monolithic structures of hierarchical database management systems (DBMS), with an object orientation.

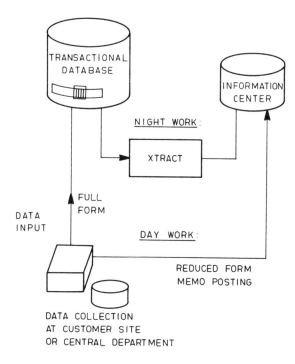

TRANSACTIONAL
DATABASE

INFORMATION
CENTER

NIGHT WORK:

XTRACT

DATA
INPUT

FULL
FORM

DAY WORK:

REDUCED FORM
MEMO POSTING

DATA COLLECTION
AT CUSTOMER SITE
OR CENTRAL DEPARTMENT

Figure 12.2 Fifteen years ago the use of Xtract was a solution, today it is an aberration

Object oriented solutions permit the design of a much more flexible and accurate system than any legacy approach ever provided. One of the better known financial institutions used classification and an objectoriented approach to support at a significant level of detail a realtime two-way sort regarding the:

- Entry of funds, and
- Withdrawal of funds.

Appropriate classification and identification help one time data input to serve multiple purposes: from general accounting, to cash flow, profitability studies, client files and relationship management. We have already spoken of the wisdom of such an approach, because of its merits.

One of the most significant benefits this financial institution has derived came from the effective use of technology in implementing interactive database mining procedures. Figure 12.2 and Figure 12.3 contrast what the old legacy systems can offer to what has been obtained through modern fully interactive solutions.

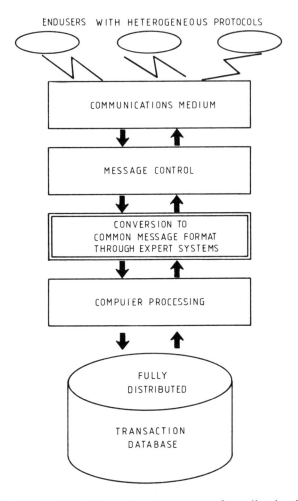

Figure 12.3 A layered structure and expert systems for online handling of heterogeneous protocols

- Fifteen years ago mainframers offered their clients an extract routine, to serve overnight for the creation of a so-called 'information center' database.

The example in Figure 12.2 comes from an IBM installation. Old hat Xtract is still used today for lack of a better approach, but it is totally uncompetitive. Yesterday's data are old stuff. They are a contradiction of the fact that managers and professionals have increasingly ad hoc queries to make – they cannot be satisfied by prestructured information elements and naive query languages.

- By contrast, Figure 12.3 shows a state-of-the-art solution. Data is received online, also online is message control and filtering as well as conversion to common message format.

The word 'message' is part of the jargon in this particular financial institution and includes transactions, messages, as well as other input. In this specific case, online computer processing is necessary (for a good part of the data flow) for netting reasons.

What should be retained from this high technology implementation reference is that the database is fully distributed, with live data accessible online. This fully current database is available for transactions and for management information purposes, with mining operations done interactively by:

- Authorized people, and
- Realtime programs.

While many issues come into database mining, specific for each application or user profile, even the generation of this relatively simple descriptive model requires a change of culture from old data processing. Just as demanding is the definition of processes able to define and handle the way by which this information database will be populated, once the model itself is well described.

As explained in preceding sections, other organizational prerequisites include the creation of a customer oriented (rather than the usual account oriented) database, and accurate profit and loss information connected to each financial product and customer account. It is most surprising how unprepared many banks are for this type of application.

Even the process of determining the right interest rate to be used in deriving the income represented by a customer's compensating balance can be a troublesome issue for banks. Numerous practices are followed, including the use of contradictory measures such as:

- A rate equal to the bank's cost of funds, which is evidently inadequate,
- The bank's average return on loans and investments, which can be meaningless,
- A rate comparable to the cost a bank would incur in obtaining funds from alternative sources,
- A rate the customer could earn if the funds had been invested directly in the money market.

Choices have to be made and they must be reflected in the solution to be chosen. An analytical approach should also pay attention to deriving the bank's expenses for servicing the customer relationship, accounting for the fact that in many respects this portion of the work can be complicated – and hence costly. High technology is key in keeping costs under control – just as it is necessary in order to obtain profitable results.

OVERCOMING THE DEFICIENCIES EMBEDDED IN LEGACY SYSTEMS

It is surprising but nevertheless true that many organizations – manufacturing companies and banks alike – find it difficult to overcome the deficiencies embedded into their legacy systems. True enough, piecemeal change will not do. A new departure is needed, and with it a change in information technology culture.

- Financial modeling is a good domain to start this change, because for many companies it is a new experience. Hence, there exist few preconceived concepts.
- But to be really rewarding, financial modeling must benefit from procedural changes, in the way we look at accounts and evaluate product as well as customer profitability.

One of the evident deficiencies of many current legacy systems is that they are based on preadvice, not confirmed figures. With *preadvices* the situation is fuzzy and therefore it cannot be handled in a deterministic way the way legacy computer programs try to do. There is a schizophrenic situation:

- While the current, quite elementary, organization stands on a *fuzzy basis*.
- Only *procedural* approaches are used which handicap visibility.

The kind of improvement which is necessary will not come as a matter of course. A major cultural change is necessary altering the abovementioned two issues and creating a situation where:

- The new organization stands on *accuracy* and *detail*.
- But data analysis permits us to account for *vagueness* and *uncertainty*.

There is no substitute for detail, provided that it is accurate and that the handling costs are acceptable, due to the use of expert systems and other artifacts. A customer mirror can be a very costly exercise unless all operations connected to the general ledger have been properly automated and the 'one-entry, many-uses' principle is observed.

Companies which have not taken care to automate their operations in an integrative way have found that ledger entry credits are more expensive to process than ledger entry debits. Organizations that do not separate the two would have only a single figure for ledger entries which typically lies between the average cost of debits and credits, but is inaccurate.

The principles which we saw in connection to relationship banking can be generally applied to all financial information. As a matter of good practice, general ledger balances should be assigned to a center for clearing reserves for profit center reporting purposes. *Capital accounts* are a good case for classification as they include:

- Capital,
- Surplus,
- Undivided profits, and
- Current net earnings.

In the case of a financial institution, these accounts constitute its true capital funds. The *collection balances* chapter in the general ledger incorporates accounts such as transit, local clearings and other items in the process of collection. These relate to cash float, most of which is attributable to deposits.

A chapter: *due from bank accounts* usually maps balances which are non-earning assets maintained for the benefit of all profit centers whose business involves the transfer of funds between banks. The difference between average bank balances and average available balances is actually *float* and should be handled as such. The reason for underlining these aspects is two-fold:

1. To bring into perspective the organizational work which is prerequisite to a sound implementation of financial models, and
2. To explain that financial modeling is not just a matter of writing equations, as many people tend to think.

One of the not-so-evident truths is how accounting balances should be handled. Available balances are often treated as *overhead assets*. Theoretically, they would be charged to applicable profit centers who would cover the cost of the funds. But lacking an equitable basis for such a distribution, they should be isolated in a center which would be charged for the funds.

Charge offs and recoveries should be assigned to profit centers, but not by arbitrary allocation using some other account as the basis. Care should also be taken in handling *miscellaneous assets* – a category which often encompasses several accounts such as:

- Employee advances,
- Accounts receivable,
- Prepaid expenses,
- Other resources,
- Other assets,
- Suspense, and
- Interbank accounts.

Generally, such accounts are not highly material in the funds computation, but they must be represented, preferably being offset by miscellaneous liabilities. Both the assets and the liabilities side should be subject to a properly conducted classification and identification.

Miscellaneous liabilities include other accrued interest and taxes, accrued expenses payable, dividends payable and other liabilities. These categories can be used in the computation of capital funds for profit center purposes, as we will see in the following section. All this is part of a functional financial model.

ACCOUNTING FOR PROFIT CENTERS AND COST CENTERS

Reference has been made in this and the preceding chapters to the profit center concept. As income earners, *profit centers* are directly affected by the pricing structure of products and services. For instance, income from *selling* bank services should be credited to the appropriate profit center which has responsibility for:

- Lending,
- Investing,
- Trading, or,
- Handling client accounts

according to the transaction being executed. By contrast, as has already been explained, *cost centers* survive through budgetary allocation. Cost centers are service providers, oriented toward other company units. Their money comes out of profits before taxes.

While the definition of which unit is a cost center and which is a profit center seems straightforward, in practice it is not that easy, mainly for political reasons. As some of the examples to be presented help document, a profit center/cost center structure should permit us to:

- Gather financial data,
- Project on future income and expenditure,
- Make budget versus actual evaluations, and
- Port expense allocation toward other centers within the *income statement* perspective.

The computation of funds charges and credits is one of the most significant factors in determining profit center profitability. Allocation should be based on the proper assignment of asset, liability and capital accounts to the centers.

The system must clarify how accounts would be handled for profit center reporting purposes, not only loans and deposits but also *cash accounts*, as well as how all:

- Income-producing, and
- Expense items

are being allocated.

The organization chart should properly identify all profit centers and cost centers and the executive accountable for each one of them. Procedural solutions must list all asset and liability accounts indicating assignment for responsibility reporting purposes.

Algorithmic approaches must focus on a flexible, parametric way of handling assets, liabilities, income and expenses. The modeling solution to be adopted should be able to represent detail but also summarize the accounts of the different centers by lines of authority:

- Emphasizing both regular and ad hoc reporting.
- Reflecting Plan versus Actual, as well as variances.
- Providing an explanation for every variance which is observed.

The assignment of expense should consider not only direct cash outlays but also fringe benefits, occupancy costs, utilities, intercompany charges and other costs. All this is part and parcel of the financial model.

In Part Two we spoke of *overhead* and said that overhead expenses should not be distributed on an individual basis. The better known example is general management overhead which is best handled through a free-standing general management account.

A similar statement can be made of other costs, such as bank examination fees. This expense is incurred for the benefit of the organization as a whole due to regulatory requirements, and has little bearing on an individual profit center. The same is true of general counsel expenses, unless the legal fees correspond to and can be identified by specific profit center business.

Once the policy decisions regarding the positioning of income statement accounts have been properly established, an algorithmic solution is not only feasible but also simple. It can be formatted along the model which is shown in Figure 12.4, or any more detailed approach management wishes to follow. The model adopted should provide a valid basis for bank-wide profit center evaluation.

A clear-cut profit center/cost center distinction is that much more important if cost control is high on management's agenda, coupled with a determination to produce results. Good examples exist in banking but are much more abundant in the manufacturing industry. An article in *Business Week* said, with reference to gains by General Electric at its power equipment plant in Schenectady, NY, and at an airplane engine parts plant in Albuquerque:

Individual profit center	Summary divisions/Regions	Summary by function	Bank–wide summary
Direct Income XXX	Direct Income XXX	Direct Expense XXX	Direct Income XXX
Direct Expense XXX	Direct Expense XXX	Direct Expense XXX	Direct Expense XXX
Funds charge/credit XXX	Funds charge/credit XXX	Funds charge/credit XXX	Funds charge/credit XXX
Indirect Expense	Indirect Expense XXX	Indirect Expense XXX	Indirect Expense XXX
By category 1 XXX	Contribution of Profit Centers XXX	Contribution of Profit Centers XXX	Contribution of Profit Centers XXX
2 XXX	Division Overhead XXX	Function Overhead XXX	Division Overhead XXX
3 XXX	Division Cost Centers XXX	Function Cost Centers XXX	Division Cost Centers XXX
Total Indirect XXX	Division Net Contribution XXX	Function Net Contribution XXX	Division Net Contribution XXX
Contribution XXX			Function Overhead XXX
			Function Cost Centers XXX
			Function Net Contribution XXX
			Bank Overhead XXX
			Reconciling Item XXX
			Bank Net Profit XXX

Figure 12.4 Format for profit center reporting

- After the power-systems unit redesigned nearly all its gas turbines, manu-facturing costs plunged by 25 percent.
- The time needed to install the machines, which are the size of a house, dropped by 70 percent.
- GE's crew also figured out how to cut the distance that parts travel by 75 percent and how to double production with 20 percent less floor space.

The entire project paid for itself in about six months. 'There is no amount of bureaucracy that stops an error,' Dr John Welch, the CEO of General Electric, aptly suggests. A profit center and cost center organization is not made just for the sake of it but in order to ensure that management has the metrics and measures which it needs in order to take action – and these are not obstructed by bureaucracy. The same is true of financial modeling.

PAYING ATTENTION TO THE DEVELOPMENT OF PROFITABILITY MODELS

Whether in manufacturing, merchandising or banking, differences in the number of discrete activities being costed can create variations in the costs for specific services. Hence the wisdom of designing a clear-cut accounts structure as it has been outlined on p. 251. Subsequently, expert systems can be used to normalize charges without losing control of real costs.

A thorough costing study should also see to it that all costs are allocated. When this is done only partially, the results are skewed. For instance, if a service organization is pricing fewer services than the whole range which it offers, it would tend to have a higher price for those services.

- *If* there is no management will or human skill available for a thorough, detailed job,
- *Then* the quality of financial modeling is dropping with evident aftermaths on costs and the P&L statement.

Some service companies find the excuse that allocating costs in a multiproduct sense is somewhat arbitrary, and they have generally practiced a policy of pricing bundled services. Under this approach the costs of all services are spread among a relatively small number of activities. In banking, for instance,

- Most often customers are implicitly charged for noncosted services when-ever they use one for which charges have been established.

- Customers using uncosted services with above average frequency would tend to benefit from this approach, while those with below average frequencies would lose.

A similar situation exists in manufacturing. Incomplete modeling biases the results to be shown in the customer mirror. This leads to the conclusion that analytical solutions are the only valid way to sound profitability calculations – even if superficially easy ways out look good enough.

A number of ill-conceived conditions are associated with profitability evaluations. For instance, at any time most bank costs appear to be fixed; plant and equipment expenses are sunk; and overhead normally shows little variance with output.

Often in the service industry the increase in total cost which a company incurs from providing a standard product to one additional customer is taken to be fairly small: supplies, postage, service proper and so on. This argument forgets about hidden costs as well as dismissing the fact that if the company were to charge the stated costs such charges would have to be very carefully set.

The base on which charges are computed greatly influences the estimated profitability. Credit and loan handling expenses provide an example. Once the total or direct costs of the loan section have been obtained, a variety of methods can be used to allocate these costs to borrowers.

- One possibility is to determine the average cost per note or per renewal.

This approach, however, could place an unduly heavy charge against the small borrower whose loan application is relatively straightforward and simple to process.

- Alternatively, costs could be allocated in proportion to the number of dollars borrowed.

This method, though, could result in overstating the costs associated with very large loans, since processing time normally does not increase directly with the size of the loan.

- A third approach is to express all costs as a function of manhours used.

If a loan officer were to maintain accurate records of the time spent on each activity, the hourly charge could then be allocated to the customer. This is the best solution but requires a standard costs system, and inexpensive capture of the time really spent on a project – otherwise it could result in higher charges for customers assigned to less efficient loan officers.

Figures 12.5 shows representative charges and collected balance requirements for standard activity services; it is the result of a survey for corporate accounts conducted by the Federal Reserve Bank of Kansas. Figures are rounded to the nearest dollar. Wide differences are seen to exist among banks in the charges for services and tend to suggest that the methods of establishing charges are often arbitrary.

A similar statement can be made about other issues, such as accounting for capital funds for purposes of profit center reporting. In a correct procedure, capital funds should be isolated in a center such as the money desk. As a result of the funds transfer policy utilized:

- The capital will in effect be *sold* to centers requiring more funds than they generate themselves.
- Therefore, the capital will *earn* a funds credit to be appropriately applied.

A model should be in place to assure that this credit should be combined with any other *profit or loss* of the internal funds trading operation, which could result if more than one funds rate were employed.

Transaction	Charge per transaction (amounts in dollars)			Percent of banks charging in account analysis
	Average	Range	Mode	
1 Annual Account Maintenance	37	2–240	36	95
2 Special Daily Statement	1	0–5	1	54
3 Ledger Entries				
• Credits	0	0–1	1	78
• Debits	0	0	0	78
4 Items Deposited				
• Encoded	0	0	0	39
• Not Encoded	0	0	0	39
5 Returned Items – 'On us'	3	0–10	5	75
6 Deposited Returned Items	1	0–7	1	79
7 Wire Transfers				
Incoming	2	0–5	2	55
Outgoing	3	1–6	2	94
8 Securities Drafts				
• Per Item	4	0–20	5	50
• Per Cent of Amount	.1%	.05%–.2%	.1%	3
9 Bond Coupon Collections				
• Per Envelope	1	0–8	1	55
• Per Coupon	0	0–1	0	35

Figure 12.5 Charges for account handling (figures rounded to the nearest dollar) *cont. overleaf*

Figure 12.5 (continued)

| Transaction | Charge per transaction (amounts in dollars) | | | Percent of banks charging in |
	Average	Range	Mode	Account analysis
10 Collected Balance Overdrafts				
• Per Occurence	4	1–8	5	20
• Percent of Amount	9%	2%–15%	10%	31
11 Stop Payment	3	.50–10	3	92
12 Certified Cheques	1	0–5	2	67
13 Audit Confirmations	3	0–13	3	16
14 Standard Wholesale Lockbox per Item	0	0–1	0	78
15 Telephone Notific. per Call	1	0–12	1	42
16 Data Transmission of Wholesale Lockbox Receipt per Item	0	0–1	0	31
17 Data Transmission of Retail Lockbox Receipt per Item	0	0–1	0	31
18 Daily Processing Charge for Zero Balance Accounts	2	0–10	.50	25
19 Bank Preparation of Depository Transfer Cheques	0	0–3	0	58
20 Account Reconciliation/ Sort Only				
• Per Item	0	0	0	20
• Flat Price Per Month	11	5–20		14

The combined net debit or credit of the trading, even if it were only the credit on capital, would have no economic meaning – being nothing more than the result of the funds transfer mechanics. But it can and should be reflected as a reconciling item on the total profit center report of the organization, assisting, in this way, a more accurate profitability evaluation.

REFINING THE COSTING STRUCTURE

We have seen that policy decisions are crucial to profitability. Both policies and solutions reached in connection to profitability modeling vary widely from one institution to the other. Even the better organized companies have found that a number of refinements in the pricing of services are essential. These typically range:

- From attempting to differentiate the costs of servicing different types of customers, at a finer grain level.
- To expanding the number of financial services reflected in analytical statements, giving greater consideration to the type of costing being used and its impact.

Both a fine grid employed in developing cost standards and a realistic appreciation of the true weight of costs can be instrumental in promoting profitability. While the costs of all transactions for a given service are not identical, few banks have attempted to base prices on a factual and documented:

- Evaluation of standards, and
- Possible alternatives.

The following are the results of analytical studies conducted by banks in London on the cost of doing business. The costs in sterling have been converted into dollars at the exchange rate prevailing when this text was written:

	£	$
• Money Market or Forex Transaction	15–20	23–30
• Cancellation	40	60
• Contract for Exchanges	30	45
• Complex Swap, per event	150	225

While these studies were well-done, a good part of the cost factors had to be guesstimated. Few banks truly account for the real cost of transactions because management fails to pay the proper attention to costing procedures. Even the simple current account transaction has a cost of about £3 ($4.5) associated with it but this is quite often forgotten.

The message these paragraphs convey is not only that every transaction has to be costed but also that this has to be done by paying attention to detail. While most banks, for example, differentiate between clearing encoded and nonencoded cheques, the method by which a cheque is cleared can also be of importance. Items which arrive stored on magnetic media are much cheaper to process:

- Virtually no additional cost is incurred if cheques are sent to local Federal Reserve Banks for collection.

- If cheques are cleared through correspondents, both the transportation charges to the correspondents and the required compensating balances should be added to the clearing costs.

Most banks use the same set of charges to analyze the accounts of retail customers, corporate customers and correspondent banks, but a moment's reflection will indicate that the cost of providing services to each is not necessarily identical. Even a financial model which is perfect in its mathematics will give substandard results if fed with data derived from such questionable procedures.

It is quite usual that costing schemes do not account for the fact that few correspondent customers, for example, make regular use of the teller lobby. Similarly, branch banks have occasionally found that the cost of transactions at the head office is different from that at branch locations.

Should correspondent customers be expected to pay for such items as floor space occupied by the correspondent department in a high-rent district of an inner city? The cost of maintaining an expensive officers' dining room? The president's salary or part thereof? Advertising expenses? Guards to police the lobby? All these are issues which impact on the financial institution's income statement.

The degree to which banks differentiate the price of services must be tempered with practicality, but failure to recognize such differences destroys some of the usefulness of the figures which are being set to guide management's hand. From an economist's viewpoint, one of the more perplexing problems in cost accounting is the *type of costs* that should be used in analyzing for profitability.

Virtually all banks have developed prices based on an average of historical records but few took the measures necessary to develop a documented standard costs of services. At the same time, the process used for cost allocation is often wanting and sometimes non-existent. No valid financial model can be made on this basis.

THE MARGINAL COST OF FUNDS

Considerations similar to those which have been made in the previous section are most relevant in determining the charges that should be made for the cost of money or funds loaned. We have already examined this case but from a different perspective – that of the risk involved in short-term and long-term timeframes. Two methods are commonly utilized for funds costing:

- The first is to base the cost of money on the bank's average cost of funds.
- The second is to use a rate representing the cost of marginal funds purchased by the bank.

Neither is wholly satisfactory. Basing the charge on the *average cost* is likely to result in underestimating the cost of acquiring loanable funds in periods of tight money, and perhaps overstating the costs in times of easy money. These two things do not average out.

During periods of rising interest rates, when additional loanable funds must often be purchased, the *marginal costs of funds* increases much more rapidly than the average cost. Unless the interest rate on loans made at such times exceeds the marginal cost of funds, losses will be incurred – and the P&L statement will tip towards the loss side.

By the same token, and for the same reasons, using the marginal cost of funds rate in evaluating the resulting profitability of all customer relationships (during such periods) will end in overstating total fund costs. It will also ignore the profits that arise from the ability of banks to lock in rate differential on some assets and liabilities.

There is, also, the possibility of hedging. Many banks seek to keep a sufficient amount of cheap core money (demand deposits and consumer time and savings deposits) to finance long-term fixed assets like mortgages. Under these circumstances, even if rates rise, a bank is still assured of a positive earnings spread on the matched portion of its portfolio.

- Accountants normally consider the cost of money to be the expense of processing demand and time deposits (including any nondeposit funds), plus interest paid on these deposits and purchased funds, minus any service charges or related fee income.
- A problem for banks using the traditional definition of the average cost of money is that this approach results in overstating the actual expenses of performing customer services, and thus tends to understate profits.

Classical approaches, as practiced with legacy systems, do not provide an ideal balance or even a sound basis for measuring the cost of funds. They take no account of the fact that costs are very dynamic, and marginal costing calculations rapidly change. Therefore, the difference costing figures in the books are quite often meaningless.

The only way to calculate the cost of funds in a dependable manner is experimentation through two different profiles, based on financial modeling and practically calculated in realtime. High technology sees to it that this job is doable:

- One will be the profile of the cost of funds, from current account deposits, to time accounts, money market and other bought money.
- The other profile will be the employment of funds, from all types of loans to off-balance sheet operations.

The figures will steadily change, but some of the cost of money might be pegged to existing commitments, leaving for the new deals a free flow which is costed dynamically. This leads to much better than marginal cost figures. Alternatively, such procedure can be seen as a refinement of marginal costs.

The implementation of financial models which account for performance indicators and the overall methodology which is necessary include major tasks required to completely automate profit and loss reporting, as we will see when we talk of critical ratios in Chapter 13. The message to be retained from this discussion is that a *profitability model* requires a golden hoard of policy decisions – not just better algorithms.

The algorithms and the heuristics are the easier part of the development of a sound financial model and should be written only after key strategic issues have been settled. Trying to substitute algorithms for strategic management decisions leads to nowhere but an abdication of responsibility.

COST OF FUNDS AND CORPORATE REPORTING PRACTICES

According to costing methods adopted by some banks, the *cost of funds* from customer deposits includes such items as the expenses of the bank lobby, tellers, proof and transit department, posting of statements, processing overdrafts and stop payments, and account maintenance. These are items over and above the money paid to depositors; they are important inasmuch as:

- Interest costs are the largest single component of the cost of funds, though at the largest banks processing costs amount to about one quarter of total costs.

These two items are often confused because they have different budgetary origins. Interest costs come out of the *interest budget* which represents roughly two thirds of the bank costs. By contrast, processing costs are part of the *noninterest budget*.

- Even if fee and service income is allocated fully to offsetting processing costs, these costs still account for about 20 percent of the total expenses for funds from different types of deposits.

The problem arises because for banks using their legacy-type cost accounting the average cost of funds would tend to charge the customer twice for certain services in the profitability analysis. The customer would first be charged for the expenses generated by account analysis. He would again be charged in the cost of funds, with the charge being proportional to loans or net funds used.

If these are general guidelines reflecting policies followed by many organizations, as well as the pitfalls such policies entail, both ingenious choices and a good analytical structure can help in improving profits by focusing on real profitability. The procedural infrastructure should include meticulous approaches to:

- Designing and installing chart of accounts,
- Making interest rate forecasts,
- Experimenting on the effects of change in basis points,
- Providing for gap analysis, as well as income variance analysis,
- Entering and keeping historical data for subsequent exploitation through analytical media.

All this should be properly integrated into an accurate management reporting practice, which is fully computer-based and incorporates the use of simulation techniques. The solution to be chosen must provide for the analysis of interest rate risk, permitting us to elaborate strategies with full understanding of repricing policies as well as of associated procedures.

The analytical approaches to profitability evaluation suggested in this chapter can never be efficiently implemented on a manual basis and even classical data processing does not attack the cost allocation and cost control problem in an effective manner. Knowledge engineering is the answer, and its usage greatly impacts on investments for the 1990s. The Industrial Bank of Japan estimated that 60–70 percent of capital budgets in Japan will be spent on:

- Labor-saving projects, or
- Developing and supporting new products.

This was published in the *Financial Times* (June 5, 1990), and the years which passed have validated such a forecast. Innovation and the swamping of costs should be our guideline for all future investments in organization and in technology, and management accounting is one of the best examples where this reference is applicable.

There exists a close link between the policies which we adopt, the tools which we are using, and the presentation of final results through monthly, quarterly and annual statements – or interactively ad hoc. Significant refinements are possible and the best results usually reflect management's will and determination.

The message is that management accounting reporting should be designed not only for the servicing of basic accounting needs but also to allow easy monitoring of the performance of the company. From customer relationships to P&L accounts, the infrastructure must be well defined but reporting must very flexible and as already underlined, interactive exploitation of data-base contents is key to successful management.

THE OLD AND NEW FRAMEWORKS FOR MANAGEMENT REPORTING

Managed through algorithms and heuristics the information elements in a distributed deductive database should make feasible the generation of a number of interactive reports, giving the enduser the option of producing only those that he needs, when he needs them. This contrasts with the old framework of management reporting which basically includes four levels of reference:

- *Monthly statement*, comparing monthly and year-to-date average balances with budgeted and historical average balances.
- *Average balances* (incorrectly, also known as analytical reports), comparing monthly average balances, average rates, and income amounts to budgeted and historical data, including non-interest income and expense items.
- *Quarterly report*, practically using the same format as the monthly report while comparing quarterly information.
- *Year-to-date report*, focusing on year-to-date information, using the same format as the monthly and quarterly reports.

Implemented in an interactive manner by high technology companies, the new framework capitalizes on algorithms, heuristics and online access to databases. Appropriate financial models assure the capability of producing daily, hourly or even split-second interactive reports such as:

1. Analysis according to any user-defined factor,
2. Statement of condition, balance sheet and off-balance sheet up to the last hour,
3. Statement of income and expenses for any unit, in any location, at any time,
4. Statement of deviations in Plan versus Actual,
5. Realtime evaluation of exposure and risk control.

An up-to-the-minute income variance analysis can provide the user with an effective way to carefully examine a particular period's interest income and interest expense. For instance, analyzing actual balances, interest, exchange rates, income performance, budget versus actual; also focusing on evaluation scenarios and explaining why they differ.

This is synonymous with the process of developing an overall business concept which is planning and control oriented – also capable of detecting deviations and trends. The best solution would compare our company to other companies; analyze the effects of changes to the Money market, to the Capital market; and incorporate prevailing macroeconomic factors as suggested in Figure 12.6.

The tools are available, but do we have the culture to utilize them? People

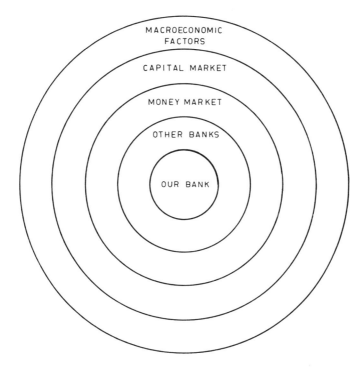

Figure 12.6 Developing an overall business concept and detecting trends

and companies with experience in financial modeling do appreciate that algorithmic and heuristic solutions permit an online, interactive examination of *variance* in respect to:

- Price(s) Variance
- Interest Variance
- Exchange rate(s) Variance
- Costs
- Volumes, and
- Product Mix.

As we will see in Part Four, visualization makes it feasible to present the results of analysis in a comprehensive manner, appreciate the results of interactive experimentation, and examine alternative approaches to necessary corrective action.

We have already underlined why the realtime evaluation of exposure for balance sheet and off-balance sheet items, and particularly for the latter, is so important. Not only must the control of risk be executed in realtime through appropriate heuristics and algorithms, but it must also become a deeply engrained company culture. The same is true of optimization.

Among the foremost organizations, currently available optimization models make it feasible to experiment on the balance sheet/off-balance sheet mix that will yield the highest level of net interest income possible – at a given level of risk. Optimization models help to compare thousands of different possible combinations of assets and liabilities.

Through genetic algorithms, fuzzy engineering or other models, we can study which course of action will produce the highest net interest income while adhering to risk standards established by the board. These risk standards can be expressed as constraints and limitations placed on the model. Management policies mapped into rules which represent constraints can be of several types:

- *Credit and market limits*, concerning upper and lower levels in connection to credit risk and market risk, parametrically expressed as a function of market and client characteristics.
- *Fund utilization*, loan/deposit ratios, capital to assets ratios, loan loss reserves versus total loans.
- *Regulatory requirements*, such as reserve ratios and liquidity plus an added safety factor established by the board.

Mathematical models can be effectively used to generate an optimized balance sheet and income statement as well as for experimentation (What-if) reasons, as the need arises. To use them effectively, however, we have to further develop our culture and quite often this is much more difficult than writing the financial model itself.

Part Four

The Board
Wants Answers
Which are
Normalized and
Comprehensible

13 How to Monitor Performance Through Critical Financial Ratios

INTRODUCTION

Financial analysts and investors have often been too simplistic in their views of income statements. This is particularly true with comments of the type: 'Revenues grew 20 percent,' or 'Expenses have been reduced by 7 percent.' Such pronouncements are not only vague but also misleading because they are often made in isolation. It is not possible to judge the health of a company:

- Without reference to what is going on in the rest of the P&L statement, by line and in a consolidated sense, and/or
- With no comprehensive notion on how the change in individual line items fits with the management's overall strategic plan.

A much sounder way is to look at individual components of a company's balance sheet, off-balance sheet and income statement not in an isolated fashion but in a way relating them to each other and to global performance. This means viewing the month-to-month changes, year-to-year variation and longer-term evolution in a strategic context.

As we will see in this chapter, the effective use of critical ratios makes it feasible to have a better understanding of how the business develops, providing insight on the way further gains can be achieved in the period ahead. At Zenith, for instance, to monitor management, the executive panel:

- Watches data on 20 variables, including production, sales, pretax profits, market share, liquidity, and productivity.
- Deviation from the corporate plan in any of these 20 variables gets fast attention, a corrective measure or a plan change reflecting the new information (*Business Week*, February 21, 1994).

As we have seen in Chapter 12, any successful approach to financial reporting will by necessity be integrative, combining applications which are already supported through classical analysis with more advanced constructs including expert systems, pattern recognition, fuzzy engineering, nonlinearities and other tools for nontraditional financial research.

THE ROLE GIVEN TO RATIO ANALYSIS

Ratio analysis will not by itself turn a financial institution or a manufacturing company into a high performer, but it can be a valuable aid in helping to review both overall performance and specific domains of activity. The use of ratios helps in pinpointing problem areas and in identifying characteristics of how a company works.

Critical ratios have been successfully used for several decades. At their origin is the desire to give special recognition to management's ability to run its business in an efficient manner. Among the better known performance ratios are:

- *Return on assets* (ROA), telling how well the assets of a company have been employed and, in consequence, how well it is managed (see also the discussion in Chapter 3).
- *Return on investment* (ROI), identifying the benefits which we get from the capital investments which we are making.
- *Return on equity* (ROE), revealing a similar story in connection with stockholders' equity – which, unlike what books and practitioners say is a fuzzy concept, and
- Ratios such as *earnings per share* (EPS), *yield*, as well as about the other factors which influence a company's financial staying power.

Not everything is, however, well with ratios. One of the problems with ROA, ROI, ROE, EPS and similar ratios is that they are based on accrual accounting information. As a result, they are subject to distortions from variations in accounting conventions such as depreciation, capitalization, and inventory valuation; neither do they reflect the extra cash flows derived from such sources as deferred taxes.

Though some of the ratios we will be reviewing in this chapter carry messages which help trigger management action, more than what is currently available is necessary to bring forward a sense of direction in decision support. Ratios, for instance, should also help as *early indicators*, being instrumental in steering the firm away from a course which could lead to catastrophic events.

The functions expected from an early indicator can be successfully achieved by means of knowledge-enriched systems which not only use artificial intelligence for key financial evaluations but also for *integrative* reasons. We have to be very careful with profitability metrics which:

- Have been originally taken separately, or
- Were defined in a way open to significant overlaps.

Not only may the financial model suffer from such shortcomings but also it will not be easy to exploit the databases. This will greatly reduce the benefits to be derived from financial analysis.

Gaps and overlaps are not accidental. They largely result from the fact that data processing applications are made in islands, lacking an open communications landscape which provides extended possibilities for experimentation. This environment reduces many of the benefits to be obtained through financial modeling.

A senior financial executive commented in the course of this research that in order to exploit the messages carried by ratios to the fullest extent, he found it necessary to implement a migration strategy:

• Its starting point was the creation of gateways between the various distinct islands of financial applications, and
• Its ultimate goal was to employ compatible presentation formats, with expert systems used for explanation and justification (see also Chapter 15).

This particular application paid due attention to the fact that the volume of traffic between the then discrete applications islands was heavy. Even more disturbing was the fact that the majority of people worked so disjointly that they often processed the same information elements or did the same ratio calculation twice or 'n' times.

The way this and many other financial executives looked at the subject of critical ratios is that they are part of a process of setting and controlling *goals*. For instance, this is the case with:

• Return on investment,
• Yield and balance sheet ratios,
• Off-balance sheet exposure, and
• Various growth indicators.

Ratios can also be of value in comparing the performance of one department against another, or of the whole organization within a national or international setting. For instance, they help to compare *our* company with other companies of similar size and product line category – as well as *our* profitability against that of the industry.

RATIOS AS A MIRROR OF FINANCIAL PERFORMANCE

Over the years, financial ratios have developed into a means of identifying and classifying performance. Few companies are content to allow themselves to remain 'average' or in the 'median' category. Most strive to be in the upper quartile or, even better, in the upper percentile. This statement is true of banks as well as of manufacturing and merchandising firms.

% Average Assets

Net Interest Income
Non Interest Income
Debt Provisions
Total Costs
Pretax Profits
Attributable Profit

Other Criteria

Attributable % Equity
EPS Growth
Dividend Cover
Gross Dividend Growth
Tax Rate (%)

Figure 13.1   Follow-up on critical ratios characterizing the operations of a leading bank over a five-year period

Investment analysts closely examine the critical ratios of the companies which they follow. The example in Figure 13.1 comes from a brokerage firm and concerns the evaluation criteria which it uses in judging the performance of financial institutions. These tests typically include a five-year period.

Critical ratios are essentially guidelines. But the calculation of a given ratio is just a stepping stone. The use of a financial model helps to pinpoint strengths and weaknesses. Thereafter, the more difficult task begins:

• Increasing yields,
• Controlling expenses,
• Reallocating assets,
• Managing risk, and
• Planning the kind of company management wants for the future.

Fourteen critical ratios are suggested by Dun and Bradstreet, the business information company, to help provide a mirror of financial performance. Focusing on the American economy, this information provider firm steadily updates ratio tables, with three figures appearing under each ratio heading.

• The center figure is the median.
• Those immediately above and below the median are, respectively, the upper and lower quartiles.

Book value per share reflects the sum of common stock at nominal balance sheet value, capital surplus, and retained earnings as shown in company accounts, divided by number of shares outstanding. Book value per share is defined as assets *minus* liabilities per share – but there is often imprecision in valuing assets. *Tangible book value* takes into account only assets and production equipment. The *price earnings (PE) ratio* is the stock price divided by estimated yearly earnings (we will examine the message conveyed by PE, and how to use it, on p. 284).

Earnings per share (EPS) are primary the per share net income, including proceeds from certain convertible securities, warrants, and options that are common-stock equivalents, but excluding extraordinary profit or loss items – divided by the number of common and common-equivalent shares.

Earnings per share estimates represent the analysts' consensus estimates and weigh heavily on how the market values the company's stock. A trend estimate is usually based on the pattern of the past five years.

Dividend rate gives the indicated annual payment rate based on latest quarterly dividend plus any recurring extra or special year-end dividends.

Yield means the indicated annual dividend as a percent of stock price.

The number of *shares outstanding* identifies the millions of common shares outstanding as of company's latest available financial report, excluding treasury shares. *Market value* is the percentage change in total market value of the company's most widely held common stock issue.

Institutional holdings reflects the percentage of outstanding common shares held by banks, insurance companies, other institutional investors (pension funds, mutual funds) and colleges. The term *turnover* indicates the percentage of outstanding shares changing hands in one year.

The term *variation* is used to indicate the percentage by which two thirds of the yearly earnings estimates are above or below the average estimate. The lower this figure is, the more analysts agree on their estimates. The fact that analysts often disagree is what makes the market. Other critical ratios include days of inventory, backlog to inventory and average Book-to-Bill.

THE MOST REVEALING FINANCIAL RATIOS

Ratios are indeed part of a traditional financial research. To properly understand their impact, and the use which can be made of them, it is important to know how they are calculated by the financial analysts whose work largely reflects the way management thinks.

• First, year-end financial statements are analyzed.

Companies in the Dun and Bradstreet survey are almost exclusively corporations with a tangible net worth over $50 million, though there exist exceptions.

• Then, each of fourteen ratios is calculated individually for every concern in the sample.

Compiled by statisticians, these individual ratio figures are segregated by line of business, and then arranged in order of size: the best ratio at the top, the weakest at the bottom.

- Ratio analysis is done under the hypothesis of a normal distribution, which is the best existing estimate.

In a statistical sense, each median is the typical ratio figure for all companies in a given line of business. The upper and lower quartiles typify the experience of firms respectively in the top and bottom of the sample – thus making feasible a comparative evaluation. An explanation of the ratios in question is given in this and in the following section.

1. *Current assets to current liabilities* (CA/CL) also called the *acid test*

This is the test of *solvency*. In our discussion on the balance sheet, in Part Three, we defined both current assets and current liabilities. However, to refresh the reader's memory in the context of ratio analysis, here is a redefinition.

Current assets (CA) are the sum of cash, notes and accounts receivables (less reserves for bad debt), advances on merchandise, merchandise inventories, and listed federal, state or municipal securities at purchase price or marked-to-market. Wise management will see to it that current assets are counted on the base of whatever *is lower*: purchase price or marked-to-market (a similar policy should be followed with off-balance sheet financial instruments).

A different way of saying *current liabilities* (CL) is current debt – the total of all liabilities falling due within one year for which the company must have adequate provisions:

- Generally, a CA/CL ratio greater than 2 is taken as satisfactory, though its exact value varies with the industry.
- A ratio of less than 1 means that the company is insolvent; and between 1 and 2 that it is bordering on trouble.

The results of the acid test are often taken as a sign of good (or alternatively bad) management. Commenting on the fate of Drexel Burnham Lambert, *Business Week* (March 5, 1990) had this to say in terms of assets and liabilities:

In the past year, as Drexel's business deteriorated, so did its financial position. Yet [CEO Frederick H.] Joseph had mismatched Drexel's assets and liabilities, leaving short-term debt covered by illiquid assets to a startling degree.

2. Net profits on net sales

This ratio is obtained by dividing net earnings of the business, after taxes, by net sales (the dollar volume less returns, allowances, and cash discounts). It is an important yardstick in measuring profitability and should be related to ratio 3 below.

3. Net profits on tangible net worth

Tangible net worth is the equity of stockholders in the business, as obtained by subtracting total liabilities from total assets and deducting intangibles. The ratio is calculated by dividing net profits after taxes by tangible net worth.

There is a tendency to look increasingly to this ratio as a criterion of profitability. Generally, a relationship of at least 10 percent is regarded as a desirable objective able to provide dividends as well as funds for future growth.

4. Net profits on net working capital

Net working capital represents the excess of current assets over current debt. This margin indicates the cushion available to the business for carrying inventories and receivables and for financing day-to-day operations. The ratio is obtained by dividing net profits after taxes by net working capital.

These are the first four out of the fourteen ratios used by financial analysts to judge business performance. The other ten ratios are described in the following section, starting with those which help in evaluating the results of marketing and sales.

EVALUATING SALES AND INVENTORIES THROUGH RATIOS

When we use critical ratios, we should carefully avoid piecemeal approaches which do not form a pattern we can understand and act upon. Financial and sales ratios are not museum exhibits, calculated to be left in a time closet or brought forward just to be admired. A meaningful approach would integrate their results and visualize them in graphical form – something that can be nicely achieved with the following algorithms.

5. Net sales to tangible net worth

Net sales are divided by tangible net worth. This gives a measure of relative turnover of invested capital, which is an important metric to many investors.

6. Net sales to net working capital

Net sales are divided by net working capital. This ratio is a guide as to the extent the company is turning over its working capital and the margin of operating funds.

7. Collection period

Annual net sales are divided by 365 days to obtain average daily credit sales; then the average daily credit sales are divided into notes and accounts receivables, including any discounted. This ratio is helpful in analyzing the collectibility of receivables.

Many people feel the collection period should not exceed the net maturity indicated by selling terms by more than 10 to 15 days. When comparing the collection period of one company with that of another, allowances should be made for possible variations in selling terms.

8. Net sales to inventory

This is obtained by dividing annual net sales by merchandise inventory as carried on the balance sheet. This quotient does not yield an actual physical turnover, but provides a yardstick for comparing stock-to-sales ratios of one firm with another, or with those for the industry.

The actual physical turnover is not part of the Dun and Bradstreet ratios and, as to be expected, it varies from one industrial sector to the other and from one company to another, though there are no generally applicable rules.

- The classical way to look at it is less than three months' turnover.
- The modern way is *just-in-time* (JIT) inventories and *fast flow replenishment* (FFR).

Both JIT and FFR can be supported by means of modeling, with the algorithms and heuristics processed in realtime to permit management to immediately apply the analytical results rather than losing precious time from study to implementation.

9. Fixed assets to tangible net worth

Fixed assets are divided by tangible net worth. Fixed assets represent depreciated book values of building, leasehold improvements, machinery, furniture, fixtures, tools, and other physical equipment, plus land (if any) valued at cost or appraised market value. Ordinarily, this relationship should not exceed 100 percent for a manufacturer, and 75 percent for a wholesaler or retailer.

10. Current debt to tangible net worth

This is derived by dividing current debt by tangible net worth. Ordinarily, a business begins to pile up trouble when this relationship exceeds 80 percent – though in highly leveraged companies it can reach 300 percent or more.

11. Total debt to tangible net worth

This is obtained by dividing total current and long-term debts by tangible net worth. When this relationship exceeds 100 percent, the equity of creditors in the assets of the business exceeds that of the owners.

12. Inventory to net working capital

Merchandise inventory is divided by net working capital. This is an additional measure of inventory balance. Normally, the relationship should not exceed 80 percent.

13. Current debt to inventory

To calculate this, we divide the current debt by inventory. The ratio yields yet another indication of the extent to which the business relies on funds from disposal of unsold inventories to meet its debts.

14. Funded debts to net working capital

Funded debt equals long-term liability minus stockholder equity. Funded debts are long-term obligations, as represented by mortgages, bonds, debentures, term loans, serial notes, and other types of liabilities maturing more than one year from the statement date. This ratio is obtained by dividing funded debt by net working capital. Analysts tend to compare capital in determining whether or not long-term debts are in proper proportion. Ordinarily, this relationship should not exceed 100 percent; let's however keep in mind that every industry has its own characteristics, and hence the wisdom of using updated industry specific tables in order to make well-documented evaluations.

With these references in mind we can add that the steady exploitation of a critical ratio system should be fully automated. Expert systems are well suited for this job, and managements who wish to have available a compass for navigating the enterprise through an increasingly competitive environment are well advised to use them.

MILESTONES IN A FINANCIAL ANALYSIS FOR INVESTMENT
REASONS

One of the values of the usage of critical financial ratios lies in the corrective action which can be triggered through their study. In the previous two sections, we have seen fourteen ratios whose industry-wide values are updated yearly by Dun and Bradstreet. There are however other key ratios, as well, whose usage is crucial in judging a company's health as well as how the market appreciates its performance.

We have seen on p. 279 that the *price earnings ratio* (PE) reflects the *market price* of a stock divided by *earnings per share* (EPS) for the previous 12 months (earnings per share is an issue on which much more will be said in the last section of this chapter). A stock selling at $20 and earning $2 per share has a price earnings ratio of 10.

This ratio is important both for an individual stock and as an indicator of the market as a whole. As the market's PE expands with (among other reasons) falling inflation, stocks with growth rates above the market average benefit from both the rise in the market's PE and an increase in their own price earnings, reflecting their growth.

The market's PE expands because the *real* value of growth is worth more when discounted by a lower required return, that is negatively affected by a lower inflation rate. It is a matter of supply and demand.

- A 9 percent nominal growth, for instance, may comprise 4 percent real growth and 5 percent inflation. Financial analysts consider this to stand at 180 percent of the inflation rate – more precisely, 9 percent growth divided by 5 percent inflation.
- If inflation drops to 2 percent then a nominal growth of 6 percent (comprising the same 4 percent real growth and 2 percent inflation) will represent 300 percent of the inflation rate.

This essentially is what happens to the market PE valuation from the framework of a classical dividend discount model. The algorithm is:

$$PE = \frac{\text{Dividend Payout Ratio}}{\text{Discount Rate} - \text{Growth Rate}}, \text{ or}$$

$$PE = \frac{DPR}{DR - GR}$$

PE ratios can differ widely and are often dependent on a number of factors such as earnings growth forecasts, the interest rate level, and economic conditions in the country in which the company is based. These go beyond the inflation rate, as we saw in the example which was given earlier in this section.

A critical question in selecting growth stocks is: 'How fast must earnings grow for a company to be considered a growth stock?' The challenge for the securities analyst is not only to answer this query but also to uncover developing trends before others do so – because thereafter the stock's price will greatly change.

Price earnings variations may also be due to a change in share price after *capital increase* which entitles the holders of old shares to acquire new shares at a certain ratio, under a specified subscription price. Since the subscription price is usually fixed below the price of the old shares, the stock exchange quotation declines after the capital increase, with the following formula helping in the computation:

Share Price after Capital Increase =
$$\frac{N \times \text{Price of Old Shares} + \text{Subscription Price}}{N + 1}$$

where N is the number of old shares for 1 new share.

This brings up the subject of *subscription rights* which are typically negotiable, since not every shareholder owns exactly as many shares as are needed to purchase one or more new shares. Furthermore, not every shareholder wants to exercise his subscription rights. The value of a subscription right is calculated by the algorithm:

Subscription Right = Price of Old Shares – Price after Capital Increase

Nevertheless, the actual stock price of the subscription right may differ from the calculated value because in the Stock Exchange it is basically determined by supply and demand.

This presents, incidentally, an opportunity for sharp traders who can capitalize upon the existing difference between real price and asked price. Even minute variations are worth exploiting and expert systems have been written for that purpose working around the clock to uncover business opportunities in the different stock exchanges.

THE CONTRIBUTION OF FINANCIAL ANALYSIS IN DISCOVERING ANOMALIES IN THE MARKET

The term 'anomalies' is not correct, but it is widely used. What it means essentially is that there is a deviation from an established pattern and the prevailing rules, on which traders and investors could capitalize. Nobody can however be sure that the old pattern will return (see Chorafas, 1994c).

- It may be that the financial market finds itself at the edge of chaos moving to a new stability.
- In this case the old order will not come back, since what has been observed is not an outlier but a new pattern.

If the anomaly hypothesis were correct, then arbitrageurs would see to it that it was rapidly corrected. Such windows of opportunity exist, but most are very small, lasting just minutes. Others, particularly in correcting changes in the price of shares, may last several days.

One important reference on the *adjustment of share price* must be brought into perspective. After a capital increase, profit distributions in the form of stock dividends (bonus shares) and stock splits, share prices are no longer comparable with those before these operations took place. This is logical since:

- The number of securities is being increased more than the company's assets, and
- Each shareholder will own fewer of the company's assets.

But the market is not necessarily 'logical'. A financial market has a community intelligence and from time to time it is capable of thinking. 'You are only logical, not really thinking,' Dr Niels Bohr used to say to his assistants and associates (see Frisch, 1979).

When other people are logical, those really thinking have the upper hand. And thinking in a market full of complexity requires a significant capability for experimentation – the way we have been discussing all along.

In terms of evaluation and experimentation, in order to obtain comparable figures, share prices need to be adjusted. One of the methods being used assumes that the capital invested remains the same over the entire period.

$$\text{Adjusted Price} = \begin{array}{c} \text{Price to be} \\ \text{Adjusted} \end{array} \times \frac{\text{Price ex-Subscription Right}}{\text{Price including Subscription Right}}$$

The ratio: price ex-subscription right over price including subscription right, is the *adjustment factor*. Since splits and bonus shares have no subscription rights, the prices are adjusted by the formula:

$$\text{Adjusted Price} = \text{Price to be Adjusted} \times \frac{N}{N + 1}$$

where N is the number of old shares for 1 new share.

This formula is rather frequently used but fundamentally there are no unique approaches to this or any other subject concerning financial evaluation. Each investment house – and sometimes each securities analyst – has proprietary algorithms which it (or he) favors. In place of earnings some analysts prefer to use cash flow which for simplicity they define as:

Earnings + Depreciation

The algorithm they choose forms a price/cash-flow ratio which is especially suitable for comparing companies with strongly varying depreciation as well as for cash inflow/outflow reasons.

These are some of the measures which have been developed by the financial industry, to help in evaluating performance. The key variables usually are:

- *Profitability*, expressed as pretax income as percent of average total assets.
- *Capital*, accounting for primary capital and expressed as percent of total assets.
- *Credit Quality*: loans less reserves, as percent of total loans.
- *Productivity* shown as net income per employee.

Still another measure of growing importance is *liquidity*. Table 13.1 shows statistics from the 1984 and 1988 timeframe based on a sample of American money center banks and regional banks in regard to the above metrics.

The years 1984–88 have been chosen to dramatize the jump in capital reserves after the Basel Committee defined the new capital requirements of the banking sector. Notice that money center banks have been much more sensitive than regional banks in terms of compliance.

It is also wise to note that in spite of higher reserves, the profitability of money center banks improved over the 1984–8 timeframe. By contrast, that of regional banks deteriorated. On the other hand, credit quality deteriorated much more with money center banks than with regional banks as a whole – while for half the regional banks credit quality held steady.

AN INTEGRATIVE APPROACH TO INVESTMENT CRITERIA

We said that financial and investment analysts have established a family of ratios to help themselves in comparative studies. Though these largely rest on assets and liabilities, each one of them underpins a particular aspect of operations or of market standing of the company.

But ratios as well as other algorithmic expressions require, in order to be calculated, some well chosen reference factors. The most important are included in the following list:

Table 13.1 Metrics from America's big financial institutions, in 1984 and 1988

	Profitability Pre-tax income as % of average		Capital Primary capital as % of total assets		Credit quality Loan-loss reserves as % of total loans		Net income per employee ($)		Liquidity Loans as % of earning assets	
	1984	1988	1984	1988	1984	1988	1984	1988	1984	1988
Money Center Banks										
Bankers Trust	1.32	1.75	6.2	9.3	1.55	5.45	27,814	51,732	64.6	51.1
Chase Manhattan	1.00	1.55	6.4	8.6	1.23	3.94	10,041	25,223	82.6	80.3
Chemical Banking	1.35	1.44	6.3	9.7	1.22	4.91	17,215	27,000	79.7	70.0
Citicorp	1.20	1.35	5.8	8.2	0.89	2.82	12,502	20,876	77.9	76.8
J.P. Morgan	1.95	1.92	7.0	9.2	1.63	5.23	41,507	64,437	65.2	41.3
Regional Banks										
Bank of New York	1.61	1.41	6.3	8.8	1.27	2.84	13,690	19,817	76.4	82.2
Mellon Bank	0.98	0.05	6.6	8.0	1.54	4.79	10,741	-3,934	76.0	70.9
PNC Financial	1.99	1.85	6.9	7.5	1.31	2.19	17,182	27,980	65.0	65.8
Banc One	4.10	2.21	7.2	8.9	1.18	1.37	12,375	20,165	706	78.0
First Bank System	1.17	-0.96	5.7	6.7	1.30	2.82	13,815	-34,425	62.9	58.4
NCNB	1.55	1.42	6.2	7.6	1.22	1.22	13,412	19,452	67.2	69.7
First Wachovia	2.09	1.95	7.2	7.9	1.34	1.15	13,882	18,109	67.6	73.8
Barnett Banks	1.43	1.47	6.2	7.8	1.02	1.11	9,611	12,764	71.3	83.3

1. Total revenues

Both operating and non-operating revenues must be reflected. The net of other income (expense), which in several instances appears as a line item in the expense portion of the income statement, should be added back to total revenues.

2. Net income

Net income is from continuing operations and before extraordinary items and preferred dividends. Major nonrecurring items included in net income should be focused on, according to the particular weight they carry by industry.

3. Profits

Though different definitions are available regarding profits, the best one is money remaining after all costs of operating a business are paid. Only realized profits should be counted – not paper profits, as it so often happens with derivatives.

4. Yield

This is a ratio and, as stated, it indicates the annual return on an equity investment expressed as a percentage of the investment's cost or current market value. Yield information must be presented in a comprehensive form, with particular emphasis on the ability to pinpoint variations.

5. Cash flow from operations

In Chapter 11 we saw in detail the importance of inflow and outflow of cash and also said that many analysts today consider cash flow a more valuable indicator than profits. A calculation method begins with cash flow from continuing operations, with preferred dividends and capitalized interest being deducted.

6. Earnings per share and cash flow per share

Both are ratios. Consistent with the treatment of net income, earnings per share is computed from continuing operations and before extraordinary items are accounted for. Since earnings per share is a much more popular barometer, we will study it in a separate section.

7. Capital and exploratory expenditures

Capital expenditures are defined as gross property, plant and equipment additions plus new investments. Exploratory expenditures aim to promote successful efforts in investments and the optimization of activities – an approach comparable to R&D along product development lines.

8. Capital and exploratory expenditures/cash flow from operations

This ratio measures the ability of a company to finance its capital and exploratory expenditures from internally generated sources. A ratio in excess of 1 indicates that external financing may be required; a ratio of less than 0.5 suggests that the company is a cash cow.

9. Pretax cash flow, coverage of fixed charges

Coverage of fixed charges is an important indicator of financial health. It is calculated by dividing pretax, preinterest cash flow by total fixed charges. Some financial analysts consider a minimum coverage ratio to be equal to 2.50.

10. Net asset value per share

This vital investment parameter provides a snapshot of what a company's underlying value might be at a given point in time. Because of the inherent limitations associated with the net asset value per share figure in a volatile price environment, securities analysts consider the ratio of market price to net asset value per share (rather than the absolute figure itself) to be a more useful statistical measure of relative valuation.

11.   Outstanding liabilities

Money and other assets a business owes to others, including amounts owed for mortgages, supplies, wages, salaries, accrued taxes and other debts. We have made a distinction between current liabilities (CL) and longer-term liabilities.

12. Long-term debt

Because their features more closely resemble those of fixed obligations, nonconvertible redeemable preferred stock, convertible exchangable preferred stock as well as convertible bonds, are classified as long-term debt in many financial analyses. This is part of longer-term liabilities.

13. Long-term debt/cash flow from operations

The ratio of long-term debt to cash flow from operations is a measure of the *debt payback* period, or the length of time required to repay a given company's long-term debt if cash flow were devoted solely to debt repayment.

14. Productivity

This is the relationship between *output*, or the quantity of goods and services produced, and *input*, or the amount of labor, material and capital expended to produce those goods and services. It is often measured in terms of output per man-hour.

15. Research and development (R&D)

The R&D budget is a measure of a company's commitment to staying in business. Therefore it is a prime indicator of survivability, particularly in a highly competitive environment, and it is often valued in this manner.

16. Investments in technology

Like R&D, a great deal of technology investment is part of the cost of staying in business. This is particularly true for whatever is associated with high technology and aims at a cultural change in the organization. The development of expert systems, interactive graphics and the use of high performance computers are examples.

We have also spoken of the wisdom of following closely *return on investment* (ROI) – the amount of pretax profit from an investment stated as a percentage of the original outlay or purchase price. ROI should be calculated for any major investment being made; it is an indicator of management's ability to derive worth from money spent on projects.

While other basic factors can also be stated, those enumerated are the more fundamental. In the following sections we will see how some of them can be used for ratio analysis purposes, taking specific examples from the banking industry.

RATIO ANALYSIS IN THE BANKING INDUSTRY

While some ratios are valid as performance indicators in a cross-industry sense, many are local to a given industrial sector where they present the better focused results identifying the quality of management. The present section discusses ratios of a more general interest.

- *Return on assets (ROA)*

As we have stated from the beginning, one of the key ratios in any industry is return on assets. This is a basic metric, able to tell how effectively the assets of a company are employed. It is calculated by taking income after taxes, divided by average total assets.

Table 13.2   Key ratios for a sample of American banks

	Upper tenth percentile	Upper quartile	Median	Lower quartile	Lower tenth percentile
Return on Assets	1.50	1.20	0.90	0.70	0.50
Tax Equivalent Yield on Earning Assets	9.80	8.80	8.30	7.80	7.40
Return on Equity	19.20	16.00	13.20	8.30	2.90
Breakeven Yield	5.20	5.80	6.40	7.10	8.20
Net Interest Margin (Tax Equivalent Basis)	69.10	61.80	56.00	47.70	35.50
Total Operating Expense as % of Operating Income	74.00	78.90	84.50	90.20	96.70

If a bank has a large amount of fixed assets or is keeping too much in cash, or correspondent bank balances, the ROA will suffer. On the other hand, if its building and their contents are substantially written down the return on assets may look better.

Table 13.2 presents the upper tenth percentile, upper quartile, median, lower quartile and lower tenth percentile for return on assets in the American banking industry. Based on a sample of banks, these are average values and are written not as a yardstick but as an example of the type of information necessary – against which to compare the critical ratios of *our* bank.

Using the values in Table 13.2 as a frame of reference, we see that to be in the upper quartile of the performance featured by the American banking industry, a financial institution had to have a return of 1.20 percent. A return on assets of at least 1.50 percent was needed in order to belong to the upper tenth percentile.

Is this yardstick fairly universal? The answer is not necessarily positive. It should be pointed out that return on assets tends to be higher in the medium-sized banks, with ROA going down in the larger banks, especially in branch banking areas.

But in the general case, this is a good ratio, able to prompt a company into action. If management is not satisfied with the bank's ROA, a thorough review should be undertaken to see whether the institution has too many nonearning assets on the books. The ratio of cash on hand and due from banks should also be studied to establish whether this category of nonearning assets is too high.

As a performance indicator, return on assets can have further refinements and also be used not only for the financial institution as a whole but also for the evaluation of its profits centers. In this manner, it becomes a common denominator for comparing profit center performance – a goal to which some banks apply the algorithm of:

• *Return on earning assets*

$$R = \frac{E}{EA}$$

where R = percentage return
  E = earnings contribution of the profit center
  EA = earning assets, *including* funds 'sold' to the Money Desk for use by other profit centers; but excluding fixed assets

This approach, however, would not apply to service oriented centers such as a trust department. For these the earnings ratio is used:

$$R' = \frac{E}{GI}$$

where R' = earnings percentage
  E = earnings contribution of the profit center
  GI = gross income of the center including funds credit, if any

The R' ratio reflects the percentage of gross income carried through to earnings. It can provide a basis of comparison with other service oriented centers as well as with past performance of the same profit center. The reader may wish to return to the discussion on profit centers and cost centers in Chapter 12 where some of the aspects of this issue have been elaborated.

• *Return on net assets* (RONA)

Another critical ratio is the return on net assets. To calculate it, the corporate weighted average cost of capital is determined, taking into consideration such factors as:

• Leverage of the firm,
• The impact of inflation, and
• Interest rates.

The aim is to maximize the spread between RONA and the cost of capital. The premise is that business units with positive spreads should be pursuing invest-and-grow strategies. Negative spread units should be shrunk, with emphasis on sacrificing growth for improved returns.

Furthermore, according to this criterion, if negative spreads cannot be turned around in short order, partial or total divestiture should be planned.

Such focus on profitability helps to isolate winners and losers in a corporate portfolio of investments.

One problem with RONA, however, is that in at least one issue it resembles EPS. This is a short-term accounting orientation rather than a focus on innovative future directions and most particularly the longer-run sustainability of performance. Quite often, tools which do not look to the future prove to be of limited service if not outright counterproductive.

- *Discounted cash flow* (DCF)

The stated limitation of EPS and RONA has been instrumental in leading some managements towards the usage of discounted cash flow in evaluating the company itself and its business units. This approach requires a careful projection of annual operating cash flows for the planning period, taking a mid-term base of, say, five years. DCF is applied to these projected cash flows to determine the:

- Net present value (NPV), and
- Internal rate of return (IRR).

DCF valuation helps manage the business with shareholder value creation in mind. It is future oriented and provides an economic value by reflecting on discounted cash flows, which are not based solely on historical information. Along a similar line of reasoning, Dr Bernard C. Reimann suggests a Q ratio:

$$Q = \frac{\text{Present Value (Cash Flow + Residual Value)}}{\text{Inflation Adjusted Assets}}$$

Reimann advances the Q ratio as a strategic measure. A Q ratio greater than one means that the value the stock market assigns to the company's net assets is greater than their actual replacement. Hence:

$Q > 1$ indicates value creation
$Q < 1$ signals value destruction

The Q ratio valuation model rests on measures which are known and appreciated, such as inflation adjusted net assets, annual cash flows, residual value, and a medium-range planning period. However, it has not been so far extensively used in order to be able to detect its weaknesses.

APPRECIATING THE MORE CLASSICAL METRICS

Other financial ratios used by business and industry are more classical. Though not all of them are being employed in the same way or at the same time, some have found significant applications. For instance, return on equity and yield to breakeven have made many managers work hard to reduce costs without cutting down on quality of service.

- *Return on equity* (ROE)

Return on equity is calculated as income divided by equity capital. The latter includes contingent reserves, surplus and undivided profits, but it does not include capital notes and debentures. Investors are often on the lookout for the top performers in ROE commensurate with the quality of products and services which give assurances of survivability.

Carefully used on a comparative basis with past years, and with other companies, ROE can be a useful tool which however is more subject to unusual variations than return on assets. As any banker will appreciate, high and low capitalization can distort return on equity. Therefore, the equity to asset ratio must be reviewed to see whether the company under examination is over or undercapitalized.

- In evaluating both return on assets and return on equity, management needs to look at the tax equivalent yield on earning assets.
- It should also be remembered that there are many companies with a relatively good return on equity that are in reality poor performers.

If the tax equivalent yield is low, it stands to reason that the company will have difficulty being a high performer. It might be possible to achieve high performance with high service charges and unusual control over expenses, but this is most unlikely – the market is not so elastic in respect to product prices and service fees.

If a company's yield on earning assets is low, some additional ratios can suggest where the problem area lies. This is for instance the case with the references made under the next two items.

- *Tax equivalent yield on earning assets*

This is a measure of income on earning assets that, for example in banking, includes interest and fees on loans, accreted discounts, interest on federal funds sold, government and agency securities, as well as interest on municipals placed on a tax equivalent basis – divided by average securities, federal funds sold and loans.

Percentiles have been shown in Table 13.2. Since these statistics reflect earning assets, nonearning assets such as cash and money due from banks as well as fixed assets have not been included. Other industrial sectors have their particular conditions with regard to this metric.

• *Yield on loans*

Though for money center banks loans no longer represent the big part of their income – this place having been taken by derivative financial products – for many other banks loans are still the largest single earning asset. For this reason, a low yield on loans will have a great effect on the total yield on earning assets.

The loan to asset ratio could show that the bank is not obtaining its share of a good yielding source of revenue. A similar ratio could be created for other products, for instance:

• *Yield on derivatives*

Yield on derivatives is not actively used today but there is no reason why it should not be, provided that it is tempered by a *risk factor*, more precisely, a factor which provides risk adjusted return on capital.

Exactly the same argument can be made with loans which, as every financial expert should know, can be a double-edged sword when interest rates are changing. When interest rates are surging, many banks are often locked into old, low rate loans. In that case the analysis will show where the problem is, but an elegant solution will be more difficult.

In the case where the yield on earning assets is low, another item to review is the tax equivalent yield on tax exempt securities. While a number of factors enter into play in this respect, from time to time – as in the 1980s – the tax equivalent yield on tax exempt securities tended to be slightly higher than the yield on loans.

Company size evidently has an impact in all these references. Even if the yield on earning assets may not vary greatly with the size of the firm, this is not necessarily true of other criteria. For example, in the financial sector the percentage of earning assets to total assets:

• Is influenced by such factors as deposit turnover and proximity to clearing banks, and
• It tends to go down as the bank becomes larger.

City banks with significant reserve typically have a lower ratio of earning assets due to their processing of many clearing and transit items, and their higher reserve requirements. Hence, to review the yield on earning assets fully, it is necessary to analyze separately the yields on *loans* and *investments*, as well as the distribution of these two categories.

If the yield on these particular assets is low, it can have a marked impact on the overall bank yield. Similarly, if the bank is not taking full advantage of tax savings assets, earnings may suffer. At the same time, management must be certain that there is enough taxable income to capitalize on tax exempt features – prior to engaging itself in this type of investment.

CAN WE ESTIMATE YIELD TO BREAKEVEN?

We have spoken rather extensively of breakeven in Chapters 6–8. Therefore, it would be redundant to return to this subject at this point were it not for the fact that breakeven studies can provide a good basis for ratio analysis in the manufacturing industry, merchandising and the financial sector.

- In a way, in measuring company performance the counterpart to earning asset yield is the *breakeven yield*.
- This ratio is a metric of the minimum yield necessary on earning assets to cover all expenses, including interest paid.

In banking, breakeven yield takes into account total operating expense less noninterest operating income, including trust department income, service charges and other operating income – divided by total earning assets, including securities, federal funds sold and loans. Percentiles have been shown in Table 13.2.

A low value of the yield to breakeven indicates high performance in the sense that the financial institution has apparently been able to control its expenses and cover a higher percentage of them through:

- Service charges, and
- Fee income.

By maintaining a relatively low breakeven yield, high performance banks usually provide themselves with greater flexibility in managing their earning assets.

Mathematically, the yield to breakeven is the yield on earning assets that is needed to cover total expenses, less revenue collected in service charges and fees. This is calculated as a function of net expense and average total earning assets, according to the following algorithm:

Net Expense = Total Expense (including interest paid)
      − Noninterest Income (service charges, fees,
       commissions, trust income)

The net expense so computed is then divided by average total earning assets to obtain the yield to breakeven ratio. It follows that total expense, noninterest income and average total earning assets must be carefully watched.

Lack of good expense control will show up initially in this yield to breakeven ratio. This includes the practice of buying asset growth with time money. Unless such money can be employed at a good margin of profit, the yield to breakeven will suffer.

The total *noninterest income* is also an issue which has attracted attention since the 1980s. Banks that feature few or no service charges and fees tend to find that the yield to breakeven is higher than the median. The realization of this fact has seen a noticeable trend away from free chequing accounts, with a number of banks discovering a 'new' source of revenue – the service charge.

- In the 1980s, the median American bank obtained between 6 percent and 10 percent of its total operations income from service charges and fees.
- This figure has tended to grow in the 1990s, after many banks realized that income from all sorts of fees had been 40–60 percent for Swiss banks.

Although the larger American banks do not do as well in return on assets as the smaller banks, they apparently do a better job of collecting service charges. Statistics indicate that the percentage of revenue from service charges goes up steadily with the size of the bank, with a significant increase in banks with over $1 billion in assets.

Larger banks feel more confident of themselves in asking for fees. But they also find themselves obliged to provide higher quality and more sophisticated services. In turn, this requires first class organization and high technology – both being served through instrumental financial models.

14 The Creative Use of Algorithmic Solutions

INTRODUCTION

As we have seen in Chapter 13, through critical ratios management provides itself with a range of facilities for describing and analyzing business results. Quantitative approaches do not need to be complex. Some rather simple algorithms like ratios and those we will see in the present chapter can be successfully employed for the performance of financial evaluations. Even simple finance algorithms can help in a creative sense.

- They provide a bird's eye view on changes concerning the most popular formulas and indices, and
- Assist in demonstrating how comprehension and conceptualization are promoted through models.

Artifacts made of algorithms and heuristics are largely *how to* tools. Their emphasis, however, is not on how to do accounting but rather on how management should look at and act in connection with the financial and accounting challenges which it encounters every day. Therefore, the fundamental notions behind the creative use of artifacts:

- Should cover different viewpoints, as they prevail in industrial practice, and
- Must be enriched with a visualization which helps to explain background notions and shows how they can be used to advantage.

Since Chapter 1 I have brought into perspective the fact that no two people have the same concept of what *financial analysis* is and is not. The same is true of *financial modeling*. Therefore, the approach which has been consistently taken has been flexible and polyvalent – given that quite varied mathematical models have been underpinning the analytical effort.

Computer literate people use models in preparing or interpreting financial statements but also as assistants in planning tax strategies. Businesses use models to analyze new product introductions, especially those in which large capital outlays are required.

We have also seen that models permit us to *experiment* on how to capitalize on our company's strengths or offset its weaknesses. Whether their users appreciate it or not, the best models are written *by management* and *for management*.

This is the basic reason why contrary to other texts on financial modeling the present book does not focus on mathematics, but works by example. Whether in setting policies or developing models, practical examples are the best way to introduce a concept and lead to its implementation.

BENEFITS DERIVED FROM SIMPLE ALGORITHMS: AN EXAMPLE WITH INTEREST INCOME

Along the line of reasoning explained in the Introduction, this section brings to the reader's attention an algorithm used to calculate *interest income*. The rate at which invested capital earns interest is usually indicated in percent per annum (% p.a.) with income calculated as:

$$\text{Yearly interest income} = \frac{\text{Investment} \times \text{Annual Interest Rate in \%} \times \text{Running Period in Years}}{100}$$

Since maturities (or interest periods) are often shorter than one year and can be in quarters, months or days, the formula for calculating in days is just as simple:

$$\text{Daily interest income} = \frac{\text{Yearly Interest Income}}{365}$$

British interest practice is customarily made with 365 days a year and 28, 29, 30 or 31 days a month. But continental European practice sees to it that the calculation of daily income is typically done on the basis of 360 days a year and 30 days a month.

Whichever approach is chosen, in a financial or commercial environment and in day-to-day operations, the capital which is earning interest can change continually through debits as well as credits. Therefore, an interest number and interest divisor are used to calculate interest income:

$$\text{Interest Income} = \frac{\text{Interest Number}}{\text{Interest Divisor}}$$

where:

$$\text{Interest Number} = \frac{\text{Capital} \times \text{Running Period in Days}}{100}$$

Table 14.1 Compound interest over fifteen years

Years	3%	5%	7%
1	1.03	1.05	1.07
2	1.0609	1.1025	1.1449
3	1.09272	1.15762	1.22504
4	1.12550	1.21550	1.31079
5	1.15927	1.27628	1.40255
6	1.19405	1.34009	1.50073
7	1.22987	1.40710	1.60578
8	1.26677	1.47745	1.71818
9	1.30477	1.55132	1.83845
10	1.34391	1.62889	1.96715
11	1.38423	1.71033	2.10485
12	1.42576	1.79585	2.25219
13	1.46853	1.88564	2.40984
14	1.51590	1.97993	2.57853
15	1.55796	2.07892	2.76903

$$\text{Interest Divisor} = \frac{360}{\text{Interest Rate in \%}}$$

Savings accounts are a special case of interest income, as income is added to the capital and the new interest income is calculated on the higher capital amount. Thus, at the end of the running period, the final capital is computed through the equation:

Final Capital =
    Initial Capital × Compound Interest Factor

As an example, Table 14.1 shows the compound interest factor for 3 percent, 5 percent, and 7 percent over a 15 year period. Annual interest should be used, if the running period is given in years; monthly interest if maturity is given in months. The computing algorithm is:

Compound Interest Factor =
$$(1 + \frac{\text{Interest Rate in \%}}{100}) \text{ Running Period}$$

The algorithm for finding the simple interest rate for investments or loans whose interest rate is not specified but income to be received (or to be paid) is known in advance, is:

$$\text{Interest Rate} = \frac{\text{Interest to be Paid} \times 100 \times 365}{\text{Capital} \times \text{Running Period in Days}}$$

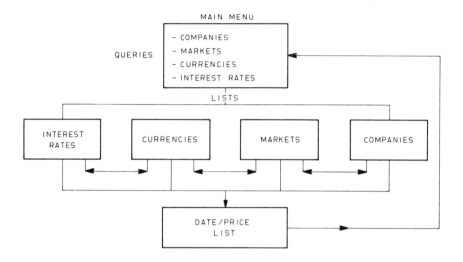

Figure 14.1 Developing a menu-base enduser interface

The following formula however applies in the case of compound interest:

$$\text{Compound Interest Factor} = \frac{\text{Final Capital}}{\text{Initial Capital}} = 1 + \frac{\text{Interest to be Paid}}{\text{Initial Capital}}$$

These are the algorithms typically used in interest calculation. The formulas are simple but even so the mathematics should be handled by computer. There exists plenty of software for this purpose.

The basic principle with analysis and modeling is that the enduser should be assisted all the way through computers, databases, communications and software. Therefore, user interfaces should be simple, agile, friendly and forgiving of possible user mistakes.

For access purposes, menu solutions are useful and Figure 14.1 presents an approach which has been applied in connection with finance algorithms and their implementation. We have been talking more about database access in Chapter 12; Chapter 15 will explain what is necessary for interactive visualization.

Effective solutions to *seamless* database access are as crucial as the validity of the algorithms which we use.

This is a fact only leading-edge organizations and learned systems specialists appreciate. The majority are mismanaging the database connection and the human interfaces – therefore only throwing down the drain any benefits there might have been.

ALGORITHMS FOR PERSONAL LOANS AND FOR YIELD CALCULATION

A little more complex in a processing sense is the computation relative to *personal loans* because of the costs associated with their handling, for which we should be watching out. Typically, personal loans are repaid in equal monthly installments which include the interest on the loan and other loan costs, as well as the repayment portion.

In addition to the bank's refinancing and administrative expenses, loan costs often have embedded in them residual debt insurance in case of death or invalidity. The factors entering into the algorithm are:

• Total Loan Cost
• Loan Amount
• Interest Rate in %
• Running Period in Months.

The Total Loan Cost is:

$$\text{Total Loan Costs} = (\text{Running Period} \times \text{Monthly Installment}) - \frac{\text{Loan}}{\text{Amount}}$$

To find the monthly installment, the total of loan amount and part payment supplement (or loan costs) is divided by the running period in months.

$$\text{Monthly Installment} = \frac{\text{Loan amount} + \text{Loan Total Costs}}{\text{Running Period in Months}}$$

Sometimes, personal loan offers indicate the installments repayable monthly or the loan costs over the entire running period of the loan, but not the annual interest rate on which their offers are based.

While *stock yield* is interest in equity rather than debt, the algorithms used for its calculation are not too different than those of personal loans. A simple formula for stock yield serves in comparing investments in securities in terms of earnings.

$$\text{Stock Yield} = \frac{\text{Dividend} \times 100}{\text{Stock Price}}$$

Sometime, the price ex-dividend of a stock sees to it that the yield seems higher after the dividend has been declared. This can be corrected by adjusting the stock price:

Adjusted Stock Yield =

$$\frac{\text{Dividend} \times 100}{\text{Stock Price} - \dfrac{\text{Dividend} \times \text{Days since last Distribution}}{360}}$$

In Chapter 13 we have spoken about the price earnings (PE) ratio which indicates price versus earnings per share – and said that it is calculated by dividing the stock price by the earnings per share. A *compound yield* helps define the total return on investment. This consists of the distribution of dividends (or of interest) and the price of capital gain or loss expressed in % of the investment amount. The algorithm is:

Compound Yield =

$$\left(\frac{\text{Distribution} + \text{Value End/Year} + \text{Value Start/Year}}{\text{Value at the Start of the Year}} \right) \times 100$$

The gain or loss is the value at the end of year minus the value at the start of year. It is rewarding to do these calculations for all positions in a portfolio and then compare the results stock-by-stock and industry-by-industry to which a company belongs.

Not only should this be done by computer, but also expert systems rather than classical data processing should be used for management planning and evaluation purposes. The solutions which we provide should incorporate a comprehensive explanation of the results in connection to the evaluations which we do.

The applications perspectives can be enlarged by expressing our problem in an algorithmic form. Examples range from day-to-day budgeting practices (which we saw in Part Two) to the interest income, personal loans and yield calculation we are discussing in this chapter.

EVALUATING THE RETURNS FROM BOND ISSUES

Related to the yield of loans, the dividends of stocks and their market fluctuation, is the *interest* and *capital appreciation* (or depreciation) of bonds. Bonds represent the securitization of debt, whether issued by a corporation or involving the productizing of other instruments such as:

- Mortgage-based financing (MBF), and
- Asset-backed financing (ABF).

Productizing is a fairly recent term, coined to differentiate between a product which is still at research and development status and one which is ready to be launched in the market. The reason for a product to stay longer in R&D, or even never come out of the laboratory, may be precompetitive research, engineering weaknesses, management inertia, and so on.

The direct yield of a bond tells the investor what income he can expect over the short term from the purchase price. The algorithm is fairly simple:

$$\text{Direct Bond Yield} = \frac{\text{Nominal Interest}}{\text{Bond Price}} \times 100$$

However, this simple equation has to be qualified in several ways. If the price is above par, the yield is lower than the nominal interest rate, as interest income is calculated from the nominal value and the bond purchaser pays a premium over the latter. If the price is below par, the yield is higher than the interest rate.

Both in the case of a higher and of a lower bond price, yield calculation is a little more complex than the algorithms characterizing the preceding examples, because we have to take into account the remaining years to the payment of the capital. Other things being equal, purchasing at, say, 93 percent a bond which matures in 1998 does not provide the same returns as buying one maturing in 2008.

- When the bond market booms and bond prices are rising, *long bonds* carry with them a premium as investors bet on the premium they will receive over, say, the next twenty years of the bond's life.
- When the bond market falls, the prices of bonds with long maturity fall faster, for exactly the same reason as it rises faster in a bull market.

Given that most bonds are repaid at par, an investor who acquires a bond at a price below 100 percent and holds it until maturity, can score price gains. At the same time, an investor who pays above nominal value will have price losses in the case the bond is repaid. The difference is calculated by means of yield to maturity:

Yield to Maturity =

$$\frac{\text{Interest Rate} + \left(\dfrac{\text{Repayment Price} - \text{Day's Price}}{\text{Period Left to Run}} \right)}{\dfrac{\text{Day's Price} + \text{Repayment Price}}{2}} \times 100$$

This algorithm, however, does not discount future payments to the current value. Yet, as stated in the preceding paragraphs, the selection of the period left to run is of crucial importance:

- If no early recall is possible, as in the case of bullet bonds, final maturity applies and the formula which we saw holds.
- If drawing by lot in exercising repurchase right is possible, then the yield to the average due date between earliest and latest possible repayment date must be used. (A more sophisticated model would be Monte Carlo simulation.)
- If a call of the issue is a strong probability, the yield to earliest possible call date applies.

When we deal with bonds of fixed interest rates, the average due date should be used for prices above par, if drawings by lot and repurchases are possible. Final maturity must be employed for prices below par.

Except in the case of the so-called *floating rate* notes, interest rates of bonds are typically fixed at the time of issue and remain unchanged throughout the entire running period. But in reality, the yield dynamically adjusts itself via bond prices to the variable interest rate levels on the capital market.

Furthermore, the simple equation we have just seen is valid in the case of *bullet bonds*, where the issuer does not retain the right to call them back after a given date which is ahead of maturity, and which are not subject to a lottery system of repayment. Should either of these conditions exist, then the establishment of the appropriate bond yield requires a much finer analytical calculation, taking into account:

- The risk that a bond purchased above par will be recalled.
- The opportunity that the same thing will happen to a bond purchased below par.
- The risk that recalling prior to maturity represents a mismatch between projected and available cash flow.
- The fact that when the capital is returned to the investor the going yields may be well below (or above) that featured by the retired bond.

As bonds are traded at any time during the year, not just at the time the interest is paid, accrued interest (broken-period interest) is normally not contained in the bond price, but is calculated separately when ownership changes.

However, in some issues – for example, dual currency loans – broken-period interest is included in the price. Such bonds are said to be traded *flat*. To calculate the yield in these cases, the broken-period interest must be subtracted from the price.

A METHODOLOGY FOR SOPHISTICATED INVESTORS

As the examples which we saw help document, financial analysts must use different approaches in their work, depending on the instrument they are handling and its particular features. Both *quantitative* methods and *qualitative* approaches are necessary to provide analytical support.

Indeed, one of the best areas of applicability of expert systems is investments in securities. This statement is based on fifteen years of experience and can be documented through lots of practical examples from the area of money management, trust management, portfolio optimization and securities trading (see Chorafas and Steinmann, 1991).

Such approaches go a long way from the macroeconomic studies of several decades ago which particularly focused on quantitative methods for regulating money supply through mathematical economics models.

- Ben Graham, who helped found securities analysis as a discipline, used to say that all financial analyses should be a combination of *quantitative* and *qualitative* solutions.
- If the financial statements represent the quantitative side of corporate performance, then the footnotes to the financial statements are the best starting point for qualitative evaluation.
- Sophisticated investors and state-of-the art dealers develop scenarios which permit them to pre-evaluate ways and means for handling assets.

The code book which gives life to the financial statements is the domain where expert systems can offer most commentable results. But let's never forget that the best solutions are those based not just on mathematics but on a valid methodology and on an intimate knowledge of how a financial product works.

Usually, analysts and traders say that supply and demand look after the proper pricing of a bond. This is true, but it is no less valid to suggest that, outside crisis periods, supply and demand adjust themselves to the characteristics of the financial product taking into account the key features through which a fixed interest security may be defined:

1. Its *face (or nominal) value*, that is the loan amount to be repaid on maturity,
2. The *coupon rate*, which is fixed at the time of issue,
3. The *maturity*, or period to repayment of the principal,
4. The *yield*, which is the return if held to maturity, and
5. The *real yield* accounting for early repayment conditions, and other clauses.

Because of the several types of bonds (there are about twenty-five different types) and their many variations, calculations can become complex, and so are the tools to be put at the disposition of traders and investors. A trading expert system by the Mitsubishi Bank classifies bonds between domestic and foreign, differentiating through its component modules between:

- Straight (bullet) bonds
- Convertible bonds
- Bonds with warrants.

This artificial intelligence construct examines the special characteristics of every issue, evaluating its *merits* and *demerits*. It also compares one bond versus another, as major companies have today in the market twenty or more different bonds each.

The effective execution of such work requires not only algorithms and heuristics but also a valid methodology on how to see the job through. No such methodology can be established through old data processing and mainframes for the simple reason that the so-called legacy approaches are the negation of efficiency.

When we think about what makes a *success story*, we find that there is a strong relationship between the level of our knowhow, our professional performance and our well-being. In this simple sentence lies the aim of a rigorous financial analysis: the new perspectives it opens to its users are an integral part of their career advancement.

ALGORITHMS AND HEURISTICS FOR LOANS AND INVESTMENTS

Clear-eyed banks have built bridges between their bond underwriting activities and their loans operations, enriching all of them with expert systems support. The output increasingly comes in graphical form, like the radar chart shown in Figure 14.2, or 3-D color graphics which permit a very effective man–machine communication.

Radar charts are popular in Japan but American companies also use them. Digital Equipment, for example, employs radar charts to evaluate *project risks*. From loan evaluation to project management, the rate of applications talks a great deal about the versatility of this visualization method.

Three-dimensional visualization is important since many analytical approaches connected with debt and equity are focusing on *conversions* and concern: *Price, Value,* and *Premium* – hence, 3 dimensions. The conversion price is the price an investor must pay for a share if he buys a convertible bond at par, and later converts it into shares.

Computation of P&L is affected by the fact that in some, albeit rare cases, the investor must also make a payment on conversion – or, alternatively, he receives a payment. The algorithm is:

$$\text{Conversion Price} = \frac{\text{Nominal Value of Convertible Bond}}{\text{Number of Shares per Convertible Issue}} \pm \frac{\text{Payment}}{\text{per Share}}$$

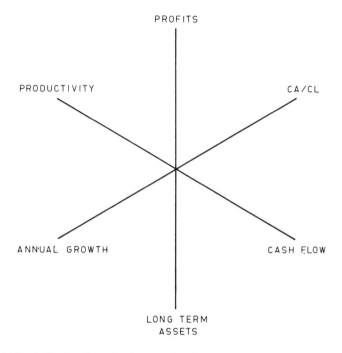

Figure 14.2 A Radar chart for loan evaluation

To protect present shareholders against a price decline of their shares, the conversion price at the time of issue is somewhat above the stock exchange price of the conversion premium. It is therefore of advantage to investors of convertible bonds if the loan terms include an automatic adjustment of the conversion price to possible capital increases or splits which might happen later.

The conversion value measures the acquisition price of the underlying share, in case the latter is bought through the acquisition of the convertible bond on the secondary market and subsequent conversion. The cost to the investor includes not only the stock exchange price of the convertible bond, but also the accrued broken-period interest which is lost on conversion. If cash payments are stipulated, further payment needs to be made.

Conversion Value =

$$\frac{\text{Convertible Bond Price being Paid}}{\text{Number of Shares per Convertible Issue}} \pm \frac{\text{Payment}}{\text{per Share}}$$

where:

Convertible Bond Price =

$$\text{Face Value} \times \frac{\text{Price of Convertible Bond in } \%}{100}$$

The conversion premium comes up in the case where the investor buys a convertible bond and wants to exchange it for shares. Depending on issue terms and price development, the shares will cost more (or less) than those bought directly on the stock exchange. Expressed in percent this surcharge (or discount) on the stock exchange price is known as the *conversion premium*.

$$\text{Conversion Premium} = \frac{\text{Conversion Value} \times 100}{\text{Share Price}} - 100$$

Such premium can vary depending on the attractiveness of the related shares or the overall market; usually rising or falling in the range of 10–20 percent.

In case the conversion premium is low or negative, conversion will involve no financial problems, with the prices of the convertible bond running parallel to the corresponding share prices. But if the conversion premium is high, such conversion is no longer attractive and the convertible bond will act like a fixed-interest bond.

EARNINGS PER SHARE AND PAYOUT

While financial institutions need critical ratios to gauge their own operations, they also use ratios extensively in order to evaluate the health of industrial companies to which they *lend* and in which they *invest*. Both lending and investing should be forward looking:

- In lending, we evaluate our customers' ability to repay – which requires both profitability and cash flow.
- In investing, we focus on the company's ability to carry the day against competition, maintaining its dividend or improving upon it.

As we saw in Chapter 13, earning per share (EPS) is a significant ratio. During the 1960s and the early 1970s a number of executive compensation and bonus plans have been designed and driven by the growth in earnings per share. As a result, corporate executives became increasingly convinced that in their decisions they should really focus on the growth in earnings.

Yet, by the mid-1970s, after the OPEC oil shock, the criteria began to change. A complex combination of factors including higher inflation, began to erode the profitability of industry and of investments at large, altering the appeal of EPS as a metric.

Inflation and interest rates pushed up capital costs while a growing competition in maturing markets and industries squeezed profits. The inevitable result has been a negative spread between returns and costs of capital, with a sharp decline in price earnings ratios and an increase in undervalued stocks.

- Quantitative approaches should however look at the fundamentals of EPS, starting with the *payout ratio* which helps in expressing what part of the profit is distributed as dividend.
- By contrast, the qualitative component of a model should reflect the psychological effects to which reference has been made.

The quantitative payout ratio shows whether the dividend is secure, as it will be if this ratio is above 100 percent. Conversely, a low payout ratio indicates that the dividend policy of the company is not very favorable to shareholders. The computational algorithm is:

$$\text{Payout Ratio} = \frac{\text{Dividend Payment}}{\text{Profit}} \times 100$$

If only one type of share exists, the calculation is easy, based on dividend per share and earnings per share. In the case the company has issued different types of shares (bearer shares, registered shares, preferred shares, participation certificates) account has to be taken of the fact that these are entitled to varying dividends. As a result, the numerator of this equation becomes the sum of the products: share type Z times the dividend it pays.

The message is that earnings per share may be one thing and the ability to give the shareholder a return for his investment might be another. A fast growing industry usually chooses to develop through retained earning rather than taking more loans, which runs contrary to what a mature industry does. A growth company typically does not have excess assets to sell in order to satisfy both its rapid development and dividend requirements.

A policy of retained earnings is acceptable to investors as long as the growth of the common shareholders' equity compensates for the dividends which are not being paid – as was the case of IBM in the early 1960s and of Xerox in the latter part of the same decade. Under these conditions, even in the absence of payout, growth in EPS generates a positive result in common equity.

However, exceptional growth conditions are not always present, hence the wisdom of a better focused analysis. The simplest equation for calculating annual EPS is:

$$EPS = \frac{\text{Average common equity} \times \text{Return on equity}}{\text{Number of common shares}}$$

$$= E \times R \times S$$

where: EPS = Earnings per share
E = Average common equity
R = Return on equity
S = 1/Number of common shares

A derivative equation is:

$$EPS = E \times A/E \times V/A \times I/V \times S = I \times S$$

where: I = Net income available for common equity
A = Average total assets
A/E = Common equity leverage
V = Average earnings assets (often written EA which is confusing)
V/A = Asset utilization
I/V = Profit margin

The ratio: I/E of net income available for common equity over average common equity will give Return on Equity. This equation can be found in the computational tables of many companies. In plain terms it states:

$$EPS = \frac{\text{Equity} \times \text{Leverage} \times \text{Asset utilization} \times \text{Profit margin}}{\text{Shares outstanding}}$$

Thus, the original EPS equation can be expanded to take into account balance sheet factors such as growth in assets and common equity, as well as to reflect changes in income statement items such as: net interest income, loan-loss provision, other income, other expenses, taxes and preferred dividends. All this impacts on profit margin which can be algorithmically expressed:

$$I/V = M \times L \times R \times P \times T \times D$$

where M = Net interest margin
L = Net revenue from assets/Net interest margin
R = Total revenue/Net revenue from assets
P = Pretax income/Total revenue
T = Net income/Pretax income
D = Net income available for common/Net income

A not very often discussed statistic is the *income value* of a share. If an investor fixes a minimum interest an investment is supposed to yield, it becomes possible to calculate from a company's earnings how much one should at most pay for this company.

$$\text{Income Value of a Share} = \frac{\text{Earnings per Share}}{\text{Capitalization Rate}} \times 100$$

The *capitalization rate* equals the market interest rate plus a risk surcharge and should not be confused with the market capitalization. Neither all companies nor all analysts use the whole range of financial models we are considering, but as this discussion documents there is plenty of material on which to base a sound analytical approach.

TAKING INTO ACCOUNT THE EVENT RISK

The bond issues and stock price of a company relate in several ways. One of the more recent to be brought under perspective is *event risk*. In case of a leveraged buyout (LBO) the price of stock increases significantly. By contrast, since many LBOs are done through junk bonds the quality of bonds which were issued by the firm can drop overnight from AAA to BB – with a corresponding loss to the investor.

Metrics, such as option against spread (OAS), have been developed to measure the risk involved in securitized financial instruments. Such metrics typically call for the use of tools from mathematical statistics, such as multiple regression analysis, binomial distribution, analysis of variance, chi-square test, operating characteristics curve and the Monte Carlo method (see Chorafas, 1960 and 1994c). Also of tools based on heuristics.

Typically, risk calculation routines will operate in conjunction with other domain oriented programs, for instance, tables for mortgages in the case of mortgage-backed financing. The latter will include:

- Annual mortgage information showing interest paid during the year, the principal repaid during the year, and the principal outstanding at the end of the year.
- Monthly mortgage calculations, showing for each month during the period requested the beginning principal outstanding, the interest paid during the month, and the principal paid during the month.

Shown at the end of each calendar year will be the interest paid during the year, the principal repaid during the year, and the principal outstanding at the end of the year. Risk oriented programs will enrich this result with the impact of properly defined risk factors on the value of the company.

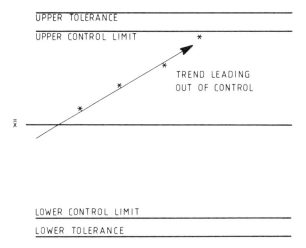

Figure 14.3   A trend line helps to identify a situation getting out of control

Astute financial institutions are keen in exploiting available graphical tools, such as quality control charts from mathematical statistics. The example given in Figure 14.3 concerns *risk evaluation*, with risk taken as normal if it fluctuates within *tolerance limits*.

Notice that the control limits are more restrained than the tolerance limits, to ensure that when a pricing (or risk) factor is in control, tolerance limits will be observed. The risk is that risk can break the upper limit.

Similar quality control charts can be plotted for *market capitalization*, with the lower limit being the value to watch. The term identifies the market value of all shares of a company and the algorithm is:

Market Capitalization = Number of Shares × Share Price

Of particular interest is the relationship between sales and market capitalization. Evidently, market capitalization should not be confused with the book value (balance sheet value) of a share which consists of the capital and reserves per share shown in the balance sheet of the company. Typically, the book value is lower than the actual value of a company in the stock market – but this is not always true.

There is no fixed relationship between book value and capitalization. Generally, however, the more the share price goes above the book value because of growth opportunities, goodwill or other reasons, the more risky the investment is.

$$\text{Book Value} = \frac{\text{Share Capital} + \text{Reported Reserves}}{\text{Number of Shares}}$$

There is also the so-called *intrinsic value* of a share, also known as real value or net asset value. This has no unique method of calculation but a frequently used algorithm is:

$$\text{Intrinsic Value} = \frac{\text{Capital Resources incl. Undisclosed Reserves}}{\text{Number of Shares}}$$

Part and parcel of capital resources is share capital, reported reserves and estimated undisclosed reserves. The intrinsic value is mainly important in connection with the takeover or liquidation of a company and is normally higher than the book value of a share.

This information is very important in terms of general company valuation as well as for leveraged buyouts – which, it should be added, are not the only major risk to the rated quality of a company's bonds. Other reasons include management performance, continuing product appeal, marketing muscle, manufacturing automation and also new factors such as the impact of health care costs for employees.

Recently, in America, Statement 106 from the Financial Accounting Standards Board (FASB), projects into the future the issue of future health care costs – and, therefore, warns investors about the damage that mounting health care costs eventually could do to corporations' balance sheets and bottom lines.

- Since it is estimated that companies face retirement health outlays, for current retirees and workers, of $228 billion.
- The implied fifteen-year write-off makes many balance sheets top-heavy with health care liabilities.

New liabilities are the result of setting aside a reserve for each present and future retiree. This means taking a hit to the bottom line (the profit figures) every year, a process which has become necessary because of reckless promises and concessions made by management, as long as future health care costs were not hitting current reported earnings. This, however, has changed.

WARRANTS AND BILLS OF EXCHANGE

A *warrant* issue typically contains a clause entitling the investor to purchase shares or participation certificates of a given company at a fixed price. Warrants can be used within a certain exercise period and, in contrast to convertible issues, the fixed-interest part of a warrant remains intact even after the subscription right has been exercised.

This reference is valid in most cases, but not in all. Occasionally, the remaining bond can be traded in at nominal value and is then voided, like a convertible bond on conversion. In the general case, the value of a warrant, which can be traded on the stock exchange is calculated through the algorithm:

Value of Warrant = (Stock Exchange Price − Subscription Price) × Number of Shares per Warrant

The concept of the *warrant premium* is important. The investor can acquire shares or participation certificates of the company concerned at a fixed subscription price in a warrant issue. This can be lucrative if the price of the equities increases. Therefore securities which can be acquired through a warrant are normally more expensive than those bought directly on the stock exchange.

The warrant premium indicates, in percent, the surcharge on the stock exchange price and is expressed through the formula:

Warrant Premium =

$$\frac{\dfrac{\text{Price of Warrant}}{\text{No. of Shares/Warrant}} + \text{Subscription Price}}{\text{Share Price}} \times 100 - 100$$

A warrant premium falls to near zero towards the end of the exercise period since the possibility of a price gain becomes continuously smaller. The warrant is worthless after that period expires. Hence the concept of *basis risk* (see also Chapter 10 on derivative financial products).

Another important reference is the *leverage factor*: a price rise of the related equity paper leads to an increase in the price of the warrant and conversely a price drop has the opposite result. The relative fluctuations in the warrant price amount to a multiple of the fluctuations in the relative share prices and this multiple is expressed by the leverage factor.

The calculation of the leverage factor aims at establishing the percentage price rise of the warrant in the case of a 1% growth of the share price. However, since there is no direct connection between the warrant price and the share price, the leverage factor cannot be measured by a simple equation. The following algorithm gives a fairly accurate estimate.

$$\text{Leverage Factor} = S \times \frac{\text{Share Price} \times \text{No. of Shares per Warrant}}{\text{Price of Warrant}}$$

$$\text{where } S = -0.5 + \frac{\text{Share Price}}{\text{Purchase Price}}$$

This formula applies to Share Price/Purchase Price proportions of less than 1.5. For Share/Purchase Price proportions of more than 1.5, S is taken as equal to 1.

There are also other metrics of interest to the financial analyst in his daily work, as well as on behalf of the investors he advises. An example is the discounting of *bills of exchange*.

Typically, in purchasing bills of exchange falling due for payment at a later date, the bank deducts from the purchase price the discount, as compensation for the early payment of the amount of the bill. The amount of this interest deduction is calculated by the algorithm:

$$\text{Discount} = \frac{\text{Bill of Exchange Amount} \times \text{Discount in } \% \times \text{Running Period}}{100 \times 360}$$

In this equation, the running period is expressed in days.

Typically, bills of exchange are discounted for a period up to 90 days, with a higher discount charged for bills with a longer running period. If the interest numbers are known, the discount can also be calculated from the interest numbers and the interest divisor.

$$\text{Discount} = \frac{\text{Interest Number}}{\text{Interest Divisor}}$$

In case a portfolio contains claims becoming payable on various dates, the *average due date* must be computed and the total of all claims entered on that date. This approach is used when a customer submits to the bank bills of exchange with various due dates, requesting the bank not to discount the bills, but credit his account with the amount of the bills on the average due date.

$$\text{Average Due Date} = \frac{\text{Total of Interest Numbers} \times 100}{\text{Amounts of Bills or Capital}}$$

As can be appreciated, the operations characterizing a number of financial transactions, as well as collection being made by banks or other companies, can be expressed algorithmically. The system can be made more sophisticated by including knowledge engineering artifacts – an issue to which we have paid considerable attention.

EXCHANGE RATES AND SWAPS

In the case foreign exchange deals are involved in a financial transaction, a currency conversion will often need to be made. Foreign exchange rates are usually indicated as units of the local currency per 100 units of the foreign currency, at the rate applicable when the conversion is done. The algorithm is:

$$\text{Base Currency Amount} = \frac{\text{Foreign Currency Amount} \times \text{Foreign Exchange Rate}}{100}$$

and conversely:

$$\text{Foreign Currency Amount} = \frac{\text{Base Currency Amount} \times 100}{\text{Foreign Exchange Rate}}$$

Base currency is the one the client is primarily treating, be it $, £, DM, SF, FF, Yen, or any other.

Foreign exchange rates are always listed from the point of view of the bank. The buying price means that the bank buys the currency in question from the customer at this price. The selling price indicates that the bank sells to the customer at this price.

The difference (margin or spread) between the two prices covers transaction costs and currency risk in the foreign exchange business. For this reason, the margin is much greater for soft currencies than for hard currencies; and within the same currency it is greater for small amounts than for large amounts.

Forex transactions might call for swaps. As we saw in Chapter 10, a *swap* may involve a combined foreign currency transaction which incorporates:

- Spot purchase of foreign exchange
- With simultaneous forward sale, or vice versa.

For instance, a customer wants to *buy forward* sterling. The bank buys spot sterling and invests the purchase on the Euromarket up to the due date. Since sterling interest rates are higher than dollar interest rates, the investment yields an interest income. The bank passes this on to the customer in the form of a discount and thus of a lower rate.

This situation is reversed for *forward sales*: in buying the funds, the bank has to pay higher sterling interest rates, and can therefore offer the customer a forward rate that is below the spot rate. Markdowns due to swap income and swap costs are calculated in simplified form through the algorithm:

Markdown =

$$\frac{\frac{\text{Spot}}{\text{Rate}} \times \frac{\text{Running Period}}{\text{in Days}} \times \left(\frac{\text{Interest Rate}}{\text{Foreign Curr.}} - \frac{\text{Interest Rate}}{\text{Base Curr.}} \right)}{360 \times 100}$$

Since the interest factor is not included in this simplified approach, it would have to be calculated separately to obtain a more precise result.

For a swap transaction, costs or income can be calculated for an entire year and expressed in percent. The annual interest rate, or *swap rate*, is computed through the formula:

$$\text{Swap Rate} = \frac{\frac{\text{Discount}}{\text{Premium}} \times 360 \times 100}{\text{Running Period in Days} \times \text{Forward Rate}}$$

In case interest rates in the foreign currency are higher than in the base (reference) currency, the forward rate has a discount. In the opposite case, with interest rates for investments in the base currency being higher than those for foreign currency investments, the forward rate has a premium.

THE USE OF INDEXED FUTURES

With floating exchange rates, the currency rates are *indexed*, but this is not the only case where an *index* is used. In the general case, for calculation reasons, an index measures various magnitudes such as prices, wages, economic conditions, inflation, and so on in relation to a base period – with the level at the time of the base period equalling 100. The algorithm has the form:

$$\text{Index Today} = \frac{\text{Magnitude Today} \times 100}{\text{Magnitude in Base Period}}$$

Indexing is done for a specific purpose, for instance to adjust income from mortgages, payment of annuities, return on savings, the calculation of real interest rates and so on. In this sense, the indexing module of a model will work in conjunction to programs useful in making calculations for, say, loans and interest.

- Calculating mortgage variables and printing monthly mortgage tables.
- Computing payment or withdrawal annuity variables and producing adjusted annuity tables.

- Estimating the total amount of money accumulated at the end of a time period at compound interest, with or without further additions of capital.
- Calculating nominal and effective true annual interest rates for installment loans, and so on.

Indexes change, and the percentage change of an index in the course of time can be calculated through the formula:

$$\text{Percentage change} = \left(\frac{\text{Index Level Today}}{\text{Index Level at Early Time}} - 1 \right) \times 100$$

The computation is particularly simple if the old index level coincides with the base period (= 100), where the equation becomes:

$$\text{Percentage Change} = \text{Index Level Today} - 100$$

Investors and wage earners are just as interested in the real percentage change. This is given by the algorithm:

$$\text{Real Percent Change} = \left(\frac{100 + \text{Nominal Increase in } \%}{100 + \text{Inflation Rate in } \%} - 1 \right) \times 100$$

Finally, *purchasing power* reflects the real value of money as compared to the cost of goods. Its calculation accounts for fluctuation of the monetary unit (where it applies) and of relative earnings levels. The purchasing power index moves contrary to the price index: if prices rise, purchasing power drops and vice versa.

Within the same country, if the purchasing power index in a given period equals 100, this purchasing power index can be calculated for other periods through the formula:

$$\text{Purchasing Power Index in Period } Y = \frac{\text{Price Index in Period } X}{\text{Prices Index in Period } Y} \times 100$$

A more complex approach is necessary in case different countries and different currencies are involved. The purchasing power index abroad indicates the value of the domestic currency in a foreign currency country at a certain time. The index starts at base period; hence $A = 100$. The index level at another period B is calculated through the algorithm:

Purchasing Power Index Abroad in Period B =

$$\frac{\text{Foreign Exchange Rate in Period } A \times 100}{\text{Foreign Exchange Rate/Period } B \times \left(1 + \dfrac{\text{Inflation Abroad}}{100} \right)}$$

Indexes can be linked, and from time to time they are revised and placed on a new basis. For instance, as consumer habits change the basket of goods and services has to be adjusted by way of a different makeup and weighting.

Through revisions, various indexes are created which start at 100 when established. But as the basket changes, the new index is no longer directly comparable with the old index. The following formula can be used to integrate successive indexes.

Old Index in Period B =

$$\frac{\text{Old Index in Period } A}{\text{New Index in Period } A} \times \text{New Index in Period } B$$

The ratio: old index in period A over new index in period A is known as the *constant factor*. Practically always we need constant factors when we are making comparisons. They are part of the methodology we apply in financial modeling.

15 The Role of Visualization with Analytical Approaches and Quantitative Methods

INTRODUCTION

In Chapter 13 we examined the role of critical ratios. In Chapter 14 we spoke of algorithmic solutions and how they assist in focusing management's attention on strong and weak points concerning the financial aspects of the business. The role of financial models is to help in evaluating basic operating issues in a relatively objective manner and to compare against industry trends.

In most of the cases which we have seen, the focal point of attention has been either a fair value calculation or how and when corrective action needs to be taken. By means of examples we have followed the results obtained from analytical approaches and how they bring into perspective the contribution of crucial factors affecting the business, also, the relationships such factors can reveal.

For instance, comparing growth rates of various firms, and estimating why some have had faster growth in earnings per share than others, it becomes feasible to answer questions such as:

- Which specific business factors contribute the most to profitability?
- What is the fair value of a financial deal and what can be expected in returns?
- How have companies with higher growth rates achieved them?
- Which decisions reflect management's success in implementing a strategic plan?
- What has been the impact of the chosen resource allocation on achieved results?

Even relatively simple quantitative evaluations assist in focusing on the problem on hand. Hence there are benefits to be obtained from the implementation of financial models and other analytical tools.

Even relatively simple solutions can offer commentable results, though competition in finance and in industry at large is today so tough that by necessity the tools used by cutting-edge organizations are getting increasingly more sophisticated. Because this book is oriented to managers and professionals, not rocket scientists, we will not discuss complex models which can be found in other references (for instance, see Chorafas, 1994c and 1992) – but we will focus on the importance of visualization.

Whether the financial model which we use is simple or complex, the results being obtained have to be communicated to the user in an easily comprehensible manner. Classically, the presentation has been done in a tabular form which time and again has proven to be inefficient, difficult to comprehend at a glance, and at times misleading.

Back in 1953, in the course of my postgraduate studies at the university of California, in Los Angeles, I had a professor, Dr Harold D. Koontz, with vast business experience. He taught me that a person reading a table always tries to convert the numbers he sees into a graph. Why not give him the results in a graphic form in the first place? This is what we are doing today through *visualization*.

GOING BEYOND THE CONTRIBUTION OF RATIOS

While, when done in a knowledgeable manner, the use of ratios in financial analysis can provide a significant contribution, there are cases where ratios alone are limited in a research and discovery sense. Therefore, they have to be supplemented by other tools such as statistical evidence.

Over the years we have often used percentiles, quartiles and median values; also range, variance and standard deviation. Ratios and statistical methods can be combined, for instance in evaluating return on assets, return on equity, the yield on earning assets on a tax equivalent basis, or the percentage of earning assets to total assets.

While the ratios themselves provide an indicator, we cannot really know if the result is too high, too low or just right unless we compare it to *our* industry's average: the median, the upper and lower quartiles as well as percentiles. This is the service of the Dun and Bradstreet tables to which reference was made in Chapter 13.

By means of statistics taken from the financial industry, we have seen that *yield on earning assets* helps in demonstrating how well management is employing the assets that are available for investment. Knowledgeable readers have appreciated that the yield is greatly influenced by such factors as:

- The cost of funds,
- Market rate levels,
- State usury laws,
- Asset mix, and
- Financial risk.

Other factors, too, contribute to the yield and should be properly accounted.

For instance, whether the bank is more retail or wholesale oriented – as well as issues pertaining to local competition.

Quite often in management decision we say: 'Other things being equal.' Starting from the premise that other companies in our area of operations face more or less equal conditions, the hypothesis is made that variation in the results is a direct reflection of management's ability. This is however a tentative statement which has to be proven.

Proof of this hypothesis cannot be gained strictly through quantitative tests. *Qualitative factors* often help in an analytical methodology, though with statistical techniques quantification is and remains the focal point.

- Algorithmic solutions are vital in terms of assisting management, but numbers alone tell only part of the story.
- The other part will be told through a qualitative analysis made feasible, for instance, through fuzzy engineering.

Yields must be shown on a tax equivalent basis to account for tax-exempt income – for instance, from state, county and municipal bonds and loans. In analyzing individual companies, situations arise where management has overinvested in one area at the expense of the others – but there may be qualitative reasons, such as market expectations, which also need to be analyzed.

In the financial industry, a bank might have overinvested in tax-exempt securities to the point where taxable income is not large enough to utilize fully the exempt interest. As a result, all of the tax benefit from deductible expenses cannot be realized. The original generalization is a failure in judgment which has both quantitative and qualitative characteristics.

Decisions relative to allocation and optimization have more to do with knowledge-based predicates than with the more general case of algorithms. This brings into perspective the role played by knowledge engineering – and, therefore, the importance of *heuristics* systems.

- Heuristics approaches are typically based on trial and errors, with trials made many times over.
- As business problems get more complex, deterministic solutions become too much computer-intensive.
- Heuristics permit us to locate optima through an experimentation which is practically fully automated.

The use of analytical solutions which involve heuristics helps in providing more personalized, tailored services to their users. But combining qualitative and quantitative approaches makes necessary efficient database access for retrieval from multiple sources, ensuring that:

- Data is timely and accurate, and
- The filtering is properly done while indexing is consistent.

As we have seen on a number of occasions, advanced analytical techniques are inseparable from an intelligent database access. One application developed by a known financial institution has paid particular attention on synonyms and homonyms: stories about mergers may include non-obvious search keys like 'share swap' and 'leveraged buyout'. But intelligence-enriched approaches can go further:

- Distinguishing between the acquisition of a product and that of a company, and
- Providing multiple indexing for persons, companies, places, and so on.

Another, similar example comes from Reuters and concerns an expert system implementation. Its development took a total of 6.5 man-years, of which 2.5 man-years were spent on rule predicates. Part of the other time was invested by two Reuters journalists, who spent approximately half a man-year categorizing 20,000 news stories for rule development and *accuracy testing* purposes.

This and similar cases suggest that today analytical techniques are not only algorithmically-based but also involve a great deal of organizational work. We have spoken of this fact since Chapter 1. The Reuters' story is important because quite often 80 percent of the problem is text and data – not equations.

CHARTS, STATISTICS AND MANAGEMENT

While ratios present reference points against which comparisons can be made, the crucial issue underlining their utilization is not a scalar unit but a trend. By permitting to go beyond a simple quantification, statistical tools:

- Effectively exhibit longer-term trends and how they develop,
- Identify variance within a process and between different processes,
- Offer performance yardsticks for control purposes, and
- Can be readily adapted to computer handling with significant time and cost savings.

In the longer term, the essence of analytical approaches is not just to provide a snapshot of a situation which existed at a given time and had a certain value. The more important contribution from financial models is that of identifying tendencies, thus serving as *early indicators*.

The search for early indicators is on from macroeconomics to

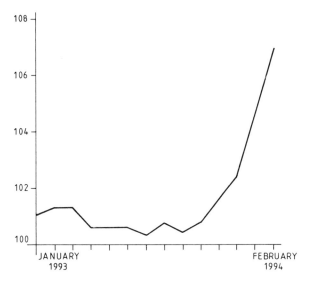

Figure 15.1   Danger signals in March 1994 by the CIBCR early indicator on inflation

microeconomics, and the rules of the game are changing. A major goal at national policy level, for example, is finding an accurate signal of inflation, which can be achieved through models.

As of 1994, the Federal Reserve is looking closely at the leading index of inflation compiled by Columbia University's Center for International Business Cycle Research. Developed in the late 1980s by CIBCR's Geoffrey H. Moore, the index is a composite of seven indicators:

* Commodity prices,
* Employment rate,
* Dun and Bradstreet's percentage of companies expecting higher prices,
* Price Index of the National Association of Purchasing Management,
* Speed of supplier deliveries,
* Public and private debt outstanding, and
* Prices of imported goods, excluding energy.

The CIBCR index is designed to predict turning points. The aim is to identify change in direction not to give information on how much inflation is likely to pick up. Over the years, this index has compiled a good record of predicting turning points in inflation six months or so in advance.

For this reason the January and February 1994 surge in the index shown in Figure 15.1, has drawn the Fed's attention. The growth rate of the index, which is more important than the level, has exceeded the 7 percent pace considered to be the trigger for a cyclical upturn in inflation.

Table 15.1 Two years of operations: computer company ABC
(millions of dollars)

	1993	1992
Net Sales	$1,580	$1.650
Cost of Sales	285	297
Research & Development	275	280
Sales & Marketing	540	544
General & Administrative	150	153
Total Operating Expenses	1,250	1.275
Income from Operations	330	374
Interest & Other Income	10	10
Pretax Income	340	384
Taxes	85	96
Net Income	255	288
Earnings per Share	$0.60	$0.68

As this and many other examples help document, what we are after in analytical techniques is insight: the ability to look into the future, not just to quantify what has happened. The accurate forecasting of trends and tendencies provides a sense of direction, permitting us to bend the developing curve in due time, before the process gets out of control. Two exhibits show the difference between snapshot presentation and trend evaluation.

- The snapshot approach is identified in Table 15.1. Over a two-year period, it reflects on net sales, cost of sales and other crucial criteria regarding Company ABC, a computer vendor.
- An example on trend evaluation is given in Figure 15.2 which maps the profit margin of American computer firms and identifies how it has been slipping for 25 years.

Both approaches are valid in terms of comparisons, but as Figure 15.2 demonstrates, economic and market trends are more effectively shown through charting: hence, visualization. Trends over a timespan of ten to fifteen years are much more effective in describing a changing environment than year-to-year comparisons can ever offer.

This statement is valid all the way from profit margins to market share, sales volumes, quality assurance and production characteristics – a fact which has not escaped the attention of management. In a production environment, for instance, line balance applications are mapped into different instruments such as:

- *The Object Chart* which addresses itself to the planned cumulative delivery schedule compared to actual deliveries.

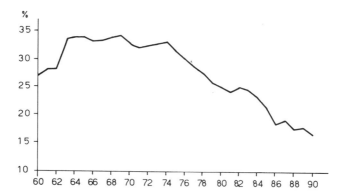

Figure 15.2 Operating margin of computer and business equipment firms over a thirty-year timeframe

- *The Program Chart*, particularly applicable to production plans, with the sequence and lead time required for each activity.
- *The Line of Balance* presentation whose goal is the comparison of program progress to objectives.
- *The Program Evaluation and Review Technique* (PERT), which has provided significant assistance in project coordination.

Among themselves, these graphical assistance tools help in avoiding omissions and duplications. They also show interrelationships in work flow and provide insight into improved utilization of resources. There is much we can learn from a graphical representation.

IMPROVING VISUALIZATION THROUGH INTERACTIVE GRAPHICS

Whether in a manufacturing or in a banking environment, graphs assist in spotlighting critical elements in time for corrective action. No wonder, therefore, that, as recent surveys indicate, a substantial number of banks have adopted graphics tools to present the results of financial models and other projects in analysis.

As the list of analytical tools being used is growing rapidly, graphics play a leading role in *interactive visualization*. In fact, the visualization tools are themselves evolving, in recognition of the fact that through graphics we can draw much more useful indicators than a simple trendline.

Figure 15.3 exploits the statistics from a sharp fall which occurred in 1990 in connection with share prices of the Adelaide Steamship Company, showing the fluctuation over a five-year period. This chart has two types of trending drawn upon it:

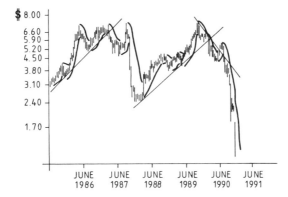

Figure 15.3 The Adelaide Steamship Company: straight and parabolic trend lines

- Simple straight lines, and
- Parabolic trend lines.

Parabolic stop lines are visualizing acceleration; they are trendlines designed to highlight changes in momentum. With derivative financial instruments we also target the rate of change with *delta* and *gamma*.

- Delta is the first derivative of the derivative product's price function with respect to the underlying.
- Gamma is the second derivative of that same function.

Some financial analysts use their own formula based on a stock's high and low prices, calculating the probability that it will stay in a specified trading range. Many chartists prefer to use logarithmic graphs as they then represent a constant rate of growth.

A growing population of financial models is written to zero-in on an overpriced or underpriced product, particularly derivatives like options. But theoretical values and real market prices often diverge, and a model which might have worked well under certain conditions can give disastrous results in other cases. There are no miracles with modeling.

As an alternative, chartists track the stock market's average closing price, over a thirty-, forty-, or fifty-week period. Then, they compare that to the current price of an index.

- Whenever the current price climbs above the XX-week moving average, they issue a call to buy.
- When it drops below, they go for a sell recommendation.

Some critics gripe that this method is too simplistic. For one thing, the recommendations are all or nothing: 100 percent in the market or 100 percent out of the market. The one-size-fits-all system fails to consider the tolerance of clients for risk.

More important than this is the fact that market data is taken at too infrequent intervals, for instance, daily, weekly or monthly. This says nothing about the way the market's heart beats.

Leading-edge financial organizations have since the late 1980s followed and analyzed market data at five-minute intervals. Minute-level frequencies are far better than hourly or daily – but we can do better than that.

The concept of *high frequency data* is very recent. It practically started in an implementation sense in 1994 and targets second-level intervals, hence 60 times faster than the minute level.

- High frequency data analysis requires innovative financial models.
- But the results which it provides can be quite revealing in terms of market trends.

Just as important is the contribution which is made by means of nonlinear financial models: chaos theory, complexity theory, fractals, fuzzy engineering, neural networks, genetic algorithms and other types of nonlinearities. The real target is the development and use of learning artifacts which can help in prediction.

- Between high frequency financial data and nonlinear models we define the domain of new, highly competitive financial research.
- The results obtained with the latest most sophisticated methods are between one and two orders of magnitude better than those characterizing the older generation of financial modeling – like that of the Adelaide Steamship Company example.

In the case of the joint effect obtained by the linear trend and parabolic lines, which we saw with the Adelaide Steamship Company, an investor who used a combination of both tools should have been able to sell out prior to the 1987 crash, to come back in for another taste in 1988 and to get out in late 1989.

Even with this generation of financial models, since June 1990, the parabolic stop line would have preserved the investor from the temptation to buy back. Such analysis however assumes that the investor was not susceptible to psychological impulses which are the undoing of most people playing in the stockmarket or in any other game.

Leaving aside the issue of psychological response which is not a main theme of this book, it is appropriate to underline that output requirements are highly linked to the goals which we wish to reach through a financial model.

- Planning, for example, involves both the development and the evaluation of alternative courses of action.
- But the financial simulator should not only be able to evaluate alternatives which have been specified but also present the results in an effective manner.

The question then arises: 'For whom are these results intended?' The answer is for the professionals; and they should be made available through an effective visualization procedure. In this simple statement lies the whole issue of designing and implementing human windows, of which we talk in the following section.

HUMAN WINDOWS: FROM GRAPHICAL PRESENTATION TO VIRTUAL REALITY

We talk of *human windows* to identify the agile, user-friendly interfaces necessary between the enduser and the computer. Cornerstone to this approach is interactive visualization, with expert systems assisting the dialog which should take place between the user and the machine.

There are multiple roles to be fulfilled in connection with output functions and all of them must have the enduser as their focal point. Practically each issue can be assisted in an able manner through technology.

- Knowledge artifacts can emulate the imaginative side of input and output.
- Just as an algorithmic model generates data, optimizes behavior, or evaluates results.

Interactive output formats must be established for an agile and comprehensive visualization. Many people fail to understand that computation is worth very little until its results are made comprehensible to the user.

Concomitant with the construction of financial models is a number of functional constraints which are posed to the builder. Among the input/output issues confronting modeling are the construction of a database system able to act as an interface between:

- The simulator itself, with its statistical analysis tools and estimation programs.
- The data sources to be chosen as well as the information providers' data streams.

Twenty and thirty years ago, output was tabular with its level of detail rarely corresponding to the layer of reporting to which it was addressed. One of the first major improvements has been *customization*. For instance, tabulation from a financial report for members of the Board and top management being limited to three significant digits.

- If last year's income was $2,353,795,610
- Then it was shown as $2.35 billion.

This is the sense of putting accuracy ahead of precision. The same is true of next year's projection. But while source and use of funds statement may be tabular, plan/actual presentation in terms of:

- Budgets,
- Sales, and
- Production schedules

are better given in a graphical form. The statement of earnings and stockholders' equity may be tabular, but the rate of return analysis should be in graphics and the same is true of financial and operating summaries.

During the mid-to late 1980s leading companies saw to it that the presentation of differences and of most statistics became graphical, with tabular information accessible interactively when detail is necessary. By the early 1990s color and 3-dimensional graphics dominated the output in leading-edge financial institutions and manufacturing organizations.

Figure 15.4 offers an example. It presents a visualization in three dimensions of shares traded to bid–ask spread versus time of transaction. 3-D color improves upon this presentation of financial information, just as it contributes most significantly to engineering design.

- PV Wave, the shell used to draw Figure 15.4, is now actively employed by Barclays Bank, Chemical Banking and National Bank.
- Other financial organizations use different tools, but among tier 1 institutions the trend is definitely towards 3-D color for mission critical applications.

The latest concept in terms of output is *virtual reality*. It provides techniques for an intuitive presentation and manipulation of *massive data* as well as of *abstract descriptions* of states and processes which reflect the financial world. A basic demand is that execution is done in *realtime*, including:

- The evaluation of the computational model, and
- The assurance of continuity for human perception.

As experience is acquired with financial models, and the demands posed in their regard are expanding, it is no longer enough to think of financial analysis, knowledge engineering and simulation as strictly computational processes. We must incorporate into the solution the possibility of generating and controlling *virtual worlds*.

This requirement places emphasis on the presentation characteristics of artifacts and the interaction with their virtual features which are essential dimensions of the representation. An interactive representation of modeling

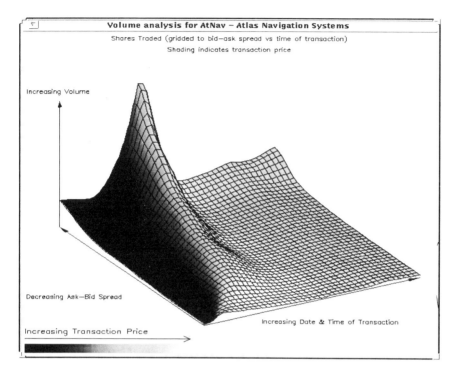

Figure 15.4   Volume Analysis for GYRT – Gyroscopic Technologies Shares Traded: gridded to bid-ask spread vs time of transaction. (Courtesy of Visual Numerics, Boulder, CO.)

results addresses the human senses, the most exploited today being the visual sense, through visualization. The presentation dimension becomes more sophisticated when:

- It is characterized by *dynamic* techniques, and
- Assures event sequences executed in *realtime*.

Among the goals of virtual reality is to exploit multi-sensory presentations requiring the synchronization of visual, auditive and other channels to promote a degree of immersion. This goes well beyond the old interaction approaches where passive computer graphics dominated (see Chorafas and Steinmann, 1995).

ORGANIZATION AND METHODOLOGY TO SUPPORT INTERACTIVE APPLICATIONS

New applications are developed continually, but an innovative strategy can be fruitful if crucial problems are identified and resolved prior to the use of mathematics. Graphs often reflect a statistical background, but managerial choices have a much broader context conditioned by a number of salient problems which include:

1. The ability to effectively integrate quantitative methods into qualitative thinking
2. The choice of qualitative tools which should accompany and enrich the use of mathematical models
3. Database contents and structure able to serve financial analysis purposes in the best possible manner

Regarding issue 1, a basic problem underlying most cases is one of efficient *communication*. Mathematics in finance and in management involves no magic, requires no special mental brilliance to understand, and its practitioners are no geniuses with a vast understanding of 'truth' in financial decision making. Their key asset is methodology.

- Few people appreciate that a valid methodology is most crucial in communication – and therefore in decision.
- Company policies are an example of methodology which assists in communicating guidelines, avoiding repetitive evaluations of already decided issues.

Any tool requires the proper *methodology* to be correctly used. The more powerful are the approaches which we use, the more this statement is true. Analytical processes have been an immeasurable aid only when management has an appreciation and understanding of their basic characteristics, their fruitful uses as well as the potential difficulties inherent in them.

A similar statement can be made about the organization necessary for the effective exploitation of the information in the database, as well as for the visualization of the results. *Organization* is the keyword common to these two references, and to many others. For instance, organizational skills are necessary for the structuring of relational and object-oriented databases (see also Chorafas, 1989c and Chorafas and Steinmann, 1993a).

The necessary organizational infrastructure is provided by a neat and efficient classification scheme, which is basically *taxonomical* in nature. Both classification and taxonomy are fundamental knowledge engineering domains. When the classification work is properly done, we can proceed with identification along the line:

<basic code>   <suffix>   <origin>

This approach permits us to identify a databased item according to its primary characteristics which created the basis for the classification, then add other factors in the suffix such as brand name. Origin makes it feasible to identify, for example, the particular factory in which a product was built – a reference which has no impact on basic classification.

I particularly underline such organizational subjects because they are fundamental in database organization and management, as it has so often been stated. The challenge of databasing multimedia information often represents the 80 percent of an analytical solution. Furthermore, once this approach is implemented, it will allow both:

- An object oriented development of distributed deductive databases, and
- The effective implementation of ephemeral hierarchies for database access which can be achieved in a seamless manner (see also Chorafas and Steinmann, 1993b).

The fundamental infrastructure of a sound taxonomical organization is invariant whether we talk of applications in finance or in the manufacturing industry. Classification is important for organizational reasons and, as we have already seen, visualization helps both the presentation and the appreciation of multimedia information.

DEVELOPING INCREASINGLY COMPETITIVE MANAGEMENT TOOLS

There used to be a time when the processing done in decision support applications primarily employed static data. Today, it requires a different kind than is found in references on past activity, such as legacy databases typically contain. Increasing competitiveness and complexity calls for a system solution able to exploit online operational information.

This reason lies behind the emphasis placed on a significant range of subjects – from databases to visualization. Expert decision support solutions are best made with dynamic but refined data. The refining and stabilizing of information used for analytical decisions necessarily means filtering out noise, that is any unwanted input. Subsequently,

- A typical enduser will access data online, manipulate it, and produce a result,
- This result will then be scrutinized through a mathematical model,
- The processed data will be refined or reformulated, through one parsing or an iteration.

Hence, we are talking of an interactive process between the user and his system. To better exemplify this reference, let's start with a system which, for the purpose of our example, contains static data. Figure 15.5 presents in a tabular form timeperiods and criteria which while already computed as ratios can further be used to compare:

- One company against another in the same timeframe, or
- The results of one timeperiod against another for the same firm.

A similar reference can be made about financial statistics such as those shown in the income statement in Figure 15.6. In both cases, we have a database which contains computed values which can further be used by different algorithms for *visualization* of current results and for *projections*.

As shown in Figure 15.7, a *radar chart* (see also Chorafas and Steinmann, 1989) can help in the effective visualization of key decision factors and their variation. Classifying ROE, ROA, ROC, EBIT, R&D and G&A in terms of performance, for instance:

		Time period			
Critical Management Ratios	*1994*	*1993*	*1992*	*1991*	*1990*
Return on equity (ROE)					
Return on assets (ROA)					
Return on capital employed (ROC)					
Sales growth (% increase)					
Gross profit margin					
Earnings before investment and taxes (EBIT)					
Earnings before taxes					
Net profit margin					
% profit increase					
% dividend increase					
Cost of goods sold					
Depreciation and amortization					
Marketing and sales (as % revenues)					
G&A* as % revenues					
Taxes as % EBIT					
R&D as % revenues					
Sundries as % revenues					
Asset turnover ratio					
Gross plant turnover					
Net plant turnover					
Asset leverage					
Inventory turnover					
Days inventory					

*General and Administrative expenses.

Figure 15.5 Critical management ratios for comparative reasons

Figure 15.5 (continued)

Critical Management Ratios	1994	Time period 1993	1992	1991	1990
Current ratio					
Acid test					
Payables turnover					
Days payables					
Years to repay debt					
Dividend coverage					
Interest coverage					
Cashflow coverage					
Long-term debt: equity ratio					
Invested capital					
• % short-term debt					
• % long-term debt					
• % common equity					
• % preferred equity					
• % retained earnings					
• % other capital sources					
Tangible net worth					
Compound Average Growth Rates					
Sales reveues					
Cost of sales					
Gross revenues					
Other revenues					
Net revenues					

- Giving high grades for high ROE and ROA
- But low grades for high G&A

financial analysts can evaluate company *A* against companies *B* and *C*, and easily visualize the results. In this example, company *A* is the worst performer of the three, while *B* leads in three of the established criteria and *C* leads in two.

Projections made through financial modeling are one of the most powerful forms of enduser computing. Such applications are forward looking but require a significant amount of data, the proper setting of initial parameters, projection algorithms and user-friendly presentation of results.

- Once the initial parameters are supplied, the real work is done by the algorithm and the computer.

Figure 15.6 Analysis of income statement

	Time period				
	1994	*1993*	*1992*	*1991*	*1990*
Sales revenue					
Cost of sales					
Gross revenues					
Other reenues (returns)					
Net reveues					
Operating Expenses:					
General and administrative					
Marketing and sales					
Research & development					
Sundries					
Total operating expenses					
Depreciation expense					
Amortization					
Total Non cash Items:					
Earnings before interest and taxes					
Interest expense					
Earnings before taxes					
Income taxes					
Net profits (loss)					
Dividends					
Increase (decrease) in ROE					

- This automation of handling routines sees to it that projections have attracted fertile minds and given significant results.

Securities is one of the fields where such analytical techniques have been successful. Other domains in finance are credit management, loan and deposit forecasting, asset management, new service evaluation, bank cost accounting, and marketing analysis.

- In the installment loan department models have been developed to improve the identification of good (and bad) credit risks and to assist in profitability analysis.
- In the area of commercial lending, the use of models made it possible to predict the cash needs and deposit decisions of corporate customers.

The net result is to assist financial officers in their decision making in an effective manner. Here again, mathematics have played a commentable role

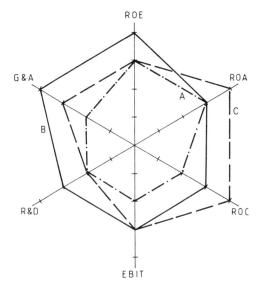

Figure 15.7   A radar chart can help in the effective visualization of key decision factors and their variation

both in clarifying complex issues and in providing the groundwork for experimentation. In this book, practical examples and case studies have been given in both areas.

CAPITALIZING ON THE POLYVALENCE OF FINANCIAL MODELS

Analytics is a polyvalent decision support tool which can be used in a variety of imaginative ways. As we saw at the beginning of this chapter, ratios can be successfully integrated with mathematical statistics and a similar statement can be made about heuristic approaches where trial and error helps in guiding management thinking.

As a matter of policy, financial modeling should be done in a manner quite similar to that prevailing in real world situations. As we have seen in Chapter 14, trends and limits provide the framework for control charts – identifying a process which tends to get out of control, thus making corrective action immediately necessary.

In a way similar to quality control charts in manufacturing industry, financial ratios have been successfully used in evaluating such diverse cases as yield at maturity, selling conditions, and financial staying power, also in making comparisons of collection period (of one concern versus another).

Control charts can also help in company valuation in terms of investments, for instance in working capital growth or shrinkage. A simple test of incremental working capital requirements over, say, a six-year period may suggest improvement or deterioration in the company's working capital and its ability to support its operations. Improvement or deterioration could be due to any of the following:

- A change in industry payment practices,
- A change in the company's own selling terms,
- Fluctuations in cash/marketable securities due to capital changes,
- Expenditures without adequate financing,
- Worsening management of working capital.

Uncovering the underlying reasons is a process of significant importance to an investment evaluation. The accuracy of the latter greatly depends on the documentation to be provided through *trend analysis*.

Trend analysis is done by comparing data as of one moment in time against equivalent data for other moments. This is, for instance, what was done with the radar chart. In other cases, it might be the comparison of:

- Daily closings,
- Monthly revenues,
- Quarterly results,
- Annual accounts, and so on.

The very essence of trend analysis is projections. But, as we have already seen, projection algorithms are very sensitive to the data fed into the program, so this data must be chosen carefully. We spoke of *high frequency financial data* on p. 330.

Both in financial institutions and in industrial organizations, the investment department has been assisted with bond-bidding and bond-switching models, as well as through studies of the term structure of interest rates. Other models have been developed to help the trust officer with the interrelated problems of:

- Equity valuation,
- Portfolio selection, and
- Evaluation of portfolio quality.

The effective use of analytics is one of the reasons why the new generation of financial decision makers is exceedingly skilled in the evaluation of investments. They are ambitious people and they are willing to take risks. But at the same time they realize that their entrepreneurial drive has not been tempered by the lessons of history; hence they use expert systems and simulation to help them in their decisions. This reference capitalizes on the fact that:

- The new generation of dealers and investment advisors is computer literate, and
- There exists an increasing inventory of analytical tools and visualization media which can be interactively exploited.

Yet it is no less true that there are very few schools of business in the United States and in Europe that focus their curriculum on the increasingly sophisticated nature of financial analysis. While the salt of the earth is learned by *doing*, formal education should be providing the best tools – not obsolete knowledge.

IMPLEMENTING SENSITIVITY ANALYSIS AND WORST-CASE SCENARIOS

In its simplest form, sensitivity analysis is a *What-if* evaluation made, for instance, to check the effects of an increase in company debt, changes in a product's price or projected sales level, also, increases in cost of production or cost of sales, and other applications.

Taking bank loans as an example, the ability of a borrower to service debt may be particularly *sensitive* to changes to one or more of the variables the preceding paragraph brought into perspective. The lender needs to be aware in advance not only of what the sensitivities are but how their variations influence the risks taken with the loan.

- A sensitivity analysis commonly made is the *worst case* scenario, which shows what would happen to the borrower's ability to repay a loan under pessimistic assumptions.

There exist, however, degrees in the sophistication of the experimentation. *If* the critical variables are changed one at a time, *then* a spreadsheet run on a PC can be the tool the banker needs for a What-if. But more complex sensitivity analyses now target the effect of a joint variation of crucial factors.

- *Complex evaluation* methods require simulators which manipulate more than one of the initial assumptions at a time, and are also able to interactively visualize the results.

Whether all the original assumptions except one are held constant, or the experimenter analyzes covariance and other effects, the success of sensitivity analysis largely rests on *database mining* and on *models*. We have spoken about both of them.

The information in the database will provide historical relationships;

management assumptions or forecasts; sales, pricing and cost data; as well as other factors needed in the experimentation. As it cannot be too often repeated, data is the largest part of the problem.

- This interaction between the model and databased information will permit us to test existing forecasts and plans, as well as to develop new ones.
- With database mining and computer forecasting models, the financial analyst can test sensitivities in *realtime* as opposed to laboriously evaluating changes by hand then waiting for the overnight batch to get numerical results.

When he works interactively, the financial analyst typically varies possibilities in a decision tree. A chosen factor may be experimented with in a linear or nonlinear program formulation. Such evaluation helps to determine how far parameters can be changed without radically altering the decision maker's selection of a preferred solution.

- The essence of What-if experimentation is the ability to perform several operations on the same data, altering the process each time.
- By contrast, with more complex simulators we are changing calculation algorithms and may as well change the basis for data selection.

Typically in the course of evaluating sensitivities the results of one operation are compared to the next to determine the effects of various changes. The background notion is to compare the same subject under different conditions – for instance, investment alternatives.

An algorithm increasingly used in yield and investment decisions is that of *anomaly processing*. We already said that, most often, what are called 'anomalies' or 'outliers' may not be anomalies at all. Yet this is the terminology being used.

This type of analysis focusing on anomalies is basically a search for unusual conditions, that is, activities or *patterns* outside the normal run of events.

- Investment banks and brokers are today analyzing massive amounts of data to determine if any one security (or market) has an unusual behavior.
- No single transaction attracts special notice, but all transactions evaluated collectively may show unusual conditions, or outliers.

Like the other types of decision support, anomaly processing begins with production data and involves the need to group, compare, summarize, and cross-reference available information. This approach is applicable both to:

- Dynamic analysis of incoming information, and
- Static data accumulating in the database.

In both cases, the goal is to detect patterns which reveal background reasons for variation, and/or to identify anomalies on which we can capitalize before our competitors become aware of them. Then we apply sensitivity tests.

Not only can the establishment of sensitivity criteria be a demanding job, but pattern analysis and anomaly processing also require much more complex mathematics than the relatively simple equations we have considered in this book. For instance: nonlinearities, chaos theory, fractals, genetic algorithms and fuzzy engineering (see Chorafas, 1994c).

ENSURING THAT SENSITIVITY ANALYSIS BECOMES PART OF THE CULTURE

In establishing strategic evaluation parameters we should appreciate that one of the major benefits of analytical financial models is that sensitivity analyses can be regularly and rather easily performed. This should be one of the goals to be outlined through a management plan.

Investment decisions are based on a number of sensitivities, some of which relate to the goals and wishes of the investor while others concern market factors. Leading financial institutions have developed proprietary sensitivity lists and the best have adopted a policy of permitting the investment advisor or underwriter to add his own:

- Constraints,
- Criteria, and
- Rules.

High performance computing can leave its mark in the tracking down of changes, and the identification of outliers, as well as of errors. With the appropriate models in place and running, errors embedded in any input or computational process can be discovered by systematically altering data and rerunning the simulator.

Alternatively, high performance computers permit attention to be focused upon critical variables and the change which they are undergoing. Thereby they are sharpening understanding of the uncertainties which exist in market behavior.

There is no better example in this connection than the evaluation of *systemic risk* resulting from highly leveraged financial transactions such as off-balance sheet operations (see Chapter 10). Systemic risk is the risk in the international monetary system due to the fact that the growth in *reserves* is tied to the creation of *new liabilities*.

The risk is that serious financial problems developing in a major institution will ultimately undermine confidence in the main reserve currencies. Their own liquidity and foreign reserves do not provide adequate comfort for central banks. In other terms:

- There should be reliance on assets that are not someone else's liability.
- That is, assets nobody can print in great quantities to suit his needs.

A steady watch for systemic risk requires round the clock risk management and this cannot be done through mainframes or PCs. It needs high performance computers and financial models able to reflect the new awareness on the part of banks, their customers, and the reserve authorities regarding:

- The importance of global risk, and
- The tools needed for risk management.

Some people might ask: 'Why is this a new culture? The financial intermediary has always been aware of risk.' This is true, but not on a global, 24-hour per day, 7-day-a-week basis. This is a new phenomenon whose impact has not yet percolated down the organizations that have a great deal to lose from systemic risk.

Sensitivity analysis can be instrumental in following systemic factors, in becoming aware of significant changes and in taking necessary measures to bring them under control. Such analysis requires making hypotheses but also testing those hypotheses to ensure that they are realistic.

- When traditional evaluation methods are employed, a considerable amount of attention is devoted to endless and heated debates concerning the effects of possible future financial developments.
- By contrast, through modeling, different current actions can be readily assessed by repeated runs of the model, evaluating whether different assumptions about the course of the economy really imply a change.

In this manner, one of the important contributions of sensitivity analysis and of economic and financial modeling at large, stems from its ability to indicate the crucial factors upon which attention should concentrate. This helps to avoid unnecessary floundering on the sea of uncertainty concerning factors which in some cases may be essentially unimportant or highly unlikely – but in other cases are crucial.

A POLICY DECISION THAT ALL RESULTS ARE COMPREHENSIBLE

One of the critical decisions top management should make and communicate to all concerned is that the results of experimentation through financial models should be highly comprehensible. At times such results are kept more or less secret, and in other cases they are communicated in very esoteric forms difficult to decipher.

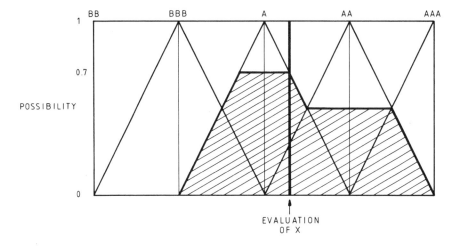

Figure 15.8 The grading of bonds is by its nature fuzzy, but possibility theory permits us to limit the area of variation.

It is possible to make comprehensible the outcome of a model even if the prevailing hypotheses and market data are full of vagueness and uncertainty. This is done through mathematical modeling using *fuzzy engineering*. Whenever it has been applied in an effective manner, fuzzy engineering essentially helps to defuzzify an unclear finance situation.

This goes beyond what other models can offer. For instance, in asset management we can obtain through linear programming models direct values for many of the decision variables. But the estimate of the worth of, say, bonds in the portfolio is essentially subjective – therefore many bankers tend to work with averages.

- The direct values linear programming provides can easily be transformed into a sequence of balance sheet positions throughout the planning horizon.
- But the effects of grading the different bonds from AAA to BB cannot be accounted for in a linear way.
- By contrast, the use of possibility theory (see also Chorafas, 1992) permits defuzzifying the quality of a bond, by defining a limited area in which its value will most likely move.

Figure 15.8 shows a grid of bond grade from BB to AAA. In reality no bond issue has an exact quality value. It may be somewhat better or somewhat worse than the grade it is given by a rating agency, while the main categories themselves overlap since they are established in a rather subjective way.

An evaluator may for instance say that a given bond X is 'somewhat better than A'. This is reflected in Figure 15.8 where through fuzzy engineering the area in which the quality of this bond will most likely fluctuate is established. Notice that since class A can reach from BBB to AA, so can the quality of bond *X*.

- If the evaluation was that *X* was 'better than AA', then its area of defuzzification extends through AA to nearly AAA.
- The possibility of *X* being BBB or AAA is zero. That of being A is 0.7 and there is a 50–50 possibility that it may be AA. (Contrary to probability theory, fuzzy engineering permits that the sum of different possibilities is greater than or less than 1.)

This brief explanation indicates the incremental benefits associated with a marginal relaxation of fixed grades and constraints. By suitable utilization of fuzzy engineering we can determine the likelihood of bond *X* being of a certain grade.

Since in each financial institution every professional thinks in terms of his own subjective and implicit conceptual models, a common basis for understanding and communication is most valuable. The output is an *explicit analytical model* which is graphically presented and appreciated by its users.

A different way of looking into this issue is that when attempting to reach asset management decisions through conventional procedures, the opinions of the most forceful rather than the most insightful analysts often carry the day. By contrast, a graphical presentation leading to defuzzification does away with this risk.

- This reference is not only true in asset management but as well in other domains, trading being an example.
- Experimentation through financial models can offer a tremendous competitive edge – and there are many cases to back up this statement.

In the race to 'buy low, sell high', banks which do not use high technology either will be frozen at the start or will jump in with incomplete knowledge. The case of competitiveness can be even better demonstrated with financial institutions which are active in the off-balance sheet markets, trading in options, futures, forwards, swaps and other derivatives.

Clarity and vision are at a premium in business at large and in trading in particular. One of the major contributions provided by mathematical models, online databases and intelligent networks is the concrete way in which they expose assumptions employed about:

- The financial market as a whole,
- Market makers and major players,

• The investment community at large.

Experimentation permits us to understand and evaluate the interrelationships among relevant variables. It also makes it feasible to provide forecasts of future economic conditions.

Careful study and analytical thinking permit us to establish a frame of reference helping astute participants in a financial market. There are many subtle and unheralded advantages from implementing models and simulation in finance. This is an issue to which top management should pay considerable attention because it is synonymous with *competitiveness*.

Acknowledgments

The following organizations, their senior executives and system specialists, participated in the 1992 and 1993 research projects which led to the contents of the present book and its documentation.

MASSACHUSETTS INSTITUTE OF TECHNOLOGY

- Professor Peter J. KEMPTHORNE, Project on Non-Traditional Methods in Financial Analysis
- Dr Alexander M. SAMAROV, Project on Non-Traditional Methods in Financial Analysis
- Professor Jean-Luc VILA, Finance Dept., Sloan School of Management
- Professor Bin ZHOU, Management Science, Sloan School of Management
- Professor Amar GUPTA, Sloan School of Management
- Patricia M. McGINNIS, Executive Director, International Financial Services
- Professor Dr Stuart E. MADNICK, Information Technology and Management Science
- Professor Dr Michael SIEGEL, Information Technology, Sloan School of Management
- Robert R. HALPERIN, Executive Director, Center for Coordination Science

292 Main Street, Cambridge, MA 02139

- Eric B. SUNDIN, Industrial Liaison Officer
- David L. VERRILL, Senior Liaison Officer, Industrial Liaison Program

Sloan School of Management
50 Memorial Drive, Cambridge, MA 02139

- Henry H. HOUH, Desk Area Network and ViewStation Project, Electrical Engineering and Computer Science
- Dr Henry A. LIEBERMAN, Media Laboratory
- Valerie A. EAMES, Media Laboratory
- Professor Dr Kenneth B. Haase, Media Arts and Sciences
- Dr David ZELTZER, Virtual Reality Project

Ames St., Cambridge, MA 02139

SANTA FE INSTITUTE

- Dr Edward A. KNAPP, President
- Dr L. Mike SIMMONS, Jr, Vice President
- Dr Bruce ABELL, Vice President Finance
- Dr John MILLER, Adaptive Computation in Economics
- Dr Blake LE BARON, Non-Traditional Methods in Economics
- Professor Dr Murray GELL-MANN, Theory of Complexity
- Professor Dr Stuart KAUFFMAN, Models in Biology
- Dr Chris LANGTON, Artificial Life

- Bruce SAWHILL, Virtual Reality

1660 Old Pecos Trail, Santa Fe, NM 87501

UNIVERSITY OF CALIFORNIA, LOS ANGELES

- Professor Dr Judea PEARL, Cognitive Systems Laboratory
- Professor Dr Walter KARPLUS, Computer Science Department
- Professor Dr Michael G. DYER, Artificial Intelligence Laboratory

Westwood Village, Los Angeles, CA 90024

SCHOOL OF BUSINESS ADMINISTRATION, UNIVERSITY OF SOUTHERN CALIFORNIA

- Dr Bert M. STEECE, Dean of Faculty, School of Business Administration
- Dr Alan ROWE, Professor of Management

Los Angeles, CA 90089–1421

UNIVERSITY OF MICHIGAN

- Professor John H. HOLLAND, Electrical Engineering and Computer Science
- Dr Rick L. RIOLO, Systems Researcher, Department of Psychology

Ann Arbor, MI 48109–2103

FINANCIAL ACCOUNTING STANDARDS BOARD

- Halsey G. BULLEN, Project Manager
- Jeannot BLANCHET, Project Manager
- Teri L. LIST, Practice Fellow

401 Merritt 7, Norwalk, CN 06856

TOKYO UNIVERSITY

- Professor Dr Michitaka HIROSE, Dept. of Mechano-Informatics, Faculty of Engineering
- Dr Kensuke YOKOYAMA, Virtual Reality Project

3–1, 7-Chome, Hongo Bunkyo-ku, Tokyo 113

TOKYO INTERNATIONAL UNIVERSITY

- Professor Dr Yoshiro KURATANI Dept. of Economics and Finance

9–1–7–528, Akasaka, Minato-ku, Tokyo 107

BANK FOR INTERNATIONAL SETTLEMENTS

- Claude SIVY, Director, Controllership and Operational Security
- Frederick C. MUSCH, Secretary General, Basel Committee on Banking Supervision

2 Centralbankplatz, Basel

BANK OF ENGLAND

- Mark LAYCOCK, Banking Supervision Division

Threadneedle Street, London EC2R 8AH

DEUTSCHE BUNDESBANK

- Eckhard OECHLER, Director of Bank Supervision and Legal Matters

14, Wilhelm Epstein Strasse, D–6000 Frankfurt 50

BANK OF JAPAN

- Harry TOYAMA, Counsel and Chief Manager, Credit and Market Management Department
- Akira IEDA, Credit and Market Management Department

2–1–1, Kongoku-Cho, Nihonbashi, Chuo-ku, Tokyo 103

SWEDISH BANKERS' ASSOCIATION

- Mr Bo GUNNARSSON, Manager, Bank Automation Department
- Mr Gösta FISCHER, Manager, Bank-Owned Financial Companies Department
- Mr Göran AHLBERG, Manager, Credit Market Affairs Department

P O Box 7603, 10394 Stockholm, Sweden

ASSOCIATION OF AUSTRIAN BANKS AND BANKERS

- Dr Fritz DIWOK, Secretary General

11, Boersengasse, 1013 Vienna

Companies visited in the United States include: Bankers Trust, Citibank, Morgan Stanley, Goldman Sachs, J.J. Kenny Services Inc., Merrill Lynch, Teachers Insurance and Annuity Association/College Retirement Equities Fund (TIAA/CREF), Prediction Company, Simgraphics Engineering Corp. Nynex Science and Technology Inc., Microsoft, Reuters America, Oracle Corporation, Digital Equipment Corporation, Unisys Corporation, Hewlett-Packard, IBM Corporation, UBS Securities, Union Bank of Switzerland.

Companies visited in the United Kingdom include: Barclays Bank, Association for

Payment Clearing Services (APACS), Abbey National Bank, Natwest Securities, Oracle Corporation, Virtual Presence, Valbecc Object Technology.

Companies visited in Scandinavia include: Vaerdipapircentralen, Skandinaviska Enskilda Banken, Securum AB, Sveatornet AB, Mandamus AB, Handelsbanken, Gota Banken, Irdem AB.

Companies visited in Austria include: Creditanstalt Bankverein, Bank Austria, Aktiengesellschaft für Bauwesen, Management Data of Creditanstalt.

Companies visited in Germany include: Deutsche Bank, Dresdner Bank, Commerzbank, Deutscher Sparkassen und Giroverband, ABN-AMRO (Holland), Media Systems, Fraunhofer Institute for Computer Graphics, GMD FIRST – Research Institute for Computer Architecture, Software Technology and Graphics, Siemens Nixdorf, UBS Germany.

Companies visited in Switzerland include: Ciba-Geigy AG.

Companies visited in Japan include: Dai-Ichi Kangyo Bank, Fuji Bank, Mitsubishi Bank, Nomura Research Institute, Mitsubishi Trust and Banking, Sakura Bank, Sanyo Securities, Center for Financial Industry Information System Sytems (FISC), Laboratory for International Fuzzy Engineering Research (LIFE), Real World Computing Partnership (RWC), Japan Electronic Directory Research Institute, Mitsubishi Research Institute (MRI), NTT Software, Ryoshin Systems, Sanyo Software Services, Fujitsu Research Institute, NEC, Toshiba, Microsoft, Apple Technology, Digital Equipment Japan, UBS Japan.

Bibliography

Black, Fischer and Karasinki, Piotr (1991) 'Bond and option pricing when short rates are lognormal,' *Financial Analyst Journal* (July–August).

Chorafas, Dimitris N. (1958) *Operations Research for Industrial Management* (New York: Reinhold, London: Chapman & Hall).

———— (1960) *Statistical Processes and Reliability Engineering* (Princeton, NJ: Van Nostrand).

———— (1965) *Systems and Simulations* (New York: Academic Press).

———— (1987) *Applying Expert Systems in Business* (New York: McGraw-Hill).

———— (1989a) *Bank Profitability* (London: Butterworth).

———— (1989b) *Handbook of Database Management and Relational Databases* (New York, TAB Books).

———— (1990a) *Risk Management in Financial Institutions* (London: McGraw-Hill Butterworth).

———— (1990b) *Handbook of Management for Scientific and Technical Personnel* (New York: McGraw-Hill/TAB Books).

———— (1991a) *Knowledge Engineering* (New York: Van Nostrand Reinhold).

———— (1991b) *Expert Systems in Manufacturing* (New York: Van Nostrand Reinhold).

———— (1992) *New Information Technologies – A Practitioner's Guide* (New York: Van Nostrand Reinhold).

———— (1994a) *Beyond LANs – Client-Server Computing* (New York: McGraw-Hill)

———— (1994b) *Intelligent Multimedia Databases* (Englewood Cliffs, NJ: Prentice-Hall).

———— (1994c) *Chaos Theory in the Financial Markets* (Chicago: Probus).

Chorafas, Dimitris N. and Steinmann, Heinrich

———— (1989) *Implementing Networks in Banking and Financial Services* (London: Macmillan).

———— (1990) *Intelligent Networks* (Boca Raton, FL: CRC Press/*Times Mirror*).

———— (1991) *Expert Systems in Banking* (London: Macmillan).

———— (1993a) *Object Oriented Databases* (Englewood Cliffs, NJ: Prentice-Hall).

———— (1993b) *Solution for Networked Databases* (San Diego, CA: Academic Press).

———— (1994a) *Off-Balance Sheet Financial Instruments* (Chicago: Probus).

———— (1994b) *Database Mining* (London and Dublin: Lafferty Publications).

———— (1995) *Practical Applications of Virtual Reality* (Englewood Cliffs, NJ: Prentice-Hall).

Frisch, Otto (1979) *What Little I Remember* (Cambridge: Canto).

Johnson, Moira (1987) *Takeover* (New York: Bantam Books).

Paulos, Allen (1990) *Innumeracy: Mathematical Illiteracy and its Consequences* (New York: Vintage Press).

Sloan, Alfred (1962) *My Years with General Motors*.

Walton, Sam (1992) *My Story – Made in America* (New York: Bantam Books).

Index

Virtual corporation, 127
Virtual reality, 332
Virtual worlds, 332
Visualization, 29, 271, 323, 336
  interactive, 74, 328
Volatility, 213, 217, 220
Volatility factor, 221
von Neumann, Dr John, 75

Wald, Abraham, 23
Walras, Leon, 54
Walton, Sam, 17, 136, 137
Warrant premium, 316
Warrants, 315, 316
Weill, Sanford I., 135, 136

What-if experimentation, 184, 191, 342
Working capital ratio (WCR), 192, 193
Work sampling, 142, 143
Worst-case scenario, 341

Xerox, 311

Yield, 279, 289
Yield on derivatives, 296
Yield on loans, 296

Zenith, 275
Zero budget, 106
Zero budgeting, 143